MICHAEL CHIARELLO'S

LIVE FIRE

MICHAEL CHIARELLO'S LIVE FIRE

125 RECIPES FOR COOKING OUTDOORS

WITH ANN KRUEGER SPIVACK AND CLAUDIA SANSONE

PHOTOGRAPHS BY FRANKIE FRANKENY

CHRONICLE BOOKS

SAN FRANCISCO

Library of Congress Cataloging-in-Publication Data available.

ISBN 978-1-4521-0181-1

Manufactured in China

Design by Michael Mabry

Prop styling by Nissa Quanstrom

Food styling by Michael Laukert

The photographer wishes to thank Ann Spivack, Claudia Sansone, Michael Laukert, Greg O'Connell, and Nissa Quanstrom for all their hard work on this book. With your help, the shoot days were pulled together and carried through with such professionalism. Thank you Eileen Gordon Chiarello for letting us take over your home; your graciousness made long photo shoots much easier. Many thanks to Ann Gaede and her team at Pro Camera—what photographer does their job well without you? Kudos again to Michael Mabry and Lilyana Bone as well as the rest of his talented design team. Your beautiful work makes it a joy to see our images in print. Chloé, my wife and best friend, tutto é possibile, grazie, grazie! And, most importantly, thank you Chef for trusting me once again to use my camera in bringing your great recipes and wonderful stories to life.

10 9 8 7 6 5 4 3 2 1

Chronicle Books LLC
680 Second Street
San Francisco, California 94107
www.chroniclebooks.com

DEDICATION

To my "Pops" Fortunato Chiarello, whose love of meat and fire was trumped only by his love for my mother Antoinette and his three boys. Thank you for your constant support and encouragement. I am forever in your debt. You will be deeply missed.

And to my wife and best friend Eileen. The biggest fire cannot equal the warmth and light you bring to my life every day.

ACKNOWLEDGMENTS

I have, by all accounts, the best book team of all time. Many thanks to my dear friend Claudia Sansone for helping me organize, test, and shoot with the greatest of ease. Thanks to my writer, Ann Spivack. My favorite part of writing a book is sharing the stories with you and seeing them come to life on the page. Frankie "Frankeninny" Frankeny…damn girl, you're good. Each and every image can almost be eaten right off the page. My heartfelt thanks to Michael "Laukey" Laukert. Twenty years later and I am blessed to have your help in bringing yet another far-flung idea to life. It only works because of you, my friend. Thanks to our hero and design guru Michael Mabry and the amazing Lilyana Bone. Seven books later and you still blow my mind with the best graphic design in the industry.

Also thanks to Frankie's assistants and stylists, Nissa Quanstrom and Greg O'Connell, who not only help us get the shot every time but do it with style, grace, and humor.

To Bill LeBlond and Sarah Billingsley of Chronicle Books, thanks for making me part of the Chronicle family and for backing me when I wanted to go beyond the ordinary BBQ book.

Thanks to all my son's friends (and their parents) who came to our home for the sleepover breakfast. Thank you Max and his mom Karen, Bryce and his mom Molly, Trevor and his mom Briana, Aidan and his mom Eileen, Lilly and Audrey and their mom Tina, Viviane and Audrey and their mom Anne-Marie, and Harper and her mom Amanda. That photo shoot will live forever in my memory thanks to your beautiful faces and your amazing energy.

Thanks to everyone who brought to life our Harvest Dinner, especially Chef Ryan McIlwraith and Judy and Denis Gordon, who helped with everything from folding napkins to hanging balloons. Thank you to my guests at the Harvest Dinner, for making this annual event such a high point and for graciously allowing the book team to document this year's dinner.

Thanks to Oscar Renteria for allowing us to photograph at the beautiful Pope Valley Beach. Thank you to Rob Hohmann, Michael Glissman, Margaret De Monte, Joel Hoachuck, and Kelly Magna, who are always ready to step in to make an event or a dinner even better.

Thanks to the staff at our Yountville NapaStyle store for their help, with a special thanks to Jennifer Flynn and Michael Bozzini for being our production assistants during the photo shoot. Thanks to everyone at V Marketplace. Thanks to Rob Hampton and J. J. Sansone for going above and beyond in lending a hand wherever it was needed.

Thanks to all our testers who cheerfully donated their time and their insight: Maria Bautista, Leigh Corshen, Leslie Crail, Paul Franson, Ken Morris, Julie Riordan, Tina Schultheiss, Betty Teller, and Chris Towns. A very special thanks to Ann Pepi, Wendy Rupprecht, and Rachael Tenerowicz.

A very loving thank you to my wife Eileen, for so very graciously allowing the book team to take over our home, and then making pizza for everyone. Thanks to Roux, Felicia, Giana, and Aidan for giving me the world's best reasons to cook over fire.

And finally, many thanks to all of you who believe, as I do, that cooking beside the people who love you will change your life. (It sure has changed mine.) I am grateful beyond words for your ongoing support.

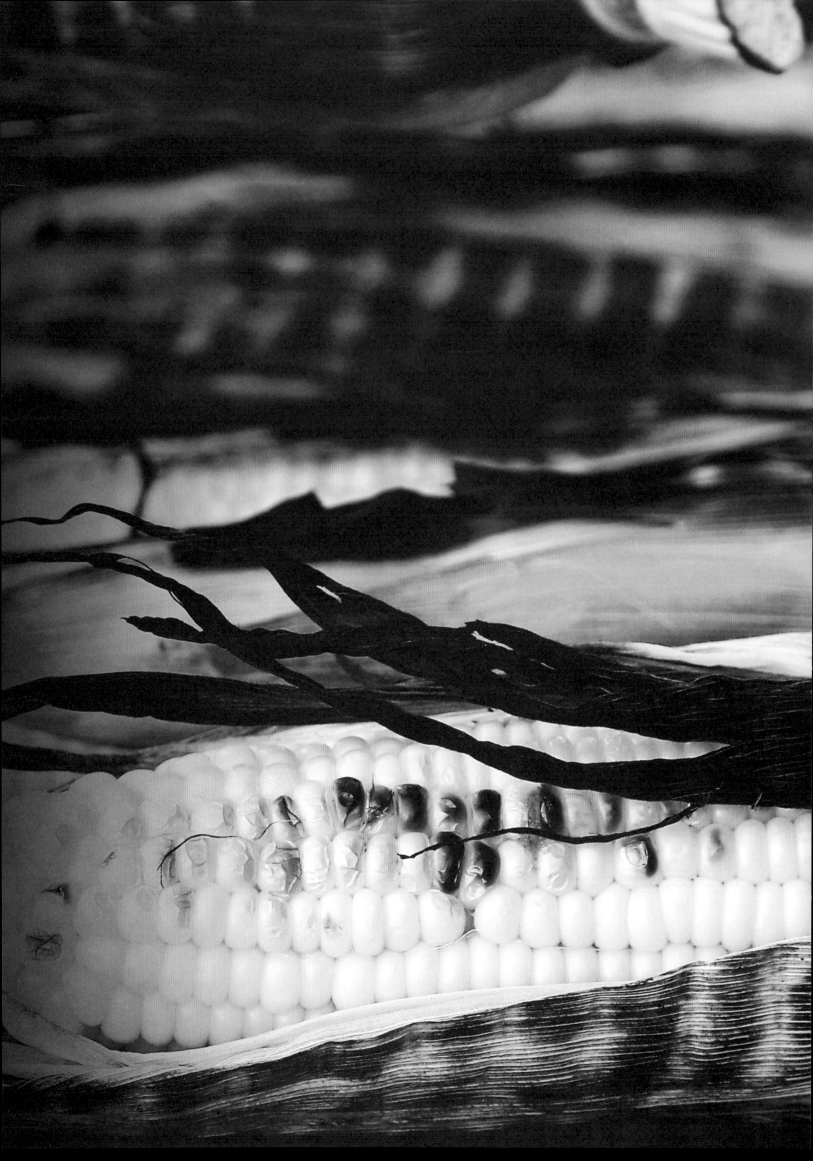

CONTENTS

AT THE END OF THE DAY, WHEN
THE FOOD HAS ALL BEEN SERVED
AND SAVORED, WHAT'S LEFT
IS YOUR CONNECTION TO THE
PEOPLE AROUND YOUR FIRE.

A fire adds flavor to your food but it's more than just a method of cooking. A live fire transforms the meal into a gathering, whether you're cooking for two people or two hundred. ❖ Italians know this at a cellular level. Ask any Italian, any time of day, if he would rather cook and eat outdoors or inside, and you'll get a "whaddya kidding me?" kind of look. Outdoors! When I have a great fire going and a gorgeous cut of meat perfectly seasoned and ready to go on that fire, I am a happy man. I can't even explain this; I just know that cooking over a live fire satisfies some deep, primal urge.

DRAMATIC FIRES AND EVERYDAY FIRES

I'll share a few restaurant techniques but this book is really about how I cook over a fire at home. My goal is to make cooking over a fire feel less intimidating, and I've written the recipes so cooks at every skill level can use them. You'll see how I use a fire to mark big occasions but also how fire can elevate a midweek family dinner or transform leftovers into a great meal (like Potato Polpette, Two Ways, page 114). I'll show you how dramatic a fire can be: Flip through the first chapter and you'll see photographs of my 2011 Harvest Dinner where we cooked two whole lambs on iron crosses—metal frames that hold the lamb over the fire. That's one extreme. To see how I use fire for everyday cooking, flip to page 93 and you'll find a pizza party that couldn't be easier. The prep work is simple, you cook the pizzas on the grill, and stay relaxed enough to visit with your guests.

THE MAIN POINT OF COOKING WITH LIVE FIRE

In this book, I'll teach you how to cook over a big fire, but also show you how to make fire the center of smaller, more intimate gatherings. Yes, the folks at a Harvest Dinner will remember the drama of a whole lamb. But don't underestimate the power of flame to light up a simple Tuesday night dinner. (See The Urban Grill, page 46, which shares where I had one of the best grilled cheese sandwiches I've tasted.)

The Harvest Dinner, pizza party, and rooftop grilled cheese are really about the same thing: *using fire to create a community*.

We humans have an affinity for fire; we're drawn to it. There's a natural rhythm to a fire that people respond to. When you cook over fire, your food tastes better and your gatherings have more warmth. My favorite part of an evening might be when the embers are dying and it's time to head home but everybody stays seated around the fire, quiet and content in the half-light and unwilling to leave the circle just yet—that's the moment you aim for when you start by building a fire.

WHAT DO I MEAN BY LIVE FIRE?

I don't mean barbecuing. While some of the foods in this book are cooked on a backyard grill, you won't find typical barbecue recipes here. This book is about live fire, which means using different types of fuel—wood, charcoal, gas—with a variety of outdoor cooking techniques and equipment. You'll see how to use a hot box to cook a whole suckling pig or a dozen chickens at one time. You'll learn how to cook a whole baby goat on a revolving spit over a fire. You'll also see how to use flame to add flavor to simple foods you usually cook indoors such as chicken and dumplings or leftover mashed potatoes or even a grilled cheese sandwich.

My friend Bobby Flay and I were discussing grilling and I caught some heat for a comment that I made: I said that grilling is not cooking. (Wait, wait—hear me out.) When I hear the word "grilling," I think of a guy sitting next to a Weber in a lawn chair, drinking a beer, and holding a spatula—and it's going to take a lot to pry him out of that lawn chair.

That guy in the lawn chair is not the audience for this book. I may cook over a grill but I am not grilling, I am *cooking*. I'm making sure the beef (or fish or chicken or vegetable) is seasoned perfectly, I'm thinking about the meal as whole, I'm thinking about my guests and coming up with new ways of using fire to get better flavor. I may be relaxed but I am not dozing in my lawn chair; I'm keeping a close watch so the meal comes off the fire at its peak.

CHOOSE WHAT TO COOK BASED ON YOUR EQUIPMENT

You choose what to cook based on where you'll cook: You cook different foods over a campfire or with a rotisserie than you would at your grill. This book is organized around that idea. Each chapter shows you what I cook over a specific type of equipment: the hearth, a gas grill, a rotisserie, a plancha, a fire pit. You can absolutely cook a recipe from the fire pit chapter at the hearth; you just have to modify it a little to work for your heat source.

STAY SAFE

This may be the most important page in this book. I hope you read it more than once. Don't get burned—follow these guidelines for keeping yourself and your family safe while cooking with fire. Look for this banner throughout the book for other safety tips.

- Don't build a fire under tree limbs, patios, awnings, or the eaves of a building. Don't build a fire closer than 30 feet to any other structure, and never build a fire indoors except in a fireplace or a wood-burning oven. (The garage? Forget about it!)

- Use extra caution when children are nearby. At our house we have one designated fire person and one designated kid person so if I'm minding the fire I know my wife, Eileen, has an eye on the kids.

- Before you start the fire, have a safe, cleared space set aside where you can place hot pieces of equipment like the grill rack or the rotisserie bar and know kids can't touch them. Make sure the ground is flat and clear of all brush where you plan to build a fire or place a grill, and check that your grill is sturdy and well-balanced. A live fire on a slant is a bad idea all the way around.

- Use the right size grill for what you're cooking. Make sure your grill and what's on it are completely stable. Don't ever rest a huge pot (like that used for the chicken and dumplings shown on page 140) on a small grill or a kettle grill.

- Don't spray anything flammable onto flames. This includes lighter fluid and even a spray can of olive oil or nonstick cooking spray. You can spray the meat or any food directly when it's not near the fire or spray the grill baskets or grill rack before you start grilling, but don't spray anything (except water in a spray bottle) directly onto flames. Because fire can travel up a stream of flammable liquid, you put yourself at great risk by spraying anything except water onto a live fire. When it's time to oil the grill rack, pour a little olive oil onto a paper towel and hold it with a pair of long tongs.

- Choose the right tools when working with fire. Make sure all your chef's tools—tongs, spatulas, roasting forks—are extra-long with grips made of wood or other material that doesn't melt or conduct heat. Choose high-quality heat-proof gloves with long cuffs. Don't skimp when buying items that keep your hands safe from flame and heat.

- When you are sliding meat or game onto a rotisserie or spit bar, keep both hands on either side of the food. Don't put your hand in a position where it can be hurt by the pointed end of the bar if the roast gives way suddenly.

- With a rotisserie, spit roast, or coal pan for the hot box, keep in mind that all these will be exceptionally hot when they come off the fire. The buddy system works here; have a friend help you lift hot, heavy items off the fire safely. Know where you will rest it before you lift something hot. Always have two pairs of good sturdy fireproof gloves before you start the fire.

- Have a source of water ready; a hose connected to a spigot is best.

- If you have a fire extinguisher, bring it outside and keep it nearby but don't let the kids touch it. Make sure your extinguisher has been inspected in the past six months. (If it doesn't have a tag showing date of inspection, take it in to be checked before you start the fire.) If you have any questions about your fire extinguisher or just fire safety issues in general, talk to the folks at your local fire department; if they can't answer your question, they'll point you in the right direction.

You can build a grill out of ten dollars' worth of bricks, and cook a meal that tastes just as good or better than food cooked on a six-thousand-dollar grill that's bigger than your car. (For proof, see the photos on pages 180 and 219.) ❖ Where grilling is concerned, the winner isn't the person with the biggest, most expensive grill; the winner is the person who uses smoke and flame to best advantage. ❖ Throughout this book, I'll show you how I aim for flavor on a grill, in a fire pit, with a rotisserie (or a spitjack), in my hearth, in a hot box, on a plancha, and using the coals left over from a fire. ❖ Please don't try to tackle all these methods at once. Choose just one piece of equipment—maybe it's your grill or maybe you want to try cooking on a plancha. Cook on it every week, every day if you can, until you know that piece of equipment and feel confident using it. Then decide which type of grilling equipment you'd like to master next.

TOOLS

You'll need these every time you cook over fire.

CHARCOAL STARTER CHIMNEY

A simple, inexpensive metal cylinder with small openings at its base, the chimney is a much better way of starting charcoal than dousing it with lighter fluid. I have two of these, so I can ignite a good amount of charcoal at one time. (See Igniting Charcoal, page 42, for directions on how to use a charcoal starter chimney.)

CUTTING BOARDS

Big cuts of meat call for oversize cutting boards. Keep your fingers safe by not carving or chopping a leg of lamb or whole pig on a too-small board. Care for your cutting boards by wiping them every 3 to 6 months with an oil specially made for cutting blocks. See Resources, page 218, for sources for cutting boards and cutting block oil.

FIRE EXTINGUISHER OR A
WATER SOURCE NEXT TO THE GRILL

A fire extinguisher is always a good idea. Make sure yours has been tested within six months and keep it where the kids can't get to it. If you don't have an extinguisher, set up a hose attached to a spigot, and test it to make sure it reaches the grill before you start a fire. If you don't have a water source, fill a five-gallon bucket with water and place it next to the grill. Chances are you won't need it, but better to be prepared. It's also wise to keep a spray bottle filled with water beside the grill to handle small flare-ups.

FIREPROOF GLOVES

Choose well-made gloves with long cuffs or gauntlets to protect your forearms. Make sure the gloves you buy are well-made and well-padded but still flexible; the gloves that protect your hands from flame are not where you want to save a few pennies. Always have two pairs ready so when you need a friend to help you, their hands are covered too.

I take good care of my grilling gloves, storing them in a drawer so I know where they are when I need them.

GRILL BASKETS

When grilling delicate fillets of fish, young asparagus, or even a dozen meatballs, a grill basket can make it easier to flip your food. A grill basket is also the best way to grill pasta (see page 61). Look for baskets with sturdy hinges and handles and evenly woven mesh when buying.

GRILL BRUSH

A clean grill rack means better grill marks and less chance for food to stick. The best way to clean the rack is with a sturdy grill brush (see page 42 for tips on cleaning the rack). If you don't have a grill brush, a wadded-up piece of aluminum foil works in a pinch, although a real brush does a better job.

LARGE, HEAT-PROOF PLATTERS

Before you put food on the grill, have platters ready for it. To keep harmful bacteria away from your cooked food, never use the same plates and platters that held raw meat, fish, or poultry for the final cooked product. I use baking sheets to hold food before grilling and then use platters after grilling so there's never any mistake about where the raw food has been.

LONG-HANDLED TONGS, FORKS,
AND SPATULAS

I invest in sturdy tools with long handles and comfortable heat-proof grips. When you're cooking with fire, flimsy tools are not an option.

MATCHES

Don't fool around with souvenir matchbooks when you're ready to cook. Buy a box of serious matches that are long enough to light the fire without singeing your fingers.

 ### METAL ASH BUCKET

Have heat-proof containers ready for ash or hot tools, and make sure they are off-limits and out of reach of any children.

PIZZA STONE

A pizza stone is usually either earthenware or ceramic, and it gives the bottom of a pizza crust its crisp, even texture. I wouldn't even try to cook a pizza over a fire without a stone.

I have pizza stones that have lasted for years but I've also cracked a few of them. To keep them intact, handle them gently and try not to place a hot stone on a cold surface or a cool stone on a very hot grill. Because a pizza stone is porous, don't ever use detergent to wash it because it will absorb the odor and flavor of the soap. Instead, wait for the stone to cool completely, then scrub with a dry brush or a damp cloth.

SMOKING GUN

I add smoke flavor to ketchup, cheese, cocktails, and salt using my smoking gun. (See The Smoking Gun, page 201, for more information about how to use one.) A smoking gun is a handheld battery-operated appliance that generates smoke by burning small wood chips that you set on top of the gun's heating element. It comes with a hose to attach to the gun's nozzle. The hose makes it easy to aim smoke where you need it.

You'll want to create a smoking chamber where the food will sit to absorb the smoke's flavor. If you have a glass bell jar, this is an ideal use for it. If you don't have a bell jar, create a smoke chamber by covering a bowl with plastic wrap. Lift one edge of the wrap, insert the smoking gun's hose, then reseal the plastic wrap around the hose to keep the smoke inside with the food.

THERMOMETERS

I use a probe thermometer to test that big pieces of meat are done. Laser and instant-read thermometers can be helpful too.

GRILLS AND GRILL EQUIPMENT

If you don't already own a grill, don't rush out and buy one; you can make your own. Live-fire cooking is about harnessing flame, not firing up your credit card. People cooked over fire thousands of years before the propane tank came along.

Having said that, here are my recommendations for grills, starting with the simplest. For sources for the following equipment, see Resources, page 218.

THE DIY GRILL

You can make your own grill using a heavy cast-iron grate and heat-proof stones or bricks.

 I've cooked at an event where we lined our fire pits with river rocks, started the fire, and put in the pork. When those river rocks started exploding, and our very well-heeled guests were dodging pork leg and river-rock shrapnel, it didn't matter how well I'd marinated the pig. Err on the side of caution and know for a fact that your rocks or bricks don't contain moisture.

THE HIBACHI OR URBAN BALCONY GRILL

The hibachi, a simple and inexpensive piece of equipment, lets city dwellers cook over charcoal. See The Urban Grill, page 46. Modern hibachis have some great features, including the ability to fold up for storage.

THE KETTLE GRILL

The next step up is a kettle grill, most commonly called by the brand name Weber. There's a reason all of us have cooked over these iconic grills at one time or another. They are convenient, affordable, and do a great job.

TOP-OF-THE-LINE WOOD-BURNING GRILL

When you're ready for a beautifully made wood-burning grill, my choice would be the Aztec Grill. The Aztec has an air-flow system that lets you control the radiant heat and burns fuel very efficiently. It reaches higher temperatures than most wood-burning grills, especially good when cooking big cuts of meat.

You'll notice I haven't mentioned propane-fueled grills. If you have one, don't worry; the recipes in this book will do your grill proud. But propane doesn't give you the same flavor as cooking over a wood fire. I own a propane grill and find myself using it when I haven't planned ahead. For an immediate fire, you can't beat propane, which is always there, no matter the weather (assuming that you've remembered to fill the propane tank). For the best flavor, you're going to want to light the wood or the charcoal.

FIRE PIT

Fire pits can be simple; the original fire pits were a hole dug in the ground. These days you have lots of fire pit options from portable to permanent and from DIY (dig-it-yourself) to beautifully crafted custom-made fire pits with grates that can be raised or lowered easily to let you move the food closer to or farther from the heat. The most important point is to set up a fire pit so you can cook over it. If you already own a fire pit, you can buy grates that let you cook over it, although in some cases they may have to be custom made. If you don't already own a fire pit and are interested in one, choose a model that has grill racks that can be moved closer to the flame or farther away. Read more about fire pits on page 128.

EQUIPMENT FOR COOKING AT THE HEARTH

Any home fireplace that uses wood (not pressed logs or gas) for fuel is suitable for cooking. Here are some tools that can help when you want to cook in your fireplace. Before you start cooking, spread out a few damp dish towels on your hearthstones to protect them from grease spatters and drops.

TUSCAN GRILL

A Tuscan grill is made up of a flat, low metal tray that holds the burning wood and coals, a metal frame with notches, and a grill rack with two wooden handles that let the cook easily adjust the rack so it sits farther or closer to the heat. You can cook in your fireplace without this type of grill (people have for centuries) but using this protects the bottom of your fireplace from food spills and gives you some flexibility in how you use the fire's heat.

HEARTHSIDE LEVER GRILL

A lever grill holds food over the fire without actually sitting in the flames. It's handy because it sets up easily, folds for storage, and you don't have to deal with ash when you want to put the hearth grill away and have a regular fire in your fireplace. (We don't have a photograph of this type of grill in the book but you can see it if you go to NapaStyle.com.)

HOOK

You'll need to install a sturdy hook to hold the Leg of Lamb on a String (page 86) but once you try this method, you'll want to cook other cuts of meat this way, too. Most hardware stores sell this type of hook, which is easy to install. Just make sure you get a hook that can hold up to 25 pounds, and install it according to the manufacturer's directions. Use the drill bit size that the manufacturer recommends to make a hole for the hook, and epoxy the hook into the drilled hole at least a few days before you hang anything from it so the epoxy has time to cure and dry.

DRIPPINGS PAN

Before basting the leg of lamb with salt water, set out pans to protect hearthstones from the drippings. A baking sheet or two will do the trick.

HOT BOX

I can't imagine cooking a whole pig or a rib fest like the one on page 149 without my hot box. I own three of them, and have been known to fire up all three at the same time.

The hot box is big enough to roast a whole pig—that's what it was designed for—but it's also ideal for a dozen chickens or a whole fish or enough ribs to feed fifty people.

This method of cooking doesn't require constant tending the way most grills do. A hot box holds in the heat, does a great job of cooking, and provides some drama when you lift out the finished product.

I also really like how portable the hot box is. Because it's on wheels and made of aluminum-lined wood, I can push it where I want it to be without needing any assistance. Bottom line: if you cook for a few dozen people on a regular basis, this might be your best live-fire tool.

ROTISSERIE OR SPITJACK

A rotisserie holds meat or vegetables (or even cake, see page 175) on a spit, rotating it over the fire for steady, even cooking. A spitjack is a specific type of stand-alone rotisserie that you can place over a fire pit or a campfire.

When buying a rotisserie, check with the manufacturer of your grill first to see if they make a rotisserie that fits your grill. See more about rotisseries on page 164.

ROTISERRIE CAGE

Most rotisserie cages cost less than thirty dollars. I've also seen folks make their own cages by punching holes in a number ten can (the largest-size commercial can) but these days some cans are coated with enamels inside that could be toxic when heated over flame, so use caution if you attempt to make a cage.

Using a cage is simple. You slide the spin rod through the cage, and secure it. (Usually they click into place.) Then snap the spin rod into place on your grill. Open the cage's hatch and pour in the Brussels sprouts or peppers, or whatever you want to cook. Close up the hatch and start the rotisserie.

PLANCHA

A plancha is a simple thick slab of metal made to rest over a flame. I use a plancha just about every time I cook with fire because it gives me a good amount of space to cook and also provides a gorgeous crust on foods, from cauliflower to steaks, that I don't get by cooking right on the grill rack. To me the plancha is like moving my stove outside.

Measure your grill before buying a plancha so you know you're ordering the right size. (For more detailed information, see Using a Plancha, page 104.)

TO ME THE PLANCHA IS LIKE MOVING MY STOVE OUTSIDE.

MESQUITE ↓

CHIARELLO FAMILY VINEYARDS
NAPA VALLEY

HILLS BROS

↓ APRICOT ↓   APPLE WOOD CHIPS ↑   OLIVE OIL ↑

DAD'S GRILLING PANTRY ☠ NO TOYS ☠ NO TOUCH ☠

Three Stars
A/S JUTLANDIA CHEESE COMPANY SKJODSTRUP
DANISH BLUE CHEESE
PRODUCT OF DENMARK

↑ OAK ↑   ↑ CHERRY

I have two kinds of pantries. The first one is outside, where I store my woods, charcoal, grapevine canes, and all my grilling equipment. The other pantry is the normal one, indoors in my kitchen.

THE OUTDOOR PANTRY

Wood smoke is the secret ingredient to outdoor cooking. With wood as the fuel, you can cook more satisfying dishes from just a few ingredients because the flavor of smoke infuses the food. When you consider that every type of wood adds its own specific flavor to your food, it makes sense to set up a pantry for hardwoods and charcoal.

You pair food and wood just as you would pair food and wine. I'll often pair a wine to the wood I will cook over as well as to the food on the menu. For wine-tasting dinners, I'll grill food over canes from the vineyards where the wines' grapes grew.

Some wood-food pairings are obvious, like cherry wood and lamb. Any protein that loves fruit flavor—ham, pork, lamb—benefits from fruit wood smoke. Oak is my go-to wood; it's my gray salt, the wood I turn to most often.

WOOD-FOOD-WINE PAIRINGS
Here are a few wood pairings that I follow.

WOOD	FOOD PAIRING	WINE PAIRING
Alder	Fish, especially salmon	Chardonnay
Apple	Bacon, ham, pork	Petite Syrah
	Wild boar	An old-vine red
Cherry	Lamb or ham	Pinot Noir
Hickory	BBQ or roasted chicken	Zinfandel
Nut	Wild game birds	Barbaresco
	Goat	Rosé
Pecan	Quail, dove	Barolo
Almond, Hazelnut	Pheasant	Merlot
Oak	Beef	Cabernet Sauvignon
	Venison	Malbec
Stone fruit	Light seafood	Sémillon Blanc
Wine canes – Cabernet Sauvignon	Beef	Cabernet Sauvignon
Wine canes – Zinfandel	Pork, ham, or lamb	Zinfandel

WOODS TO NEVER COOK OVER
- Pine, cedar, fir, or wood from any resinous tree: These give off a bitter smoke that leaves a bad taste on food.
- Willow: Contains too much water.
- Oleander: Poisonous.
- Mountain laurel: Poisonous.
- Bay: Imparts a bitter flavor.
- Wood that's been treated with any kind of paint, finish, lacquer, or chemical.
- Wood that's been stored near gasoline, turpentine, or other flammable liquids.
- Damp or moldy wood that hasn't been protected from rain.

CHOOSING AND STORING WOOD

For cooking it's best to use seasoned hardwood. Seasoned wood is simply wood that has had at least six months to dry. Wood seasoned for six months to two years offers the most consistent, hot, long-burning flame. Wood that is unseasoned (or green) has a higher moisture content, doesn't burn as hot or evenly, and lets off more smoke. For the cooking fires we'll use in this book, seasoned hardwood is the way to go.

Firewood needs to be stored in a dry spot. If storing wood indoors, keep it away from anything that emits fumes such as paint, gasoline, or power mowers. Don't store wood near a heat source such as a water heater.

Whether storing wood indoors or outdoors, keep it elevated off the floor or ground, either on shelving or palettes. You can create your own palettes by resting solid two-by-fours on bricks, and then stacking the wood on the two-by-fours. The goal is to let air circulate beneath the wood.

If storing wood outdoors, protect it from rain or snow by covering it with a tarp. If you're starting with green wood that you want to season yourself, leave it uncovered during the summer months and let the sun and wind help dry the wood.

If you live someplace where wood can't dry between showers, store firewood under cover.

WHEN TO SEEK
OUT FRUIT TRIMMINGS

All fruit farmers have to prune their trees, generally in the fall or spring. That's when to head out to the country. (And every town has country at some point. If you live in New York City, call your favorite winery out on Long Island and ask when they'll be pruning their vines. Choose that day to go taste their wines, buy a case, and ask for some trimmings.)

These days many farmers use chippers. If you see wood being chipped, stop and ask if you can gather up a few bags of chips. Keep wood chips in cloth or burlap bags stored elevated on shelving or palettes, in a spot where they're protected from moisture.

CHOOSING AND
STORING CHARCOAL

All charcoal is not created equal. For example, chunks of mesquite charcoal from Texas add a richer, smokier flavor than charcoal briquettes.

I rarely use briquettes. I prefer lump charcoal, and tend to buy Lazzari brand (see Resources, page 218). What's the difference between lump charcoal and briquettes? It's like the difference between gray salt and table salt. Just as gray salt is less refined, so is lump charcoal closer to its natural state. For lump charcoal, wood (and only wood) is heated to a temperature high enough to drive out all the volatile chemicals, leaving behind big chunks of carbon. In making briquettes, the carbon chunks are then ground up, mixed with fillers (such as corn cobs), and pressed into the familiar pillow shape.

The advantage to briquettes is they're cheaper than lump charcoal and they burn more consistently. Because lump charcoal comes in chunks of varying size, it won't burn quite as evenly as briquettes. On the other hand, briquettes can't reach the high temperatures you can get with lump charcoal, and briquettes leave a lot more ash. Lump charcoal burns more cleanly (leaving less ash) and imparts a better taste than the briquettes I've cooked with.

Charcoal is a valuable resource. I store my charcoal just like I'd store my wine—in a cool, dry spot. If you leave your charcoal outdoors, sitting in the half-empty bag it came in, exposed to sun, air, and moisture, your fire won't burn as hot and your cooking won't be as consistent.

When you're done grilling for the day, wrap up your unused charcoal in a plastic garbage bag or store it in an airtight bin so the next time you grill, the charcoal burns cleanly and steadily.

FOR AN ITALIAN, A WELL-STOCKED PANTRY MEANS A SENSE OF WELL-BEING.

THE INDOOR PANTRY

For an Italian, a well-stocked pantry means a sense of well-being. It's not just being prepared for any kind of contingency that makes my full pantry so satisfying. For me, there's a sense of accomplishment when I open the door and see the stocked shelves. My full pantry inspires me, comforts me, and makes me feel ready to handle whatever gets thrown my way.

Don't forget that your pantry extends beyond the cupboard door. My freezer is a valuable part of my pantry, and I know I can always find stock, bread crumbs, compound butter, and my nonna's tomato sauce waiting in my freezer until I need them.

ANCHOVIES

I prefer salt-packed anchovies. When you open the container, hold the fish under cold running water and use your fingers to coax apart the two fillets down the back. Lift out the skeleton, toss it, rinse the fillets, and pat dry.

BEANS, DRIED

Seek out unusual heirloom varieties at farmers' markets and in specialty stores. I store all my beans in airtight containers and date them, noting when I purchased them. Beans are best when cooked within a year from the time they're dried.

BREAD AND BREAD CRUMBS

I like country-style bread, which means loaves with a good, sturdy crust and a dense, chewy interior. Buy breads that contain nothing but flour, water, yeast, and salt. You can typically find this bread at a bakery, although premium grocery stores often carry good breads as well.

When your bread grows stale, make bread crumbs by slicing the bread into cubes and then grinding them in your food processor to the coarseness you want. I spread them on a baking sheet, freeze them, and then seal them up in the bags. Frozen bread crumbs keep for up to 1 month.

CALABRIAN CHILE PASTE

This has a smoky flavor and a warm rich spiciness that isn't overwhelmingly hot. Look for the words *silafunghi, specialità dalla Calabria,* or *peperoncino tritato piccante* on the jar. If you can't find these, seek out chiles from Calabria. See Resources, page 218.

CAPERS

I prefer salt-packed capers. Rinse them in cool water and let them drain in a fine-mesh strainer before using.

CHEESE

Whenever you see the word *Parmesan* in this book, know that I'm using the real thing, Reggiano. Look at the rind of the cheese for those two words: Parmigiano-Reggiano. You cheat yourself when you buy poor substitutes; the taste and texture of true Reggiano is one of life's great pleasures.

Don't think of this as just a grating cheese—it's a cheese tray choice as well. I bring wedges of Parmigiano-Reggiano to room temperature and serve it to guests.

CHOCOLATE

Whether buying milk or dark chocolate, bring the best flavor to your desserts by choosing a premium brand such as Scharffen Berger, Callebaut, or Valrhona. Wrap chocolate well and store it in a cool dark spot.

MUSHROOMS, DRIED

I always keep dried porcinis on hand. The ones from Italy are the best. Soak the mushrooms in warm—not hot—water for 15 to 30 minutes before using them. After soaking, strain the liquid through a paper coffee filter and add it to your recipe for a woodsy flavor that I love. Store dried mushrooms in an airtight container for up to one year.

NUTS

I buy both raw nuts and roasted nuts. Some nuts, such as pine nuts, I toast myself just before cooking (see page 58). I also always have walnuts, hazelnuts, and pistachios, as well as Marcona almonds from Spain in my pantry, already roasted and ready to serve. I know many folks like to store their nuts in the freezer. I don't. I keep my nuts in airtight containers in my pantry because I go through them fairly quickly.

OLIVE OIL

I mainly use three types of olive oil in my kitchens: everyday extra-virgin olive oil, special-use extra-virgin olive oil, and "pure" olive oil. Throughout this book, in each recipe I've noted whether you should use extra-virgin olive oil.

My everyday extra-virgin olive oil is relatively inexpensive, especially if you buy by the jug and store in a cool, dark place.

I save pricier extra-virgin olive oils for use as a condiment, drizzling it on steaks, white beans, or pasta just before serving.

A third type of olive oil, called "pure," has a lighter, milder flavor. This olive oil doesn't have the words "extra-virgin" on the label; it generally comes in 3-liter tins like the ones you see on page 134. This oil can reach a higher temperature without smoking and adds a lighter flavor to foods that I don't want to overwhelm with a stronger olive oil. Paler than extra-virgin oils, and straw-colored, this is the oil to use if a recipe in this book calls for "olive oil" (with no mention of extra-virgin).

OLIVES

I like kalamatas from Greece, gaetas from Italy, and picholines from France, all brine-cured. I also like the wrinkly dry-cured olives (also called oil-cured) that you find in every country circling the Mediterranean Sea.

I buy olives with pits, because the pits help preserve the olive's flavor and texture. Most olives can be pitted easily; if a pit is stubborn, use a cleaver to lightly smash the olive, which should loosen its hold on the pit.

Once you open olives, store them in an airtight container in your fridge, and keep them submerged in brine.

PASTA, DRIED

I love making fresh pasta dough but I also keep dried pasta at home. The trick is to buy good-quality dried pasta. Lower-quality dried pasta is bland and becomes soggy and overcooked too quickly while good pasta gives you some leeway with its cooking time.

I buy dried pasta from artisan producers such as Rustichella d'Abruzzo. Pasta from Barilla, another Italian producer, can be found in many grocery stores and is better than most of what you'll find on the shelf.

Both Rustichella d'Abruzzo and Barilla shape their pasta with bronze dies, rather than the Teflon-coated dies used by most pasta producers in the United States. The bronze gives the pasta a very faintly textured surface (you can see this if you look under a magnifying glass). This lets the pasta "hold on" to sauces better. Both of these producers also air dry their pasta very slowly, which means pasta still has some "chew" when it emerges from the water. This gives the cook some flexibility: you can leave a high-quality pasta in hot water for an extra minute or two while you finish a sauce and it won't lose shape or texture.

SALT

Salt is the only ingredient that goes in everything you cook and bake. The simpler your food, the more important it is that each ingredient be stellar, and this is especially true of your salt.

I use gray salt every single day and even take it on the road with me when I travel. What is gray salt? It's an unprocessed sea salt from Brittany that retains all the minerals found in the sea. Gray salt is moist and almost lavender in color and it's collected by hand just as it has been for centuries. Gray salt is worth seeking

out because its natural flavor is much more than just "saltiness." True Brittany sea salt has flavor notes of algae and violets. Those flavor notes benefit everything you cook.

Because gray salt is moist and coarse, it's more of a challenge to distribute evenly. I dry it by spreading 2 to 4 cups of salt on a baking sheet and letting it sit in a 200°F oven for 2 hours, then I pound the salt or grind it in a spice grinder until it's medium-coarse. I store the salt that I've dried and pounded in airtight containers in my pantry until it's time to replenish my salt box that sits next to my stove.

TOMATOES

I always have cans of plump Marzano whole tomatoes in my pantry. In the summer, I don't use these often; I pick tomatoes off the vine as needed. But in winter, these cans are opened every week.

I never buy diced or puréed tomatoes and rarely use tomato paste, preferring to push whole canned tomatoes through a food mill just before cooking. It takes about 1½ pounds of fresh plum tomatoes to make 2 cups of purée. A 28-ounce can of whole Marzano tomatoes makes about 3½ cups purée. If you find *passata* (Italian tomato purée) in jars or bottles imported from Italy, buy a case and stock up. Otherwise, you'll see a recipe for passata on page 213.

I'm a big fan of Muir Glen's organic canned tomatoes. Because Muir Glen uses enamel-lined cans rather than unlined tin, there's no worry about off flavors.

VINEGAR

Invest in high-quality vinegars; the wrong vinegar can ruin a beautiful salad. Taste vinegars and find brands that you like. Bad wine vinegar (and there are a lot of bad vinegars out there) taste harsh, with an unpleasant aroma. Good wine vinegar is fruity, aromatic, and mellow.

Balsamic vinegar is one of my kitchen essentials. I keep an aged *aceto balsamico tradizionale* for sprinkling sparingly over Parmesan cheese or a grilled steak. I also stock a moderately priced, younger balsamic vinegar to use more freely in vinaigrettes. Avoid inexpensive balsamic vinegar—it's often nothing more than wine vinegar and caramel. Look for reputable brands from Modena, Italy, and taste vinegar until you find one that's rich, dark, and glossy, with hints of wood from the casks in which the vinegar aged, and an almost sweet flavor and depth. Check the label to see how many years a balsamic vinegar has been aged. Don't buy balsamic vinegar that has been aged for fewer than 12 years. A vinegar aged for 25 years should have a creamy, full-bodied flavor, and a hundred-year-old *balsamico* is a thing of beauty.

A HUNDRED-YEAR-OLD BALSAMICO IS A THING OF BEAUTY.

CHAPTER ONE

BUILDING THE FIRE

Every family has iconic events: a family reunion, a daughter getting married, a fiftieth wedding anniversary. You want the memories from these events to last a lifetime. A rented hall, a caterer hired for the big event—these are sometimes necessary. But if you can, I urge you to bring the meal outside and let the time spent building the fire become part of the day's memories.

Fire is itself an icon. To center a meal around a fire marks an occasion, and sears the day into your memory. No single food can bring light, warmth, and meaning to a gathering the way fire can.

THE FIRE
AND THE
CROSS

THE FUEL

The best fire for cooking is a wood fire. All things being equal—time, resources, the weather—I would cook over a wood fire all the time if I could.

It's hard to be spiritual about a six-burner restaurant-grade stove, but when a fire warms your face and the stars fill the sky overhead, small worries vanish and wonder takes over.

There's a flavor edge to cooking with wood that you don't get anywhere else. If I burn apple wood or the kiln-dried Cabernet canes from my own vineyards, these contribute their character to a great cut of beef or a whole game bird.

For big parties, I'll often combine wood and charcoal, starting with a charcoal fire and adding wood later. Charcoal forms a more even, longer-lasting coal bed than wood alone, so a combination fire can give you the best of both worlds.

Don't start cooking over wood until the fire has burned to coals. Decades ago, I was smacked down by a critic, and rightfully so, when I cooked over wood that hadn't burned down far enough. The critic wrote that my food had a "creosote flavor." Thinking about that review still makes me wince. Be sure your wood has transformed to glowing coals before you put any food on the fire. Add new wood to the back of the fire, and rake it forward when it's ready.

ONE IMPORTANT POINT: Always have a good supply of dry kindling and small and large logs nearby. It's not optimal to be hunting for fuel when your meat is on the fire.

HOW TO START A FIRE

Before you start any fire, read Stay Safe, page 10. Stand in the spot where you plan to build the fire and make sure the ground is clear, with no brush, grasses, or trees within 30 feet.

Check the direction of the wind. If the wind blows straight from your fire pit to where your guests will sit, consider locating the fire so the smoke will blow away from your dining table—or move the table.

I start a fire with the smallest, most easily ignited fuel first. I crumple up four or five sheets of newspaper, and then put down tall, thin pieces of kindling so one end rests on the ground and the other end rests on the crumpled paper. Then I add larger pieces of kindling, again leaning them so they touch the ground at the bottom and the tips come together at the top above the paper. You're aiming for a kind of teepee shape. Add a few thin logs the same way, and then light a long piece of kindling and use it to set the paper at the fire's center ablaze. Wait until the fire is really going before you add medium-size logs, and wait until those catch and are burning well before adding big logs to the fire.

DON'T START COOKING OVER WOOD UNTIL THE FIRE HAS BURNED TO COALS.

USING AN
IRON
CROSS

An iron cross works as a frame, holding a whole lamb open beside a fire so it cooks evenly and thoroughly. For this book, we've used an iron cross made of a vertical iron bar with two horizontal crossbars welded in place. (I've also seen a frame that looks like an X, with each of the lamb's legs secured to one branch of the X.) ❖ Roasting a lamb on an iron cross is not a one-man operation. Have at least one buddy (male or female) ready to help you; having two or three friends nearby is even better. Read The Lore of the Night Before, page 36, if you hesitate to ask for help. Being asked to take part in the big lamb dinner prep is an honor, not a chore.

FINDING AN IRON CROSS
See Resources, page 218, for where to order an iron cross. You could save yourself some shipping charges if you find a metal worker near you to fabricate one (do an Internet search for "blacksmith" plus the name of your town). If you know any horse people, most good farriers should be able to make an iron cross to these specifications: 7-foot vertical bar (about 2 inches wide) with 1⅛-inch-diameter holes. The crossbars should be 3 feet across, 1-inch outside diameter to fit the holes in the vertical bar. Take this book, show them the photo, and have them weld a cross. Long before the day of the party, you should check to make sure the crossbar is welded firmly to the vertical bar.

You could dig a deep, narrow hole and stand the iron cross in the ground like a fencepost right over the fire. I prefer to use metal stands made of heavy cast iron to hold up the highest end of the cross because they give me more flexibility to adjust the meat over the heat (see photo, facing page). The stands I use have brackets to hold the top of the cross firmly. Look for this type of metal stand in hardware stores or photography supply stores, or see Resources, page 218.

SEEKING OUT A WHOLE LAMB
It's worth visiting a farmers' markets to find someone local who raises lambs. You also can order whole or half lambs from Heritage Foods (see Resources, page 218), and be confident that the lambs were raised in a way that considers the planet as well as the animal.

When you order whole lamb, plan on slightly less than 1 pound per person. During a recent wine auction dinner, I ordered 130 pounds of whole lamb for 150 people. (The average 100-pound lamb yields about 35 pounds of meat.)

If you're serving fewer than thirty people, go with one or two baby lambs; they're much easier to truss and handle than a full-size lamb.

WHOLE LAMB ON AN IRON CROSS
WITH MINT PESTO AND CHILE-FENNEL TZATZIKI

Serves 30 to 40

When I consider all the people, throughout centuries, who have used this method to cook a lamb, I feel like one small dot in a very long timeline. This is a 30-log kind of a fire. To be safe have 3 dozen logs, each about 6 inches in diameter and each completely dry, stacked, and ready before you bring home the lamb. For more information on finding an iron cross, see Using an Iron Cross, page 28, as well as Resources, page 218. ❖ The basting liquid makes enough for two 20-pound lambs or one lamb or pig up to 45 pounds. I love the flavor butcher's salt adds to the basting liquid. Butcher's salt is a blend of salt and spices from France made especially for meat. See Resources, page 218, for butcher's salt, or use a smaller amount of black pepper in its place. ❖ In a perfect world, you'd baste the lamb while it cooks using a branch of rosemary as your brush. Silicone basting brushes—as big as you can get—do the job just fine too.

Two 20-pound lambs or 1 lamb or pig up to 45 pounds

BASTING LIQUID
1 loosely packed cup fresh sage leaves
½ cup fresh rosemary sprigs
½ cup fresh thyme sprigs
4 cups fresh flat-leaf parsley
2 cups fresh mint
1½ cups fresh oregano
8 garlic cloves
1 tablespoon kosher salt
1 tablespoon butcher's salt (see headnote)
   or ½ tablespoon coarsely ground black pepper
2 cups olive oil
2 cups dry white wine
6 bay leaves, fresh or dried
Mint Pesto (see page 32)
Chile-Fennel Tzatziki (see page 32)

FOR THE BASTING LIQUID: In a food processor, or in a blender in batches, combine the sage, rosemary, thyme, parsley, mint, oregano, garlic, kosher salt, and butcher's salt or pepper. Process to a coarse purée. With the machine running, add the oil and wine and purée until smooth. Transfer the liquid to a container with a lid, add the bay leaves, and refrigerate until the lamb goes on the fire.

SETTING UP FOR THE LAMB: When you're ready to start cooking, clean the lamb, but don't tie it to the cross until you've started the fire. (See How to Start a Fire, page 26.) When the fire is ready for the big logs, add them and then fasten the lamb onto the cross while the fire burns down a little. Look at the fires I have under my lambs in the photo on page 29; the fire you need to build won't be the size of a bonfire but just big enough to provide steady, even heat for the 4 hours that the lamb will cook.

Have one or two friends hold the lamb up against the vertical bar, with the lamb's shoulders toward the ground, while you tie each of the four legs to a crossbar (see the photo on facing page). The back of the lamb should be against the cross; the ribs should be facing out toward the fire. Use a heavy-gauge wire (at least 16-gauge, found in any hardware store) to securely tie each leg to a crossbar and then use the wire to fasten the neck to the center, vertical bar.

When the fire has died down slightly so it's not raging flames, maneuver the iron cross into place so it's close to the fire but not right on top of it. Use your hands to test that the lamb is close enough to the heat to cook. You'll want to allow at least 4 to 5 hours for a lamb that weighs 30 to 45 pounds and 6 hours for a lamb that weighs more than 45 pounds.

Check the fire periodically. If it begins to cool, add logs but always add new wood to the edge of the fire farthest from the iron cross; you don't want flaming logs under the lamb. When the new wood glows red and is no longer emitting lots of smoke and flame, then rake it forward closer to the lamb.

Don't rely on time alone to determine when the meat is done. For medium-rare lamb, it's done when the meat registers 145°F on a meat or probe thermometer. Take the lamb off the fire and let it rest for 15 minutes before you begin to carve.

If you have an iron cross with rings, slide each of the animal's legs through the rings. Secure each leg by twining 16-gauge stainless steel picture wire around the leg and the crossbar. (You can find wire in your local hardware store.)

 Don't use a wire that's too lightweight to hold the animal and don't use wire with any kind of coating on it.

Have a large heat-proof surface ready for the lamb. A butcher block table is ideal. Ask a friend or two to help plate the lamb as you carve.

TO CARVE: First untie the wire from the lamb and discard it. Cut away the hind legs at the joint; the meat should be tender enough so this is easy. Next, carve at the shoulder, working down toward the front legs. Cut away the front legs, and then carve the lamb one section at a time, working from the ribs toward the backbone.

MINT PESTO

Makes about 1¼ cups

There's a reason mint jelly has been served with lamb for generations: it's the ideal complement to the rich, savory roasted meat. This delicious pesto has a much stronger fresh mint flavor than any store-bought jelly. ❖ You can find ascorbic acid in health food stores. It works better than anything I've found to keep this pesto bright green.

SIMPLE SYRUP
½ cup water
½ cup granulated sugar

3 cups fresh mint
½ cup packed fresh flat-leaf parsley
1 tablespoon toasted pine nuts (see page 58)
½ teaspoon minced garlic
¹⁄₁₆ teaspoon ascorbic acid or finely ground vitamin C
½ cup extra-virgin olive oil
2 tablespoons Simple Syrup
¼ teaspoon coarse sea salt, preferably gray salt
⅛ teaspoon freshly ground black pepper

FOR THE SIMPLE SYRUP: In a small pan over high heat bring the water and sugar to a boil. Stir until the sugar is dissolved, and then take the pan off the heat and set aside.

Bring about 2 quarts of water to a boil in a stockpot over high heat. While the water heats, set up an ice bath—a large bowl full of ice and water. When the water boils, blanch the mint for 30 seconds. With a slotted spoon transfer it from the hot water to the ice bath. Blanch the parsley for 30 seconds and then transfer it to the ice bath. Remove the herbs from the cold water and squeeze into a ball to remove excess moisture. Roughly chop them.

In a large, heavy-duty blender or a food processor, blend the mint, parsley, pine nuts, garlic, and ascorbic acid, pulsing just until combined. With the machine running, pour in the olive oil very slowly. Pour in 2 tablespoons of the simple syrup. (Refrigerate the remaining simple syrup and use it for cocktails or to sweeten coffee or tea.) Add salt and pepper to the pesto, taste, and season with more salt and pepper or simple syrup if you like.

CHILE-FENNEL TZATZIKI

Makes 3 cups

In Greece, whenever you're served lamb, it comes with the refreshing yogurt sauce known as tzatziki. The rich hot lamb and the cool, creamy sauce are made for each other. I gave this an Italian twist by adding fennel, roasted lemon juice, and Calabrian chiles. Use a traditional thick Greek-style yogurt, such as Fage, and use the green fronds at the top of your fennel to give this extra flavor and color. ❖ For more flavor grate the cucumber, catching all the juices for the tzatziki. I like to make this at least an hour ahead of time so it can chill before serving.

1 juicy lemon, halved
1 small fennel bulb with green fronds
2 cups Greek-style yogurt
1 teaspoon minced garlic
1 large whole peeled cucumber or 2 small whole
   peeled cucumbers
1 teaspoon Calabrian chile paste, or ¼ teaspoon
   red pepper flakes
¼ teaspoon coarse sea salt, preferably gray salt
⅛ teaspoon freshly ground black pepper

On a hot grill or in a cast-iron pan over a fire or on the stove, place the lemon halves cut-side down. Cook until the lemon shows some char, 4 to 5 minutes. When the lemons have cooled, juice them and then strain the juice to get rid of some of the char. Measure about 1 tablespoon of the roasted lemon juice and reserve the remaining juice.

Trim the fennel. Cut the white part into ¼-inch dice (about 1 cup); coarsely chop the green fronds (about 1 tablespoon).

In a medium bowl, mix the 1 tablespoon strained lemon juice with the diced fennel, yogurt, and garlic. Grate the peeled cucumber into a measuring cup, catching all the juice that you can. Add the grated cuke and its juice to the bowl when you have about 1 cup. (A little less or extra is fine.) Stir in the chopped fennel fronds, chile paste, salt, and pepper. Taste and then add another few teaspoons of roasted lemon juice or more salt and pepper if you like.

Cover with plastic wrap, refrigerate, and chill for at least an hour or overnight. Stir just before serving.

ROSEMARY PARMESAN FLATBREAD
WITH
BURRATA AND TORN FIGS

Serves 6 as an appetizer

Use the pizza dough recipe on page 94 or buy dough from your local pizzeria. Once the dough is on hand, this couldn't be easier or faster to make.

Two 6-ounce balls of Pizza Dough (page 94)
1 teaspoon fresh rosemary
2 tablespoons finely grated Parmesan
½ pound Burrata
6 whole ripe figs
Coarse sea salt, preferably gray salt
Freshly ground black pepper

Press together the balls of dough and, with a rolling pin, roll into a large, thin round. Carefully transfer to a hot pizza stone, close the grill lid, and bake until very crisp, 1 to 2 minutes. Take the flatbread off the pizza stone with a pizza peel or two large spatulas. Sprinkle the rosemary and parmesan over the top while it's just off the fire.

Drop spoonfuls of Burrata on top the flatbread. Tear each fig into pieces with your fingers, add to the flatbread, and finish with salt and pepper. Slice into 6 pieces with a pizza cutter.

STRAWBERRY PAZZO CAKE
WITH
HERBED CRÈME FRAÎCHE

Serves 8

Twelve years ago, I made a simple bowl of "strawberries pazzo"—*pazzo* means "crazy" in Italian—for my friend Ann Spivack (this book's co-writer). The combination of strawberries, balsamic vinegar, and black pepper has been part of my repertoire for decades. Ann thanked me by baking me this *pazzo* cake. ❖ This dessert—while easy to make—is a cut above a standard strawberry shortcake. The cake batter is very forgiving and comes out well when baked on your grill or in your oven. Bake this in a standard 8-by-8-inch baking pan in your oven; if baking inside a covered grill, pour the batter into a cast-iron skillet, enameled cast-iron baking dish, or Dutch oven. ❖ The key to the herbed crème fraîche is a light touch with the fresh herbs. You don't want to overwhelm the cake. We used rosemary but small tender basil leaves are delicious too. ❖ We dressed up this cake for our Harvest Dinner by drizzling on a balsamic glaze, spooning Roasted Strawberries (page 90) onto the plate, and finishing with an herbed crème fraîche. You can serve all three with the cake, any one of them, or forget all three of them and just serve the cake simply with a light dusting of confectioners' sugar.

HERBED CRÈME FRAÎCHE

1¾ cups Crème Fraîche (page 217)

1 tablespoon minced fresh rosemary leaves
   (or minced fresh basil leaves)

PAZZO CAKE

6 tablespoons unsalted butter, at room temperature,
   plus more to grease the pan

1½ cups all-purpose flour

1½ teaspoons baking powder

½ teaspoon coarse sea salt, preferably gray salt

½ cup granulated sugar

¼ cup packed dark brown sugar

1 egg

½ cup whole milk

1 teaspoon pure vanilla extract

1 pound fresh strawberries, hulled and halved

BALSAMIC GLAZE

4 tablespoons balsamic vinegar

1 tablespoon plus 1 teaspoon granulated sugar

A few grinds of fresh black pepper

Confectioners' sugar for dusting, optional

1 cup Roasted Strawberries with syrup
   (page 90), optional

FOR THE CRÈME FRAÎCHE: Stir together the crème fraîche and the herbs. Refrigerate and let sit for 30 minutes or overnight.

FOR THE CAKE: Butter a 9-inch cast-iron skillet or 8-by-8-inch enameled cast-iron baking pan (if cooking in the grill) or standard 8-by-8-inch baking pan (if baking in your oven). (Don't put a standard baking pan inside your grill or over a fire.) Ignite the coals, turn a gas grill to high, or preheat an oven to 350°F.

Whisk together the flour, baking powder, and salt. Set aside. In the bowl of a stand mixer fitted with the paddle attachment or with an electric mixer, cream the butter and sugars on medium speed until the mixture looks creamy, about 3 minutes. Slowly add the egg, milk, and vanilla and mix just until combined. Gradually add the flour mixture, mixing just until smooth with a creamy texture.

Pour the batter into the buttered pan. Arrange the strawberry halves, cut-side down, on top of the cake batter. Don't overlap the berries; use just enough strawberries for one layer and set aside the rest to use as garnish.

TO BAKE IN A GRILL: When the grill reaches 350°F, slide in the cake, resting the pan on the grill rack, close the grill's lid and let it bake for at least 20 minutes with the grill lid closed. Test the cake: It's done when a skewer inserted into the center (but not in a strawberry) comes out clean and the cake is golden brown on top.

TO BAKE IN AN OVEN: Bake for 10 minutes and then decrease the heat to 325°F and bake for an additional 45 to 50 minutes. The cake is done when a skewer inserted into the center (but not in a strawberry) comes out clean and the cake is golden brown on top.

FOR THE GLAZE: While the cake is baking, in a small pan combine the balsamic vinegar, sugar, and black pepper. Bring to a boil over high heat and remove from the heat right away. Set it aside until the cake has baked. It should be the consistency of maple syrup; if it thickens too much before the cake comes out of the oven, stir in a few more spoonfuls of vinegar. As soon as the cake comes off the heat, drizzle the top with about three-fourths of the balsamic glaze.

When the cake has cooled, cut it into wedges if baked in a skillet; if baked in a standard baking pan, cut it into squares. To garnish simply, top with a light dusting of confectioners' sugar. To dress up the cake, spoon several tablespoons of the Roasted Strawberries onto one side of each plate; on the other side of the plate drizzle a small pool of the balsamic glaze, and smear it lightly with the back of a spoon. Drizzle more balsamic glaze over the cake if you like. Set a cake slice on top the strawberry syrup, and top the cake with a spoonful of Herbed Crème Fraîche. Spoon any remaining crème fraîche into a bowl and set on a platter with leftover halved strawberries to pass so guests can add extra if they like.

THE LORE OF THE NIGHT BEFORE

Maybe you don't need to get up in the middle of the night to start the fire. Maybe you don't need two bottles of Napa's finest Cab for the evening to be seared into your memory. Probably you don't need the fifth of Maker's Mark to wash down the smoke.

What you do need is the story of what comes before the meal.

When Wayne Badovinus, who's a larger-than-life Montana man, had us up to his Sonoma house for a pig pickin', we showed up at 7 P.M. the night before. We divvied up the chores, building the pit from cinder blocks and rebar and shoveling a six-foot pile of sand into the center.

Wayne lit the wood, and we gathered around the pit. Hunting and fishing adventures were shared as the fire roared, the wine flowed, and the whiskey was passed from hand to hand. Everyone around the fire knew not to let the truth get in the way of a good story.

As the flames died down, so did the talking, and one by one the people around the fire dropped off. Not me. I was in it for the long haul along with Wayne and his son Nick. Four hours later, the pig started its trek to a great meal, and we put coffee on the fire to brew.

Nick readied what may be the best baked beans I've ever had in my life, in a gigantic Dutch oven, and those of us still awake stayed near the fire, breathing in the aromas of smoke, simmering beans, and crackling pork.

Something about a fire in the middle of the night gives you permission to tell a story for the hundredth time. A fire makes a joke funnier than the last ten times you heard it. The lore of the night before becomes part of the meal, savored as a first course before the pig comes off the fire.

HARVEST DINNER

Every autumn we host a harvest dinner, pouring wines from our Chiarello Family Vineyards and serving foods that best complement those wines. We invite one hundred people and set a hundred-foot table in the vineyards. We've had guests come from every continent. Some guests come every year, which means every year I try to outdo the meal I cooked the year before. Family makes the party better. That's me with my brother, Kevin, in the pink-striped shirt.

For this dinner, we're cooking whole lambs on iron crosses, each set over a fire begun hours before. Read pages 28-31 to see how to use an iron cross and for the complete recipe for the lamb. You'll find the recipes for the rest of the Harvest Dinner throughout the book. We've noted page numbers so you can find them easily.

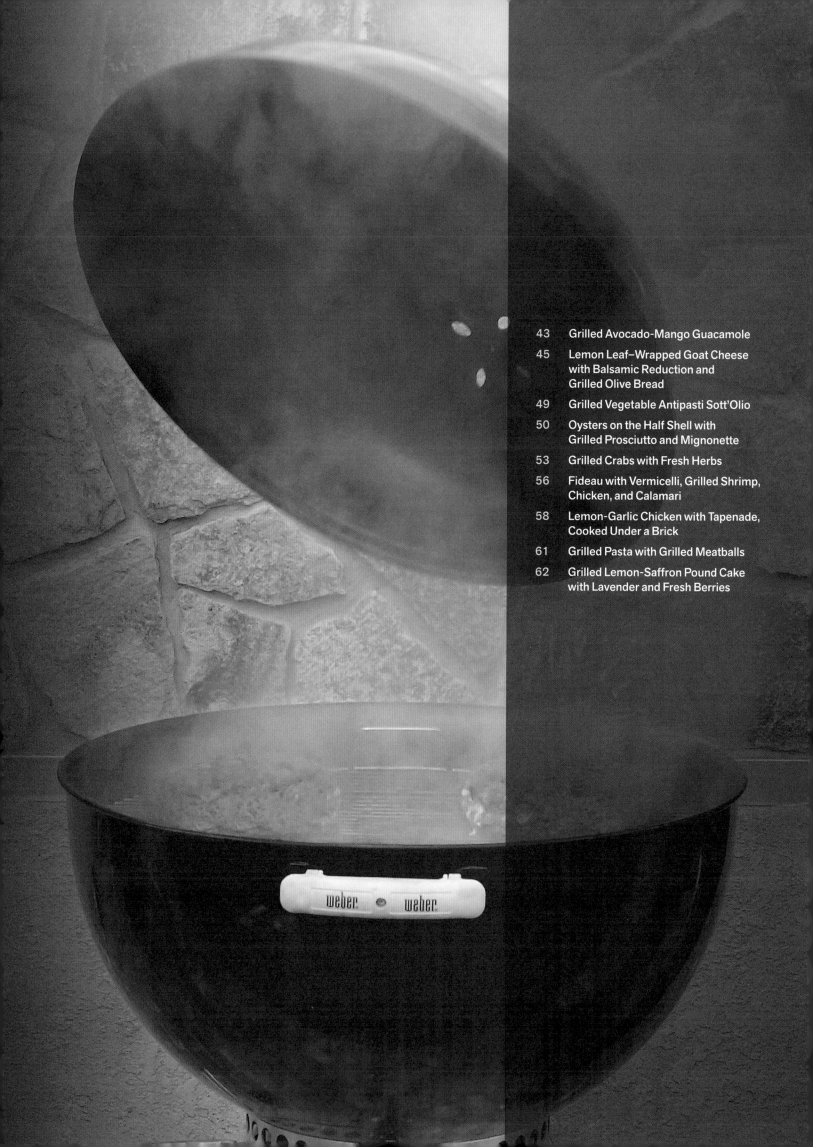

CHAPTER TWO

FIRE CONTAINED: THE GRILL

I sometimes think that fancy grills take us a step away from what matters—what matters is the fire. I read an article about a man who'd been preserved in a glacier in the Tyrolean Alps for more than 5,300 years. He was carrying a small box containing charred wood wrapped in maple leaves. The man had no fire-starting tools, like flint, so experts think he carried smoldering wood to start his next fire. That guy comes to mind whenever I cook over charcoal; I wonder what he was planning to cook over his next fire. For him, the fire was as important as—or more important than—the meal itself.

Don't let the grill come between you and the fire. The fideau (see page 56) is a good way to bring all your guests into the action. Set chairs around the grill and have everyone help snap the raw pasta into pieces. As the ingredients go into the pan—the onion and garlic, the wine, the stock, the tomato sauce—everyone experiences the sizzle of the pan, the way the aromas rise up. Plus the host gets to sip wine and chat with friends during the process. This is the best part of cooking with fire.

For all you burger aficionados, burgers get some love in this chapter. A burger bash is one of my favorite parties to throw (flip to the end of this chapter, page 65, to see recipes for the entire party).

GETTING READY TO GRILL

Before starting the fire or heating up the grill, take a few steps so your food cooks faster and tastes better. Make sure you're stocked up on fuel, with one or two bags of fresh charcoal and a spare full canister of propane if you don't have a direct gas-line hook-up.

IGNITING CHARCOAL

I avoid lighter fluid because it leaves a bad taste on my food. Instead, I ignite charcoal using a chimney starter (see page 13), which can generally be found for under twenty bucks. If you have to choose between a big chimney and a small one, choose the big one. You can always fill it just halfway with charcoal.

To use a chimney, first take the grill rack off your grill and set it aside. (You don't want to rest the chimney on your grill rack.) Crumple two full pages of newspaper or a large brown paper bag, and lightly push the paper into the base of the chimney. Set the chimney on the bottom of your grill and pour charcoal into the chimney. Strike a match and hold it through one of the openings at the bottom of the chimney until the paper ignites. The paper will light the bottom layer of charcoal, and the fire will spread upward until all the coals ignite.

If you have any trouble lighting the coals in the chimney, douse a brown paper bag or some crumpled-up newspaper with vegetable oil and push it into the chimney's base from the bottom. Most of the time you won't need to resort to oil.

When most of the coals begin to glow red but still show some gray and black on the edges, don a fireproof glove, grab the handle of the chimney, and carefully pour the burning coals into the bottom of your grill. Use a poker or tongs to spread out the glowing coals, and add a few more lumps of black coal to the coal bed.

GRILL TEMPERATURES

We've used the following notations for grill temperature. On a gas grill it's fairly easy to reduce or increase the heat. On a charcoal grill, use a thermometer to check the heat. If you need to raise the temperature, make sure the vents are open or take off the lid for a minute. To lower the temperature, close your top grill vent partway.

High 500°F to 600°F
Medium-high 450°F to 500°F
Medium 400°F to 450°F
Low 350°F to 450°F

CLEANING THE GRILL RACK

Here's my routine, which I do each time before grilling on a gas or charcoal grill: First I get my grill hot, 500°F or hotter. Let it heat for at least 10 minutes. If you're using a charcoal grill, get the coals flaming (see Igniting Charcoal, to the left) and let the fire burn with the rack in place for at least 10 minutes. When the rack is hot but the flames have died down a little, use a grill brush to scrub the bars. (Note: Don't use any brush except one made for hot surfaces. If you don't have a grill brush, wad up some foil and scrub the grill with that—a trick my mom taught me.)

After scrubbing, gather a good, thick wad of paper towels—at least 8 to 10 sheets. Dip half the wad in water—it should be wet but not dripping—and then use long-handled tongs to rub the wet towels along your grill rack.

I do this every time I grill, on any grill I use, gas or charcoal. A clean grill rack means you have clear, distinct grill marks and you're less likely to have to pry stuck-on burgers from the rack. A disciplined cook learns to clean the hot grill within a few minutes after the last food is taken off and then wipe the rungs with oil so the grill is prepped ahead for the next use.

USING YOUR GRILL VENTS

The air vents in the lid of your charcoal grill help you control the temperature inside the grill. Here's how you use them.

Open the vents all the way just before you start the fire. Once your coals are glowing, close the vent on the top just a little to lower the temperature inside. Basically, more air means higher heat. If you ever have a fire inside the grill that's out of control, close all the vents and the fire will burn itself out.

On a windy day, turn the grill's lid so the breeze flows through the vent, making your fire hotter.

The vent at the bottom should be fully open and should stay open during cooking. Close it only after you're done cooking, when you want the fire to go out as quickly as possible.

GRILLED AVOCADO-MANGO GUACAMOLE

Serves 8 to 10

At our flagship NapaStyle store in Yountville, we serve sandwiches, soups, and small bites for people to try while they're wine tasting. This version of guacamole—we actually call it "Rockamole" on our menu—flies out the door when we serve it at lunchtime. Grilled avocados and mango make this guacamole a great topping for a turkey burger (see page 70) but it's also fantastic as a chip dip or a spread for bruschetta. ❖ I add a lot of garlic. You can tone yours down by halving the garlic amount if you prefer a less garlicky guacamole.

8 ripe avocados

2 lemons, halved, for drizzling (reserve 1 tablespoon of juice for the onion)

¼ cup extra-virgin olive oil, plus more for drizzling

¾ teaspoon coarse sea salt, preferably gray salt

¼ teaspoon freshly ground black pepper

2 mangoes

½ large red onion

2 tablespoons finely minced garlic

¾ cup chiffonade of fresh basil leaves (see Chef's Note)

½ cup sour cream or Crème Fraîche (page 217)

½ cup freshly grated Parmesan cheese

Turn a gas grill to high or ignite charcoal. When the grill is hot, for both gas and charcoal grills, clean your grill rack. Decrease the temperature to medium-high (on a gas grill only), and brush or wipe a little olive oil on the grill rack.

Halve, peel, and pit the avocados. As you peel each avocado, put the flesh in a bowl and squeeze fresh lemon juice on top to keep it from oxidizing. Drizzle the avocado halves with about 1 tablespoon of the olive oil and sprinkle with salt and pepper.

Peel the mangoes and have them ready for the grill.

Halve the red onion lengthwise into 2 equal pieces (wrap one piece in plastic wrap, refrigerate, and save for another use). Cut the remaining piece crosswise into thin half-moons. Place the onion slices in a small bowl and pour over the reserved 1 tablespoon of fresh lemon juice. Toss and set aside.

With tongs, place the peeled avocados and mangoes on the grill rack. Grill until you see some grill marks, about 1 to 2 minutes, and then turn them over and grill for another minute on the other side. Take the avocados and the mangoes off the grill and set them aside to cool.

Preheat a 10-inch sauté pan at the stove or a cast-iron pan on the grill. Add ¼ cup of olive oil to the pan, add the minced garlic, and sauté until it begins to show some color. Add the basil and sauté until wilted. Transfer the garlic and basil to a large glass or ceramic bowl and allow to cool.

With a fork, mash the grilled avocado into the basil mixture. Add the sour cream or crème fraîche and stir. Add the Parmesan and stir. Dice the grilled mango after cutting away and discarding the pits. Gently stir in the mango and the red onion with its lemon juice. Taste and add more sea salt and pepper if you like.

Serve right away or cover with plastic wrap, smoothing it across the top of the guacamole to keep it from discoloring, and refrigerate until you're ready to serve. This is best served on the same day it's made.

CHEF'S NOTE: A chiffonade of fresh basil means cutting the leaves into very fine ribbons. The easiest way to do this is to align the whole washed leaves before cutting. Stack the leaves with the center vein facing down, and all the tips pointing in the same direction. Roll up the stack of leaves tightly from the side as if you were rolling a cigar, and then, starting at the tip, slice into thin ribbons.

VARIATION: Sometimes the grilled avocados and mangoes are too nice to mash. Make a salad instead with 2 cups of organic baby greens and some arugula. Toss the greens with ¼ cup of the Grilled Red Onion Dressing (page 213). Slice the grilled avocado and mangoes and arrange on top of the greens with slices of red onion.

LEMON LEAF–WRAPPED GOAT CHEESE WITH BALSAMIC REDUCTION AND GRILLED OLIVE BREAD

Serves 8

If you have a lemon tree in your yard, use the leaves to wrap up soft, creamy goat cheese before grilling. The leaves will flavor the cheese but you don't actually want to eat them. Please use leaves that have never been sprayed. If you don't have a lemon tree, beg some off a neighbor or buy grape leaves in jars from your supermarket and use them in place of the lemon leaves (see Chef's Note). ❖ Finer lemon zest is better for this recipe; I use a fine microplane grater for a light, clean zest. ❖ This recipe is simple but presents beautifully. Serve with ice-cold Falanghina (a white wine from Campania) or a rosé from your favorite wine region.

One 8-ounce log goat cheese, sliced into
   8 equal rounds (1 ounce each)
2 tablespoons finely grated lemon zest (from about 2 lemons)
½ teaspoon coarse sea salt, preferably gray salt
4 teaspoons Fennel Spice Rub (page 208)
16 large flawless lemon leaves, preferably from an
   organic source
Extra-virgin olive oil for brushing

BALSAMIC REDUCTION
½ cup balsamic vinegar

One 16-ounce loaf olive bread, cut into ½-inch-thick slices
8 small clusters sweet grapes

Line a platter with parchment paper. Set the goat cheese slices on the parchment.

In a small bowl, mix the lemon zest and salt. Sprinkle the top of each goat cheese round with the lemon-salt mixture. Turn the rounds over and sprinkle the other side with the spice rub.

Sandwich a goat cheese round between 2 lemon leaves with the shiny sides of the leaves facing away from the goat cheese. Secure the leaves at each end with toothpicks or forego the toothpicks and just turn the leaves and cheese very carefully when they're cooking. Refrigerate the cheese bundles until you're ready to grill, at least 1 hour or overnight.

FOR THE REDUCTION: I like the Chef's-Style Balsamic Reduction method (page 209). If you don't want to deal with inverted sugar, you can reduce the old-fashioned way: Heat the balsamic vinegar in a small saucepan over medium-high heat. Bring to a boil and let the liquid cook until reduced by half, 6 to 8 minutes. (The process speeds up toward the end, so don't walk away from it.) Take the pan off the heat and let the mixture cool. Skim off any foam. You should have a generous ¼ cup of balsamic syrup.

Turn a gas grill to high or ignite charcoal. When the grill is hot, for both gas and charcoal grills, clean your grill rack. Decrease the temperature to medium-high (on a gas grill only), and brush or wipe a little olive oil on the grill rack.

Before grilling the leaf-cheese bundles, grill the bread. Brush the bread slices lightly with olive oil, and heat on the rack until grill marks show, 1 to 2 minutes. Set the bread aside.

Brush each side of the leaf-cheese bundles lightly with olive oil. Place the bundles on the grill and cook for 1 to 2 minutes on each side.

Set four bundles on each platter, and add pieces of grilled bread and a cluster of grapes. Open the bundles, discard the top leaf, and spoon a little balsamic reduction over each round of cheese. Pour extra reduction into 2 small dishes or ramekins and add to the platters. Have guests spread the soft cheese on the grilled bread and drizzle on more reduction if they like (but tell them not to eat the leaves).

CHEF'S NOTE: Grape leaves work well with this method also. You can use fresh (unsprayed) grape leaves if you have access to them or use a jar of grape leaves from the market. You'll need just 1 grape leaf for each bundle. Rinse the leaves in water. With the underside of the leaf facing up, place a goat cheese round in the center of the leaf and fold over each side, then fold the tip and stem of the leaf to form a small packet. Brush with olive oil, place on a hot grill rack, and grill until you see distinct grill marks on the leaf, but not longer than 2 minutes per side.

THE URBAN GRILL

We were creating some live-fire cocktails for this book and grilling some of the drink ingredients on Frankie Frankeny's rooftop in San Francisco. (Frankie's my photographer and a great friend.) While we grilled and tasted cocktails, we were looking out over the city lights—a really breath-taking scene. When we needed a little sustenance, Frankie got some bread and cheese, and made us the best grilled cheese sandwiches I think I've ever had in my life, right on her small rooftop grill.

This struck me as the best possible example of how the grill can make the simplest food memorable. And you don't even need a backyard. It's not the size of your grill that matters; it's the light and warmth of a friendship—as reflected by the fire—that makes a meal great.

You city dwellers out there, write me on Facebook and let me know which recipes in this book you're trying out on your urban grill.

Thanks for the grilled cheese, Frankie.

GRILLED
VEGETABLE ANTIPASTI
SOTT'OLIO

Serves 8

Sott'olio means preserved in oil in Italian, but the English translation falls short. To preserve something in oil is to give it its due. My mom's sister, my Aunt Rose, would use this method to preserve tuna caught by my cousins or local fishermen; it was a treat for us to get a few jars after a visit to their coastal Oregon town. We also used olive oil to preserve sun-dried tomatoes, salt-brined green tomatoes and eggplant, and vegetables right out of our garden. ❖ My mom never grilled her vegetables before canning but I love the smoky, summery taste it gives them.

6 large Yukon gold potatoes (about 1½ pounds total)

5 tablespoons kosher salt

6 medium peeled carrots (about 1¼ pounds total)

2 large fennel bulbs

3 small green zucchini

1 large eggplant (about ¾ pound)

1 tablespoon coarse sea salt, preferably gray salt, plus more for sprinkling

1 pound small button mushrooms or large cremini mushrooms (leave the button mushrooms whole but halve the cremini from dome to stem)

¾ cup extra-virgin olive oil, plus more for drizzling

Freshly ground black pepper

Fill a large stockpot with about 5 quarts of cold water. Bring the water to a boil over high heat. Peel the potatoes while you're waiting for the pot to boil. Add the kosher salt to the boiling water, then add the potatoes. Decrease the heat to keep the water at a good simmer but not a hard boil. Cook until the potatoes are about half done and still very firm, about 10 minutes. With tongs or a slotted spoon, take the potatoes out of the water (leave the water in the pot) and set them aside to cool.

Add the carrots to the hot water, adjusting the heat if necessary to keep the water at a strong simmer. Cook until the carrots are about half done, 3 to 4 minutes. Transfer them to a plate to cool, leaving the water in the pot for the fennel.

Halve the fennel lengthwise and then cut each half into six wedges. Add the fennel to the pot of simmering water and cook for about 3 minutes. Remove the fennel, and allow it to cool. At this point you can drain the water in the pot.

Cut each zucchini lengthwise into 3 long slabs. Set them aside.

Trim the stem and bottom from the eggplant and slice into ¼-inch rounds (approximately 10 slices). Rinse each slice in cool water and pat dry with paper towels. Sprinkle the one tablespoon sea salt over the eggplant rounds. Let the slices rest for 15 minutes, then rinse them in cool water and pat dry again with paper towels.

Turn a gas grill to high or ignite charcoal. When the grill is hot, for both gas and charcoal grills, clean your grill rack. Decrease the temperature to medium-high (on a gas grill only), and brush or wipe a little olive oil on the grill rack.

Cut the potatoes into ¼-inch rounds and halve the carrots lengthwise.

With a brush, give each vegetable a light coat of olive oil and then a sprinkling of salt and pepper. You'll cook the vegetables separately and then either serve them immediately or refrigerate them.

Grill the potatoes for about 10 minutes, the carrots for about 8 minutes, the zucchini for 7 minutes, the eggplant slices and mushrooms for 6 minutes, and the fennel for 5 minutes, turning with tongs about halfway through the grilling time.

As each vegetable comes off the grill, transfer to a serving platter. Serve while warm or keep them covered with oil and refrigerated for up to 1 week. If you cover the vegetables with olive oil, save the olive oil and use it in the Smoked Oil Dressing (page 210).

OYSTERS
ON THE HALF SHELL
WITH
GRILLED PROSCIUTTO
AND MIGNONETTE

Serves 8

Forget shucking raw oysters. If you place whole closed oysters on the grill, not only do they open easily, but you add a little drama to the party. If you have already-shucked oysters, you can grill them too: just wipe the grill with olive oil, and grill the naked oysters for a bare 2 minutes. ❖ Kumamotos and Bluepoints are both good choices for grilling. I love our local Hog Island oysters, which you can order by mail, or seek out great oysters from a fish-monger near you. See Resources, page 218. ❖ A traditional mignonette (a classic vinaigrette for oysters), calls for shallots, but I like the bolder flavor of red onion with the grilled prosciutto. Substitute 3 tablespoons of diced shallots for the red onion if you prefer a more subtle flavor. ❖ Ask your butcher for a whole piece of prosciutto (not cut into thin slices the way it is normally). You'll grill the prosciutto chunk and then cut it into strips for the top of each oyster (as shown in the photo, facing page). ❖ A brunoise dice is a restaurant kitchen technique in which the onion is diced into tiny, neat squares.

24 oysters in their shells

MIGNONETTE
4 tablespoons extra-virgin olive oil
1 tablespoon minced fresh flat-leaf parsley
3 tablespoons red onion, cut into brunoise dice (tiny cubes)
4 tablespoons freshly squeezed lemon juice
1 teaspoon grated lemon zest
½ teaspoon Calabrian chile paste,
 or ¼ teaspoon red pepper flakes
¼ teaspoon coarse sea salt, preferably gray salt
⅛ teaspoon freshly ground black pepper

2-ounce chunk prosciutto (not sliced)
½ tablespoon whole peppercorns, for garnish

Place the oysters in a large bowl and fill it with cold water. Clean each oyster with a brush, scraping off any loose particles that may be attached to the shell. Once the oysters are well rinsed, drain off the water, make sure each oyster is arranged so the deep-cup side of the shell faces down, and store the oysters in the refrigerator, covered with a towel. Never store oysters sub-merged in water.

FOR THE MIGNONETTE: Whisk together the oil and pars-ley in a bowl. (If you combine the herbs and oil first, the herbs don't brown as quickly.) Add the onion, lemon juice and zest, chile paste, salt, and pepper. Cover and place it in the fridge to cool for at least 30 minutes or up to 4 hours.

Turn a gas grill to high or ignite charcoal. For both gas and charcoal grills, when the grill is hot, clean your grill rack. For a gas grill, decrease the temperature to medium-high, and brush or wipe a little olive oil on the grill rack.

With tongs, lay the chunk of prosciutto on the grill and cook until the bottom shows distinct grill marks, 1 to 2 minutes. Turn and grill the other side until marked, about 2 minutes. Remove the prosciutto from the grill and allow it to cool while you grill the oysters.

Make sure the gas grill is hot or that your charcoal has burned to a hot pile that shows some red glow beneath gray ashy coals.

Wipe each oyster with a towel and place the shell directly on the grill rack. When all 24 oysters are on the grill, close the grill lid. Allow the oysters to cook just until you hear them popping open, 3 to 4 minutes.

With tongs take the oysters off the grill, and snap off and discard the top shell, taking care not to lose the liquid inside the shell. Using an oyster knife, gently scrape the bottom shell to release the oyster, without spilling any liquid if you can help it.

Cut the prosciutto chunk into strips, each about ¼ inch thick and ¾ inch long. Fill several serving dishes (unless you have one big enough for 24 oysters) with crushed ice and sprinkle peppercorns over the ice for contrast.

Transfer the oysters, still on their half shells, onto the bed of ice, and top each oyster with a few strips of grilled prosciutto. Spoon mignonette over each oyster, and pour the remain-ing mignonette into a small serving bowl, which gets passed around the table.

GRILLED
CRABS
WITH FRESH HERBS

Serves 6

Fresh Dungeness crab, in season, is one of the best things you can throw on the fire. I call this "grill and chill," because I like to grill the crabs, refrigerate them, and serve them cold. You can serve them hot off the coals or chill them; both ways are good. ❖ Start with whole, not cracked, crabs, and get them live if you can. I boil the crabs in water before putting them on the grill; the grilling adds a smoky flavor that complements the sweetness of the crab meat. ❖ When you're ready to serve, pile the chilled crab on a big platter and serve with sliced cucumbers and tomatoes, dressed with a simple vinaigrette or the Smoked Oil Dressing (page 210).

6 whole Dungeness crabs (about 1¼ pounds each), cleaned

6 tablespoons extra-virgin olive oil

HERB MARINADE

1 lemon

¾ cup extra-virgin olive oil

½ cup minced fresh tarragon

¾ cup minced fresh flat-leaf parsley

1 teaspoon whole black peppercorns

CUCUMBER SALAD

4 large cucumbers

4 medium tomatoes

½ cup Smoked Oil Dressing (page 210)

Bring a pot of water to a boil in a pan on a stove indoors. (It takes a long time to bring this much water to a boil on the grill; unless you're at the shore and not near a stove, heat the water indoors.) Pick up the crab by its two hind legs. Hold them together firmly and stroke the top of the crab's head just behind the mouth until the crab goes quiet. Lower the crab into the pot slowly so you don't splash yourself. Decrease the heat to medium-low (adjust the heat to keep the water at a simmer) and cook until the crabs turn pink, about 10 minutes. With tongs, take the crabs from the pot and let them cool on their backs on a plate.

Turn a gas grill to high or ignite charcoal. While the grill heats, coat each crab with olive oil, front and back. When the grill is hot, clean your grill rack. For a gas grill, decrease the temperature to medium-high, and brush or wipe a little olive oil on the grill rack.

Grill the crabs for about 3 minutes; turn them over and grill another 3 minutes.

Take the crabs off the fire and let them cool. Clean the crabs by grasping the legs and twisting them off the body. Crack them lightly in several places with a nutcracker. Pull the shell apart where it attaches to the back of the crab. Hold the body with the back side up and put your right thumb in the joint between the upper and lower shell on the side opposite the mouth. Your palm will then be stretched across the top of the shell. Hold the bottom of the crab in your opposite hand. Force your thumb in and pull up and back to your right. The shell will snap off.

Remove the lungs and reproductive organs before marinating.

FOR THE MARINADE: Cut the lemon into slices about ⅛ inch thick. Discard the seeds, put the slices in a bowl, and add the olive oil, tarragon, and parsley. With the back of a heavy knife, crack the peppercorns and add them to the marinade. Pour the marinade over the grilled crabs and refrigerate for at least 30 minutes or until ready to serve.

FOR THE SALAD: While the crabs are chilling, peel, seed, and slice the cucumbers and quarter the tomatoes. Toss together the cucumbers and tomatoes with the Smoked Oil Dressing or any vinaigrette you like. You can refrigerate the salad until you're ready to serve the crab.

Serve crabs and salad well chilled.

FRESH CRAB

Crabbing doesn't require anyone to be a fisherman. In fact, in my family the twelve-year-olds were pretty much in charge of the crab operation. The entire extended family met up on the Oregon Coast every year to visit Aunt Rose, Uncle Dick, and their nine children. We'd set crab traps and then go clamming, stomping on the sand and digging furiously when a clam shot up a jet of water.

Every half hour or so, one of my cousins would pop his head up like a prairie dog and start racing for the crab traps, and then all of us would run, toting our clam buckets, with water sloshing, because we didn't want to leave the buckets behind and have someone take our clams. The first cousin to the pier would yank up the trap rope as fast as his (or her) skinny arms could pull. If there were crabs in the trap, you'd turn them out onto the pier to measure them; meanwhile, they're scuttling toward freedom and dropping off the pier into the water while you're scuttling along the pier in a low crouch chasing them.

By this time, the aunts and uncles have come up to see what we've caught and the Italians have taken over the pier. We'd measure and they'd all be too small except for one crab—the rest would go back into the water. The traps were baited and tossed back in and that one big-enough crab went into a bucket of sea water.

For me, at ten years old, in the middle of a herd of cousins, feeling the sun hot on my shoulders as I raced to the traps and then leaning over the frigid Oregon water to pull up the rope—this made crabs taste all that much sweeter when we finally had enough good-size ones to eat.

Don't miss out on this simple pleasure. Crabs that you've caught yourself waiting in a bucket of sea water until you're ready to cook—this belongs on everybody's bucket list.

FIDEAU
WITH
VERMICELLI, GRILLED SHRIMP, CHICKEN, AND CALAMARI

Serves 8

From the Valencia region of Spain, *fideau* is like a paella, with the same combination of seafood, chicken, and spices. Instead of rice, a fideau calls for broken bits of uncooked vermicelli pasta. ❖ You'll need a paella pan for this dish, 17 to 21 inches wide. You can rest it right on top of the charcoal in your grill or in a fire pit. This recipe doesn't translate well to a gas grill; having the pan resting on hot coals works a certain magic that propane can't duplicate. ❖ Your guests gather round while you toast the broken pasta in olive oil, adding spices, chicken broth, tomato sauce, and wine, and then finally the chicken, shrimp, and calamari (that you've given a quick grill beforehand). This takes about 60 minutes from start to finish but it's a relaxed hour. All the while, the fragrance keeps getting better and better and the people sitting around the fire get more and more eager to have a taste. This is what cooking around a fire is all about. ❖ One piece of advice if you're making a fideau for the first time: when you pour in stock after the first pour, add just a little at a time and let it cook away before you add more, just as you would when making risotto (although with fideau, you don't stir after a certain point). ❖ I like a spicy fideau; if you want a milder version, just halve the amount of red pepper flakes and chili powder. ❖ And please let your guests help you break the pasta into 1-inch pieces. The pieces don't need to be even and, especially if there are kids around, breaking uncooked spaghetti is just plain fun.

½ **loosely packed teaspoon saffron threads (about 20 threads)**

2½ **cups dry white wine**

6 **chicken thighs, skin left on**

¼ **cup extra-virgin olive oil, plus more for coating the chicken and seafood**

2 **teaspoons coarse sea salt, preferably gray salt, plus more for seasoning the chicken and seafood**

½ **teaspoon freshly ground black pepper, plus more for seasoning the chicken and seafood**

1 **pound shrimp (12 to 16 shrimp)**

1 **pound calamari, tubes and tentacles, cleaned (ask your fishmonger to clean it for you)**

1 **large yellow onion, cut into medium dice**

1 **heaping tablespoon minced garlic (about 3 cloves)**

1 **pound uncooked vermicelli or spaghetti, broken into 1-inch pieces**

6 **cups Chicken Broth (page 217), fish stock, or store-bought stock, plus ¼ cup more at the end if needed**

2½ **cups Grilled Tomato Sauce (page 215, or substitute tomato Passata, page 213), plus ¼ cup more at the end if needed**

1 **teaspoon ground cumin**

2 **teaspoons Pimentón de la Vera (sweet, smoky Spanish paprika)**

1 **teaspoon dried oregano (or ½ teaspoon minced fresh oregano)**

½ **teaspoon red pepper flakes**

½ **teaspoon chili powder**

1 **heaping tablespoon finely chopped fresh flat-leaf parsley**

Place the saffron threads in a small bowl and pour the white wine over them. Set aside.

You can grill the chicken and seafood over a charcoal fire or over a fire in your fire pit. Ignite charcoal or start a fire in a fire pit (see page 42). Spread out the charcoal when it's ready and put the rack in place on the grill. When the rack is hot, clean it and brush or wipe a little oil on the rack.

Rub the chicken thighs with a little olive oil all the way around and place on the grill skin-side down. While they're on the grill, season with about 1 teaspoon of sea salt and ¼ teaspoon of black pepper. Grill for about 4 minutes, then turn the thighs over and grill for another 4 minutes. You want the chicken to be just short of done—not white all the way through but a little pink in the center so it finishes cooking in the paella pan. While the chicken is grilling, rub the shrimp and calamari pieces with a little olive oil.

When the chicken is not quite done but has good grill marks—when an instant-read thermometer inserted in a thigh but not touching the bone reads 130°F to 140°F—take the chicken off the grill and set it aside on a platter. Put the shrimp and calamari on the grill rack, and season with salt and pepper. Again, you don't want to cook these all the way through because you want them to absorb the sauce and spices while in the paella pan. Cook the shrimp for less than 2 minutes per side, and the calamari just for 1 to 2 minutes per side. Take them off the grill and set them aside with the chicken.

Lift the rack off the grill and put it in a safe spot where no children can get close to it. If cooking over charcoal, add another 2 to 3 pounds of charcoal to the charcoal already burning. You want the fire to stay hot the entire time the fideau is cooking. Give the charcoal about 5 minutes to burn and then rest a paella pan right on the coals. It's okay if a little of the charcoal shows some black at this point.

When the paella pan is hot, pour in the ¼ cup of the olive oil. When the oil is hot, add the diced onion and cook until the onion is soft, about 2 minutes, stirring occasionally. Add the garlic and let it cook for 30 seconds, then add all the broken pasta pieces. Toast the pasta in the pan until it's just past light brown, stirring all the while, and then pour in the reserved saffron-wine mixture. When almost all the wine has evaporated, pour in 2½ cups of the broth. Cook until most of the broth has evaporated, about 5 minutes. Add another cup of broth, and cook again until most of the liquid is gone. Add another cup, let cook until almost dry, and so on, until you've used all the broth, except for the last ¼ cup of broth, which is set aside until the dish is finished. Pour in 2 cups of the tomato sauce. Add the cumin, paprika, oregano, red pepper flakes, and chili powder. Add the 2 teaspoons salt and ½ teaspoon black pepper. Stir. Pour in another ½ cup of the tomato sauce. Let it cook down a little before adding more, just as you did with the broth. If you notice any hot spots—areas that are boiling more vigorously—rotate the pan on the coals.

Add the chicken and seafood to the pan; once you place the chicken and seafood on top the pasta, you won't stir any more. For a better-looking finished fideau, arrange the chicken thighs, shrimp, and calamari this way: Add the chicken to the pan in an even circle about halfway from the edge of the pan with the grill marks facing up. Add the cooked shrimp in a circle a little closer to the center of the pan with all the tails pointing in the same direction. Finally, add the calamari to the very center. At this point you are done stirring. You're just waiting and sipping some wine while the pasta, chicken, and seafood absorb all the flavors.

It's done when the pan is just about dry, but don't wait so long that the pasta burns. Just as with paella, you want a little crust on the bottom of the pan. If the noodles seem too dry at this point, pour in the remaining ¼ cup of tomato sauce and ¼ cup broth, but only add these if the pasta seems dry and the pan isn't too full.

Take the pan off the fire, and sprinkle parsley. It will continue cooking and absorbing the juices but should be ready by the time you coax everyone to the table. Place the fideau at the center of a big table, gather people you really like to join you, and serve.

LEMON-GARLIC CHICKEN
WITH
TAPENADE COOKED UNDER A BRICK

Serves 4

I predict this will become a regular part of your repertoire. It's the perfect weeknight meal to cook at the grill because it doesn't require much time or effort, and the lemons, black olives, and garlic come together to make this chicken a standout. Whether cooked in a wood-fired oven or over a grill, cooking the bird under a weight (in this recipe, a brick wrapped in foil) keeps it moist and flavorful. You'll need to remove the backbone and the breastbone from each bird so it lies flat during cooking. Save yourself some time by asking your butcher to do this for you. ❖ Marinate the bird for at least 4 hours or overnight, and let the chicken warm for at least 20 minutes at room temperature before grilling.

KALAMATA TAPENADE

2 tablespoons pine nuts

2 cups pitted kalamata olives

2 teaspoons chopped fresh flat-leaf parsley

¼ teaspoon minced fresh rosemary

1 garlic clove, chopped

¼ teaspoon grated lemon zest

1 teaspoon extra-virgin olive oil

¼ teaspoon coarse sea salt, preferably gray salt

⅛ teaspoon freshly ground black pepper

LEMON-GARLIC MARINADE

¼ cup extra-virgin olive oil

2 tablespoons grated lemon zest (from 2 large lemons)

⅓ cup freshly squeezed lemon juice

2 tablespoons minced garlic (about 6 cloves)

1 tablespoon minced fresh rosemary

1 teaspoon kosher salt

1 teaspoon freshly ground black pepper

One chicken (4 to 5 pounds)

2 teaspoons coarse sea salt, preferably gray salt, plus more for sprinkling

2 lemons, halved

FOR THE TAPENADE: Toast the pine nuts in a small dry sauté pan on the stovetop over medium-low heat just until they begin to show color, 2 to 3 minutes. Immediately transfer them to a plate to cool.

In a food processor, blend the olives, parsley, rosemary, garlic, lemon zest, olive oil, salt, and pepper. Add the cooled pine nuts and process until smooth. You can make this ahead if you like; store tightly covered in the fridge for up to 1 week.

FOR THE MARINADE: In a small bowl, combine the olive oil, lemon zest, lemon juice, garlic, rosemary, salt, and pepper. Stir well and set aside while you prepare the chicken.

Place the chicken on a cutting board. Using a boning knife or poultry shears, cut along either side of the backbone. With your fingers, lift the backbone away from the bird and set it aside. With a boning knife or a paring knife, cut around the breastbone all the way around, working your knife under the bone until you can pull the bone out of the bird with your fingers. Wrap the bones tightly and store them in your freezer. Add them to the pot the next time you make chicken stock.

Taking care not to tear the skin of the bird, lift the skin by gently running your hand between the skin and the meat. Place 1 tablespoon of tapenade under the skin of each leg. Place about 4 teaspoons of tapenade under the skin of each breast. Gently massage the tapenade under the skin to distribute evenly.

Place the chicken in a ceramic or glass dish just large enough to hold it flat. Pour the marinade over the chicken, turning the bird to coat with marinade. Cover the dish with plastic wrap and refrigerate for at least 4 hours or overnight. Turn the chicken two or three times while marinating.

Turn a gas grill to high or ignite charcoal. When the grill is hot, clean your grill rack. Decrease the temperature to medium-high, and brush or wipe a little olive oil on the grill rack.

Sprinkle the outside of the chicken with about 1 teaspoon salt on each side, and place it, skin-side up, on the grill. Set a cast-iron skillet on top of the bird, and place a foil-wrapped brick in the skillet. Cook for 10 to 13 minutes, then remove the skillet and the brick, turn the bird, put the skillet and brick back in place, and cook for another 11 to 13 minutes. Add the cut lemons to the grill, cut-side down, during the last few minutes of cooking.

The bird is done when it's golden brown and crisp on the outside and an instant-read thermometer registers 170°F when inserted in a thigh but not touching a bone. Transfer the chicken to a cutting board, cover with aluminum foil, and allow it to rest for 5 minutes. Cut in quarters, sprinkle with salt, and serve with the grilled lemon halves for squeezing over the bird.

GRILLED PASTA WITH GRILLED MEATBALLS

Serves 8 as a first course

This is an old-school pasta cooked a new-school way. Grilling the pasta makes it entirely new, adding a smoky flavor and the occasional browned crunchy bit of pasta, which is delicious. ❖ For my Harvest Dinner, because I was cooking pasta for 100 people, I vac-packed the meatballs the night before the party. I've given instructions for this method of cooking for those of you who have vac-pack equipment; it's a great way to cook for a crowd. ❖ Don't worry if you don't have sous-vide equipment or a vac-packer; we've also included steps for cooking meatballs the usual way. ❖ This recipe makes a lot of meatballs. You can halve it if you like; I never mind having some meatballs in my fridge the next day.

2 pounds ground sirloin

2 eggs

4 tablespoons freshly grated Parmesan cheese

4 tablespoons finely chopped fresh flat-leaf parsley

2 teaspoons dried oregano

1 tablespoon finely chopped fresh basil leaves

2 cups finely chopped yellow onion

2 cups finely ground dried bread crumbs

2 large garlic cloves, minced

2 teaspoons coarse sea salt, preferably gray salt

¼ teaspoon freshly ground black pepper

2 cups water, plus more if needed

5 tablespoons kosher salt

1 pound dried spaghetti

4 tablespoons extra-virgin olive oil

2 cups Grilled Tomato Sauce (page 215)

4 tablespoons grated pecorino cheese

In a large bowl, mix together the meat, eggs, cheese, parsley, oregano, basil, onion, bread crumbs, and garlic, and season with salt and pepper. Add 1 cup of the water. Knead the water into the meat mixture with your hands. Knead and form meatballs into about 1½-inch balls with a 2-ounce scoop (see Chef's Note) or roll into balls with your hands.

VAC-PACKED COOKING METHOD: Seal the meatballs with just a teaspoon of extra-virgin olive oil and cook them in 130°F water for 35 minutes.

OLD-WORLD COOKING METHOD: Place the meatballs in a large saucepan or skillet on the stove (use 2 pans if they don't all fit in a single pan), add ½ cup of the water over them (½ cup water to each pan if using 2 pans), and cover. Steam the meatballs over medium heat for about 25 minutes. Transfer to a platter and refrigerate until you're ready to grill them.

Turn a gas grill to high or ignite charcoal. When the grill is hot, for both gas and charcoal grills, clean your grill rack. Decrease the temperature to medium-high (on a gas grill only), and brush or wipe a little olive oil on the grill rack.

In batches, grill the meatballs in a cast-iron pan or plancha on the grill until they're well-browned all the way around, 4 minutes total for the vac-packed meatballs and about 6 minutes total for the pan-cooked meatballs. Remove from the heat and reserve.

Fill a large pot with about 5 quarts of water, add the kosher salt, and bring to a boil over high heat on your stove. Add the pasta and cook until just al dente, 6 to 8 minutes. Drain the pasta, reserving 1 cup of the pasta water.

Spread the pasta on a baking sheet and drizzle with 2 tablespoons of the olive oil, so it won't stick together.

Lightly oil a long, flat grill basket or spritz with nonstick cooking spray. With tongs, add half the pasta to the basket, arranging it in a thin even layer. (If you have two grill baskets, cook both batches of pasta at once.) Place the basket on a rack over hot coals and turn frequently, until the pasta turns a golden color. You'll hear it crackling during grilling.

Empty the grill basket into a large heat-proof bowl. Toss the pasta with 1 to 2 cups of Grilled Tomato Sauce. If it needs some moisture, add ¼ cup of the reserved pasta water and toss again. Add the remaining 2 tablespoons olive oil, and 2 tablespoons of the pecorino cheese. Toss. Transfer to a serving bowl, top with the remaining pecorino cheese, and serve immediately.

CHEF'S NOTE: It's so much faster to make a meatball with a scoop than with your hands. Scoops make such quick work of certain tasks—shaping meatballs, gougères, or cookie dough, for example—that I keep a variety of scoop sizes at home as well as at work. If you don't have a 2-ounce scoop for the meatballs, try using a ¼-cup measure instead. You'll find scoops in most restaurant-supply stores or cookware stores.

GRILLED
LEMON-SAFFRON
POUND CAKE
WITH
LAVENDER AND FRESH
BERRIES

Serves 8 to 10

I love a dessert that isn't too sweet; this pound cake is just right. It gets its golden color from lemon and saffron, which adds a deep, almost savory flavor note that I really like. It's baked in the oven; after baking, slice the cake and then finish the slices on the grill until they're toasted. This is ideal with fresh summer berries or grilled figs with local lavender honey in the fall. Because you're going to grill the cake slices, you can make it the day before if you like. ❖ I gather lavender flowers from my backyard for this dessert (yes, I have a history of running outside to gather flowers for my cooking). If your lavender doesn't come from your own yard, be sure the person who grew it didn't use harmful sprays.

4½ tablespoons freshly squeezed lemon juice

1 loosely packed tablespoon saffron threads

1 teaspoon lavender (flowers only), plus extra for garnish

1 cup plus 1 tablespoon sugar

½ cup (1 stick) unsalted butter, at room temperature

4 teaspoons grated lemon zest

2 eggs, at room temperature

1½ teaspoons pure vanilla extract

1½ cups all-purpose flour

¼ teaspoon coarse sea salt, preferably gray salt

¼ teaspoon baking powder

¼ teaspoon baking soda

½ cup buttermilk

Olive oil for brushing

1 pint blackberries or 1 pint of any sweet summer berry

In a small saucepan over medium heat, combine 3 tablespoons of the lemon juice with the saffron and lavender. Bring to a simmer, take it off the heat, and let the juice infuse with flavor. Set aside.

Preheat the oven to 350°F. Butter the inside of a 9-by-5-inch loaf pan or spray with nonstick cooking spray. Line the pan bottom with a strip of parchment paper that extends up and slightly beyond the two narrow ends of the pan. (You'll use the long ends of this paper to lift the loaf out of the pan after baking.) Lightly butter the parchment paper or coat with a nonstick spray. Pour the 1 tablespoon of sugar into the pan, and tilt the pan so the sugar coats the sides and bottom. Dump out any excess sugar and set the pan aside.

In a stand mixer fitted with the paddle attachment or with a hand mixer, cream together the butter, lemon zest, and remaining 1 cup of sugar until the mixture is fluffy and much lighter in color. Add the eggs one at a time, beating for 30 seconds after each addition and scraping the sides of the bowl. Add the vanilla and beat for 10 seconds.

In a large bowl, whisk together the flour, salt, baking powder, and baking soda. With the mixer on low, gradually add the dry ingredients to the batter. Beat for another 30 seconds after the last of the dry ingredients go in.

With the mixer on low, add the remaining 1½ tablespoons of lemon juice, the saffron-lavender-juice mixture, and the buttermilk. Mix for 1 minute.

Pour the batter into the prepared pan. Bake until the cake is golden-brown on top, about 45 minutes. Let the cake cool in the pan. When it's cool and you're ready to grill it, lift it out by the parchment paper handles, and carefully cut lengthwise into 3 equal slabs of cake, as shown in the photo.

Ideally you'd be using the tail end of a fire you'd built for the main course. If not, ignite charcoal or turn a gas grill to medium. Brush the grill rack with olive oil and brush the cake slices lightly with olive oil on both sides. Grill approximately 2 minutes on the first side and 1½ minutes on second side. (Note: Grill marks are nice but don't make them your goal; it's more important that the cake slices be slightly toasted and not too dark.)

Serve each slice with berries and fresh lavender flowers if available.

BIG BURGER BASH

This is an over-the-top burger party with three recipes for regular-size burgers, each made with a different kind of meat, and one recipe for a *gigante* beef burger because what's a big burger bash without a big burger? If you're cooking for a smaller group, make just one or two of the burger recipes in this section.

This is not a tablecloth kind of party. I bring the tables outside and cover them with butcher paper. If you run out of platters just pile the sliced tomatoes and crisp lettuce leaves right on the paper.

THREE-POUND BEEF BURGER FOR SIX ON COUNTRY BREAD

Serves 6

SHAPING BURGERS

You want burgers to be tender, and that means not overhandling the meat. Here's how I shape burgers: I lightly press the ground meat into a form—a 4½-inch-diameter ramekin for standard-size burgers and a 9-inch-diameter cake tin for the big burger. If you don't have the right ramekins, use the lid from a wide-mouth canning jar or even the lid from a large jar of peanut butter.

For burgers of either size, line the container with plastic wrap, and use your fingers to *gently* press the ground meat into shape, using the form as a mold. Lift the plastic wrap to pull the shaped burger out of the mold (invert the normal-size burgers on a baking sheet until you're ready to grill; follow directions in the recipe on this page.)

See the Big Burger on page 68. Here's a fact: turning the big burger without it breaking is a feat. Here's a more important fact: it's not that big of a deal if it breaks. You can arrange it on the loaf of bread after cooking and it won't matter all that much if it's one piece or in several pieces. It's a showstopper either way.

I use two pizza peels (one above, one below the patty) to turn the burger. If you don't have peels, use large spatulas. A quick wipe of olive oil or spritz of nonstick cooking spray on the peels or the spatulas can't hurt.

This burger is messy in the best possible way. Eat chunks of it with your fingers, dip the bread into the cherry sauce, and enjoy every bite.

3½ pounds ground beef
    (see A Great Burger Begins with
    the Meat, facing page)
1½ teaspoons coarse sea salt,
    preferably gray salt
½ teaspoon freshly ground black pepper
6 ounces soft, fresh goat cheese (such
    as Laura Chenel), at room temperature
One 16-ounce round loaf country bread
Grilled Bing Cherry–White Balsamic
    Sauce (facing page)

Turn a gas grill to high or ignite charcoal. When the grill is hot, for both gas and charcoal grills, clean your grill rack. Decrease the temperature to medium-high (on a gas grill only), and brush or wipe a little olive oil on the grill rack.

To shape the big burger, first divide the ground meat into two equal portions. Line a 9-inch round cake tin with plastic wrap. Place one of the portions of the ground meat in the cake tin on top of the plastic wrap and *gently* push the meat into the tin. Don't press too hard. Place another sheet of plastic wrap on a work surface and invert the tin so the

shaped patty pops out onto the plastic wrap. Line the cake tin again with plastic wrap. Form another big burger in the cake tin with the remaining portion of ground beef but keep it in the cake tin for the moment.

Sprinkle the top of each patty with ½ teaspoon of the salt and ⅛ teaspoon of the pepper. Spoon the goat cheese onto the patty not in the tin. Spread to cover the meat, but leave about ½-inch margin uncovered around the edge. Use the lining of plastic wrap to remove the patty still in the tin out of the tin and flip it onto the cheese-covered patty (you want the seasoned sides of the meat facing together, with the cheese sandwiched between). Lightly press the 2 patties together all around the edge. Sprinkle the top of the burger with the remaining salt and pepper.

Wipe a pizza peel with a little olive oil and then use the peel to transfer the burger to the grill. Close the grill lid and cook until the bottom of the patty shows grill marks, 8 to 9 minutes. Spritz a little nonstick spray on the top of the burger, then flip and cook for another 8 to 9 minutes.

Have a large platter waiting next to the grill. Gently transfer the cooked burger to the platter and let it rest for at least 15 minutes.

Halve the bread loaf straight across horizontally so it forms a bun. If you like, you can toast both halves lightly on the grill. Transfer the beef onto the bottom half of the loaf, spoon on enough of the cherry sauce to cover the meat, and close the burger with the top half of the bread. Slice the burger into 6 wedges (as if you were cutting a pie) and serve.

YOU WANT BURGERS TO BE TENDER, AND THAT MEANS NOT OVERHANDLING THE MEAT.

GRILLED BING CHERRY–WHITE BALSAMIC SAUCE

Makes about 2 cups

Summer fruit, when given a quick turn on the grill, gets a smoky, sultry tang that works well with the goat cheese inside the big burger. This also works well as a topping for a turkey burger (see page 70), or a grilled pork chop or pork loin.

Dark red Bing cherries are beautiful in this sauce but you can also use a combination of cherries with apricots, peaches, or any stone fruit. I like to grill cherries and then pit them; you lose less juice that way. For stone fruit, cut the fruit in half, remove the pit, give the fruit a light rub of olive oil on both sides, and then grill for 2 minutes on each side.

Use a fine-mesh grill basket to hold the cherries over the fire (an all-metal strainer will work in a pinch), and don't cook them for longer than 4 minutes. You want them bright and smoky, not charred.

2 cups whole Bing cherries, stemmed
2 tablespoons unsalted butter
2 tablespoons finely chopped shallots
2 tablespoons brown sugar
6 tablespoons white balsamic vinegar
¼ teaspoon coarse sea salt,
    preferably gray salt
Pinch of freshly ground black pepper

Pour the cherries into a grill basket, and place the basket over a medium-hot gas grill or a charcoal grill in which the coals glow red under gray ash. (Alternatively, grill the cherries in a hot grill pan over high heat on the stove.) Give the basket a good shake every 20 to 30 seconds, so the cherries heat through. After 3 minutes, taste a cherry to see if it's smoky enough. Don't let them cook longer than 4 minutes. Take the basket off the heat and let the cherries cool for at least 5 minutes.

Halve the cherries over a bowl, reserving all the cherry juice you can. Discard the pits. In a large saucepan or skillet, either on the grill or inside at the stove, melt the butter over medium-high heat. When the butter is done foaming, add the shallots and stir. Cook until the shallots begin to show some color, about 2 minutes. Add the brown sugar and the vinegar, and stir. Add the cherries to the pan with any reserved juice. Cook until just slightly syrupy, about 3 minutes. Add the salt and pepper, taste, and add more seasoning if you like.

This sauce can be stored in the fridge, tightly covered, for 3 to 4 days.

A GREAT BURGER BEGINS WITH THE MEAT

You'll never get a great burger from meat in a tube. Good burgers come from freshly ground steaks with a good percentage of fat. There's no such thing as a great super-lean burger. As a rule of thumb, choose beef with 20 to 25 percent fat content for your burgers.

A fresh grind is just as important. Choose chuck steaks from your butchers and ask them to grind the meat while you wait, the same day you plan to cook the burgers if possible. Even your local supermarket butcher will be happy to do this for you.

GRILL MARKS AREN'T THE GOAL

Don't accept good grill marks as the sign of a perfect burger. The perfect burger is juicy and tastes great, end of story. Don't let the pursuit of grill marks distract you from the goal.

BLUE CHEESE-STUFFED BEEF BURGERS WITH ZIN-ONION MARMALADE

Serves 6

Sweet onions cooked in Zinfandel—hard to top this as a topping for a burger. For all its rich, complex flavor, this marmalade is fast and easy to make. The combination of blue cheese and Zin onions makes this one of my favorite burgers. Serve with a good Zinfandel. (Duh.)

ZIN-ONION MARMALADE

2 medium red onions

¼ cup extra-virgin olive oil

½ teaspoon coarse sea salt,
   preferably gray salt

¼ teaspoon freshly ground black pepper

2 teaspoons finely chopped fresh thyme

2 cups Zinfandel

3 pounds ground chuck
   (see A Great Burger Begins with
   the Meat, page 67)

¾ cup (about 6 ounces) crumbled
   blue cheese

About 1 tablespoon coarse sea salt,
   preferably gray salt

About 1 teaspoon freshly ground
   black pepper

6 sourdough or small levain rolls

FOR THE MARMALADE: Slice off the ends of the onions, halve the onions from end to end, then peel them. Slice each half into thin half-moons. You should have about 4 cups of sliced onions. Set aside.

Heat a large saucepan over high heat. When the pan is hot, pour in the olive oil. When the oil is hot, add the onions, salt, and pepper. Decrease the heat to medium-high, and cook, stirring occasionally, until the onions are caramelized, 8 to 10 minutes. Sprinkle in the thyme and cook for 1 minute more. Pour in the Zinfandel and cook until the sauce has reduced by about two-thirds, 4 to 5 minutes. Take the pan off the heat and let the marmalade cool while you make the burgers.

Turn a gas grill to high or ignite charcoal. When the grill is hot, for both gas and charcoal grills, clean your grill rack. Decrease the temperature to medium-high (on a gas grill only), and brush or wipe a little olive oil on the grill rack.

Shape the ground beef into 12 thin patties (see Shaping Burgers, page 66). On each of 6 of the patties, spoon 2 tablespoons of blue cheese, leaving ½-inch margin free of cheese all the way around. Cover with the remaining patties. Lightly, lightly press the edges of each burger together while keeping its shape. Season both sides of each burger with salt and pepper.

Place the burgers on the hot grill and close the lid. After 5 to 6 minutes, flip the burgers, close the lid, and cook for another 4 minutes for medium-rare burgers, another 6 minutes for medium burgers.

To serve, place each patty on a roll and top with a few spoonfuls of the marmalade.

CHEF'S NOTE: You can freeze the Zin-Onion Marmalade, which makes it a great way to use leftover wine the day after a party. Store the marmalade in an airtight container in your freezer for up to 1 month.

WHY IS THE CHEESE INSIDE THE BURGER?

Cheese on the outside of a burger is tricky. The cheese can get too well done while the burger's not quite ready. It can slide off the burger. Even worse, when the burger has been off the heat for a few minutes, the cheese can get a little weird—rubbery, crusty, saggy, or just plain old and tired-looking. That doesn't work for me, so I put the cheese inside the burger. As long as the burger is warm, the cheese inside the burger is always at the right temperature and texture. Delicious!

MONTEREY JACK-STUFFED TURKEY BURGERS
WITH GRILLED AVOCADO-MANGO GUACAMOLE

Serves 6

Ground turkey doesn't have the fat of ground beef or pork so choose toppings—such as guacamole—that bring in some fat and complement the turkey's lighter texture. The mild flavor of Jack cheese lets the guacamole and turkey have a say.

Grilled Avocado-Mango Guacamole (page 43)

3 pounds ground turkey

¾ cup grated Monterey Jack cheese

About 1 tablespoon coarse sea salt, preferably gray salt

About ½ teaspoon freshly ground black pepper

6 sourdough or levain rolls

Make the guacamole and have it chilling before you start the burgers. Turn a gas grill to high or ignite charcoal. When the grill is hot, for both gas and charcoal grills, clean your grill rack. Decrease the temperature to medium-high (on a gas grill only), and brush or wipe a little olive oil on the grill rack.

Shape the ground turkey into 12 thin patties (see Shaping Burgers, page 66). On 6 of the patties, spoon 2 tablespoons of grated cheese, leaving a ½-inch margin free of cheese all the way around. Cover with the remaining patties. Lightly, lightly press the edges of each burger together while keeping its shape. Season both sides of each burger with salt and pepper.

Place the burgers on the medium-high grill and close the lid. After 6 minutes flip the burgers, close the lid, and cook the burgers for another 4 to 5 minutes. If you like, slice your buns in half, and grill them cut-side down on the grill for the burgers' final 1 to 2 minutes.

To serve, place each turkey burger on a roll and top with a few spoonfuls of the guacamole.

LAMB BURGERS
WITH EMBER-ROASTED ONION PURÉE AND GRILLED PEACH-NECTARINE MOSTARDA

Serves 6

A purée made from onions that have been slow-roasted in the coals adds incredible sweet, rich flavor to lamb burgers. See page 186 for two different ways of roasting onions for this purée.

For the final touch, I love the sweet-hot mustard flavor of a good fruity mostarda, a condiment that many Italians (including me) make in large batches. If you don't have mostarda on your pantry shelf, and time is short, you can top these lamb burgers with the quick-to-make Grilled Bing Cherry–White Balsamic Sauce (page 67).

Grilled Peach-Nectarine Mostarda (page 132)

3 pounds ground lamb

6 tablespoons Ember-Roasted Onion Purée (page 186)

About 1 tablespoon coarse sea salt, preferably gray salt

About ½ teaspoon freshly ground black pepper

6 sourdough or levain rolls

Turn a gas grill to high or ignite charcoal. When the grill is hot, for both gas and charcoal grills, clean your grill rack. Decrease the temperature to medium-high (on a gas grill only), and brush or wipe a little olive oil on the grill rack.

Divide the ground lamb into 6 equal balls. Mix 1 tablespoon of the onion purée into each of the balls. Form 6 patties (see Shaping Burgers, page 66). Season both sides of each patty with salt and pepper.

Place the burgers on the hot grill, and close the lid. After 5 to 6 minutes, flip the burgers, close the lid, and cook for another 3 to 4 minutes. If you like, slice the rolls in half, and place them cut-side down on the grill for the burgers' final 1 to 2 minutes.

To serve, place each lamb burger on a roll and top with a few spoonfuls of the mostarda or the cherry sauce on page 67.

SMOKY PAPRIKA BBQ POTATO CHIPS

Serves 8

Yes, homemade potato chips are great but if you don't feel like deep-frying, instead try spicing up a few bags of regular store-bought chips. The quality of the spice is the most important thing, so make sure your paprika is fresh and intensely fragrant. I like to use the very smoky Spanish paprika called Pimentón de la Vera.

I'm not sure how it does this, but ascorbic or citric acid (another name for vitamin C), works to keep the spice flavors bright. You can find ascorbic acid in most health-food stores.

For online sources for fresh spices and ascorbic acid, see Resources (page 218).

Two 10-ounce bags high-quality potato chips (such as Kettle Chips)
2 tablespoons Pimentón de la Vera
1 tablespoon plus ½ teaspoon garlic powder
1½ teaspoons turbinado sugar
½ tablespoon coarse sea salt, preferably gray salt
¼ teaspoon ascorbic acid

Preheat the oven to 300°F. Line two baking sheets with parchment paper. Place the chips on the baking sheets, and bake until hot, about 5 minutes. When you can smell the chips, take them out of the oven.

While the chips are baking, in a small bowl mix the paprika, garlic powder, sugar, salt, and ascorbic acid.

As soon as you pull the chips from the oven, pour into a bowl off the heat, then pour the spice mix into a sieve and sprinkle over the hot chips. With a spatula, carefully toss the chips to coat them in spice, being careful not to break them.

Serve the chips warm or let them cool before serving.

SMOKED OLIVE OIL–MANCHEGO POTATO CHIPS

Serves 8

For the thin potato slices needed for great chips, you need a mandoline. Even if you have very good knife skills, it's time-consuming to do the task with a knife. An inexpensive Japanese mandoline does a fine job.

You can smoke your own olive oil (see page 210) or buy it (see Resources, page 218). Smoked olive oil has a bold flavor that I love, but you can use other flavored oils with these chips. For white truffle oil, use 1½ tablespoons instead of 2 tablespoons.

6 large Idaho potatoes (about 1½ pounds), cleaned but with peel left on
Peanut oil, for frying
2 tablespoons Smoked Olive Oil (page 210) or 1½ tablespoons truffle oil
½ cup grated dry Manchego cheese
2 teaspoons coarse sea salt, preferably gray salt
½ teaspoon freshly ground black pepper

With a mandoline, shave the potatoes into paper-thin slices. Soak the slices in cold water for 30 minutes.

While the potatoes soak, fill a large pot with 4 inches of peanut oil. Turn the heat to high, and let the oil heat. Line a baking sheet with paper towels.

After 30 minutes, drain the potatoes and pat the slices dry with paper towels.

When the oil registers 375°F on a deep-fat thermometer, add the potato slices, a handful at a time. Cook until the potatoes turn golden and crisp, 2 to 3 minutes. With a fry basket or slotted spoon, transfer the potatoes to the towel-lined baking sheet, and add another handful of potatoes to the hot oil. Continue until all the potato slices are deep-fried.

Sprinkle the cooked potatoes with half of the smoked oil, cheese, salt, and pepper, gently toss, and then sprinkle on the remaining oil, cheese, and seasonings. Serve warm or at room temperature.

ROASTED POTATO SALAD
WITH ROASTED GARLIC DRESSING

Serves 6

Grilling adds flavor to familiar dishes; when you grill the potatoes, green onions, and garlic for this pretty potato salad, the flavor is much bolder than your standard potato salad that comes to the picnic wearing Tupperware.

You can cook these potatoes lots of ways: on the grill, wrapped in foil in the coals, and even roasted in the oven, but whatever the method, be sure you boil them first in salt water so you get salt flavor inside the potato.

It's best to make the Roasted Garlic Dressing (page 212) a day or two ahead if you can.

5 tablespoons kosher salt
2 pounds medium red potatoes,
    peel left on
½ cup extra-virgin olive oil, plus more
    if needed
1 medium red onion
2 tablespoons freshly squeezed
    lemon juice
6 whole green onions
2 cups finely sliced celery (about
    1 whole head; shave on a mandoline
    or slice very thinly)
1 tablespoon minced fresh tarragon
2 tablespoons Roasted Garlic Dressing
    (page 212)
Coarse sea salt, preferably gray salt
Freshly ground black pepper

Fill a large pot with 4 to 5 quarts of water and bring to a boil over high heat. Add the kosher salt to the water. While the water heats, quarter the potatoes, from end to end.

When the water is boiling, add the potatoes, decrease the heat to medium, and simmer until tender, 15 to 20 minutes. Drain the potatoes, and spread them out on a baking sheet so the steam evaporates. Taste them for seasoning, and add more kosher salt if they need it. Toss the potatoes with ½ cup of the olive oil and set aside.

Turn a gas grill to high or ignite charcoal. When the grill is hot, for both gas and charcoal grills, clean your grill rack. Decrease the temperature to medium-high (on a gas grill only), and brush or wipe a little olive oil on the grill rack.

Trim the ends from the red onion, halve the onion from end to end, then peel. Slice each half into thin half-moons; place the onion slices in a medium bowl and pour the lemon juice over them. Toss the slices in the lemon juice, and set aside.

When the grill is hot, place the oiled potatoes on the rack. (You can put them in a grill basket if you like.) Grill, turning every 2 minutes, until the potatoes are tender inside and golden brown all the way around, 15 to 17 minutes. When the potatoes are done, take them off the grill and set aside.

Drizzle the green onions with a little olive oil and sprinkle with sea salt and pepper. Grill for 1 minute, turn, and grill for 1 more minute. Take the green onions off the grill, let them cool, and then slice on the diagonal. Set aside.

When the potatoes have cooled slightly, cut them into bite-size chunks.

Gently toss the potatoes, red onions, green onions, celery, tarragon, and Roasted Garlic Dressing. Taste, and season with sea salt and pepper, if needed.

Serve at room temperature or chilled. Because there's no mayo in this, it will keep in the fridge for 3 to 4 days, and travels well for picnics.

SIMPLE LIME-CILANTRO SLAW

Serves 6

Lime and chopped cilantro brighten up this simple slaw, which is crisp, cool, and easy to make. It's just right served alongside a burger that's hot off the grill.

Mix up the dressing beforehand but to keep the cabbage crisp, don't pour on the dressing until you're just about to serve.

6 cups thinly sliced green cabbage
    (about ½ large head)
¾ cup coarsely chopped fresh cilantro
    (see Chef's Note)
1 teaspoon coarse sea salt, preferably
    gray salt
¼ teaspoon freshly ground black pepper

¼ cup freshly squeezed lime juice
2 tablespoons freshly squeezed
    orange juice
3 tablespoons extra-virgin olive oil
    plus more if needed

In a large bowl, toss the cabbage and cilantro with the salt and pepper.

In another bowl whisk together the lime juice, orange juice, and the olive oil.

Toss the slaw with the dressing just before serving. Taste, and see if you'd like more oil or citrus juice.

CHEF'S NOTE: You don't need to pick the leaves off cilantro for this salad. Just slice off the top of a bunch of cilantro and chop it, stems and all.

YOU DON'T REALLY
TASTE THE PICKLE OR
THE GARLIC IN THIS
MUSTARD. IT'S JUST THE
BRIGHTEST, FRESHEST
MUSTARD AROUND.

THE CONDIMENT BAR

I love homemade condiments but I understand when people are reluctant to switch out their favorite ketchup or mustard.

The next time you invite friends over for burgers, try this: Ask each guest to bring a favorite condiment. Set up a condiment station and watch as your guests react. At first, just out of habit, they reach for a familiar plastic bottle. Then they take a second look at the crock of home-spiced mustard or the homemade pickles from cucumbers picked fresh from the garden. You can stand by and watch as a condiment attitude shift takes place.

PICKLES ALLA PRESTO

Makes 5 cups

My mom and I used to fight over the pickle juice left in the jar when all the pickles were gone; we would elbow each other out of the way to try and win that final dip of a heel of bread into that vinegary, spicy juice.

I love homemade pickles but these days I'd rather spend weekends with my six-year-old son, and with my daughters when they

come to visit. *Alla presto* means "as soon as possible" and these pickles are. Forget about canning jars. You cook these in 9 minutes in your microwave, chill them overnight, and they're ready for the party. And if you're sitting next to me, don't think you're going to win that pickle juice final dip.

2 medium cucumbers, peel left on
1 cup thinly sliced yellow onion
    (about half of 1 medium onion)
1 cup thinly sliced fennel
½ cup apple cider vinegar
¼ cup sugar
¼ teaspoon red pepper flakes
½ teaspoon coarse sea salt,
    preferably gray salt
½ teaspoon mustard seed
¼ teaspoon coriander seed
½ teaspoon celery seed
¼ teaspoon whole cloves
1 teaspoon ground turmeric

With the peel left on, slice the cucumber into rounds, making the slices as thick as you like. (I like them very thin, but you might prefer them a little thicker.) In a microwave-safe bowl toss the cucumber slices with the onion and fennel slices, and set aside.

In a separate bowl, whisk together the vinegar, sugar, red pepper flakes, salt, mustard seed, coriander seed, celery seed, cloves, and turmeric. Pour over the cucumbers, onion, and fennel. Cover the container with plastic wrap or a microwave-safe cover. Microwave at full-strength for 4 minutes. Take the bowl out of the microwave (careful, the contents will be hot), stir, and put the cover or plastic wrap back in place. Microwave for an additional 5 minutes. Let the bowl cool in the microwave. Transfer the pickles to glass bowls or jars, cover, and refrigerate overnight or for at least 4 hours. These will keep for up to 3 months in your refrigerator.

BOCCE COURT MUSTARD

Makes 2 cups

Chef Michael Laukert and I were making Consorzio Oils back in the 1990s, and we were trying to figure out what to make with the roasted garlic paste left over from a batch of roasted garlic oil.

Michael decided to make garlic mustard. He did some research and found that there are two types of mustard: milled mustard, which is ground mustard seed, and prepared mustard from mustard powder.

This one is prepared mustard, and very easy to make. Mustard powder is very mild until you add vinegar, which kicks up its spicy flavor. Laukert had the brilliant idea of using pickle juice instead of plain vinegar with this mustard.

Don't use fancy, highly seasoned pickle juice; choose the juice from a high-quality but plain dill pickle—most likely what's already in the jar in your fridge right now.

1 teaspoon superfine mustard powder
    (such as Colman's)
1 tablespoon plus 1 teaspoon pickle juice
1 tablespoon Roasted Garlic Paste
    (page 212)
½ cup yellow mustard (such as French's)

Whisk the mustard powder, pickle juice, and garlic paste into the mustard. Serve or refrigerate for up to 3 weeks.

CHEF DAD'S NOTE: Here's a good experiment to do with kids: Have them put a little mustard powder on their tongue and see how mild it tastes. Then add just a few drops of pickle juice, and see how it changes flavor on your tongue. Mustard is sweet until acid is added.

MY DAUGHTER GIANA
ABSOLUTELY LOVES THESE,
AND THEY'VE BEEN A
MAINSTAY ON HER BURGERS,
STEAKS, AND OMELETS
FOR MANY YEARS.

SMOKED HOMEMADE TOMATO KETCHUP

Makes 3 cups

This has much more flavor than a bottled ketchup. If you want a smokier ketchup, add a little more smoked olive oil.

You can also use a smoking gun to add flavor to any ketchup. See directions following the recipe.

½ cup white balsamic vinegar

½ cup sugar

½ teaspoon coarse sea salt, preferably gray salt

½ teaspoon freshly ground black pepper plus 2 teaspoons for onions

¼ teaspoon ground nutmeg

¼ teaspoon ground allspice

1 teaspoon ground cloves

½ teaspoon mustard powder

1½ pounds vine-ripened tomatoes

½ medium yellow onion, peeled and sliced into ¼-inch rounds

4 tablespoons extra-virgin olive oil

1 tablespoon coarse sea salt, preferably gray salt

1 teaspoon Roasted Garlic Paste (page 212)

2 to 3 tablespoons Smoked Olive Oil (page 210)

Turn a gas grill to high or ignite charcoal. When the grill is hot, for both gas and charcoal grills, clean your grill rack. Decrease the temperature to medium-high (on a gas grill only), and brush or wipe a little olive oil on the grill rack.

In a small pan on the stove, heat the vinegar just until warm. Add the sugar and stir until dissolved. Add the salt, pepper, nutmeg, allspice, cloves, and mustard powder and take the pan off the heat. Set it aside to let the herbs steep in the warm vinegar.

Grill the tomatoes following the steps on page 215. Lightly drizzle the onion rounds with olive oil and a sprinkle of gray salt. Grill until they show distinct grill marks, 2 to 3 minutes on each side. Let the vegetables cool.

When cool enough to handle, purée the tomatoes and onions in a blender. Pour the purée into a pot with the Roasted Garlic Paste. Strain the vinegar, and pour the liquid into the pot. (Discard any spices left in the strainer.) Place the pot over medium-high heat; as soon as you see bubbles around the edge of the pan, reduce the heat to low and let the mixture simmer for 20 to 30 minutes. Let it cool, and then stir in the Smoked Olive Oil.

See page 201 for how to use a smoking gun. Pour the ketchup into a large baking dish or pot and cover the top with plastic wrap. Turn on the smoking gun and run the nozzle under the plastic wrap. Add a good layer of smoke, take out the nozzle, replace the plastic wrap and let the ketchup absorb the smoke's flavor for at least 15 minutes.

Store the ketchup in a covered bowl in your fridge.

GRIDDLED ONIONS

Grilled onions never get cooked enough for me. I prefer to griddle my onions, preferably in a cast-iron pan or plancha on which I've just cooked steaks or burgers.

Cut the onions as you would for onion soup: Slice off the ends of the onions and then peel them. Halve them lengthwise, end to end, then slice each half into thin half-moons. Toss them with a few teaspoons of olive oil, gray sea salt, ground black pepper, and a bay leaf. When the meat comes off the fire and is resting, toss the onions into the hot pan. (Decrease the heat if you're cooking on a gas grill or use long tongs to spread out the charcoal a little if cooking on a charcoal grill.) Cook the onions, stirring occasionally, until they're completely caramelized, 10 to 12 minutes.

A QUEST FOR THE PERFECT BURGER

In an era when the sesame seed bun and the sauce get a lot of attention, I beg you to make the meat the hero of your burger. My own quest for the perfect burger began when I met Leo Iacoppi in San Francisco in the early 1980s.

Tra Vigne was being built when my future partners asked me to step into Fog City Diner in San Francisco to work alongside one of America's best chefs, Cindy Pawlcyn. I'd grown up with Italian food and been trained in classic French techniques but true American cuisine was new to me.

Once I had tasted Fog City's stellar burgers, I made it my mission to get to know the butcher who supplied the meat. Every week between lunch and dinner service, I'd make a pilgrimage to Leo's shop in North Beach, hiking the two hundred steps over Telegraph Hill.

Leo opened my mind about what a burger could be—but he never revealed his secrets. Every time I'd come up with a new theory about what went into his burger meat and I'd tell him my thought, he would smile and wink but neither confirm nor deny. Years later, the closest I can come to Leo's formula is three parts beef to one part pork fat with a little short rib meat for added flavor.

Leo's burgers revealed how much care he took. He ground the fresh meat while it was very cold so the pork fat stayed pristinely white. Leo confirmed what I already knew from the Italian butchers in my family: that the best burgers went from grinder to flame with little handling in between.

Because of Leo's influence my burgers have gotten steadily better over the years. I keep in mind his feather-light butcher's touch and something greater: the pride of a man who sets the bar high, and then keeps working to meet his own standards.

CHAPTER THREE

ROMANCING THE FIRE: THE HEARTH

Until just a few generations ago, the hearth—the fireplace—was a home's lifeblood: You cooked there, washed there, shared stories by it, and stayed close for warmth. You may have a state-of-the-art kitchen but you're missing out if you don't cook at the hearth on occasion. You rekindle the spark of a romance or brighten a family dinner if you cook next to the hearth. There's a ceremony to starting and tending a fire in your living room that is very pleasing. Turn the page for a few good reasons why this method of cooking is worth a try.

Even if you choose not to cook in your fireplace (all of these recipes can also be prepared on an outdoor grill), carry the plates over and sit in front of the fire. A simple spread of wine, cheese, and nuts is a romantic feast when you're looking into a fire. You can buy all the ocean tracks you want for your iPod. For me, nothing comes close to the sound of a fire when the lights are low and the people you love most in the world are within arm's reach.

WHY I COOK IN MY FIREPLACE

The hearth is the most romantic place to cook, no question. I proposed to my wife, Eileen, over a dinner that I cooked for her, just the two of us sitting in front of the fire. ❖ But cooking in front of a hearth works for family dinners and casual entertaining too, even if you have just a small fireplace. All of my kids have loved sitting in front of the fire during dinner. I'll tell my six-year-old, Aidan, to bring a log and help me start a fire for dinner, and he stays right there to help me cook. I never have to call anyone in my family to the table when I'm cooking beside the hearth. ❖ I like how, after a hearth dinner, my youngest daughter, Giana, even as a teenager, would come out of the bath with her hair wrapped in a towel and sit quietly by the fire until bedtime. I even love the way my house smells the next morning when we've had a fire the night before.

BUILDING A COOKING FIRE

Don't use charcoal in your fireplace. Use only hardwood, and check Woods to Never Cook Over, page 19, to be sure you're using only wood that works for food.

Start a fire in your hearth the same way you build any fire. Build up a loose pyramid structure of kindling with paper underneath (newspaper and brown paper bags are both smart choices). Light the paper. When the kindling is burning well, add larger pieces of kindling. Once the large kindling ignites, add small logs.

You don't want to cook over a roaring fire. Let it burn for at least 20 minutes or until the flames have died down and the glowing wood is providing a steady heat source. Don't walk away; you need to sit by the fire to keep an eye on it. Don't waste the moment but open a bottle of good wine and enjoy the flames until it's time to cook.

Make the fire a good size to start. When you add a log to a fire, it will flame when it ignites—not optimal for cooking. Just build a good-size fire, let it burn down, and then cook while the temperature is stable. If your fire is big enough at the beginning, you won't need to add more wood until after you're finished cooking.

TIPS FOR SAFE COOKING IN A FIREPLACE
If your fireplace is safe for a roaring fire, it's safe for food, which is cooked at a lower temperature than the fire's hottest point. For more information about setting up your fireplace for cooking, see Equipment for Cooking at the Hearth (page 17).

Before you begin cooking, take a few steps to ensure that you and your family stay safe.

- **Never use charcoal.**
- **Be sure the chimney flue is open before you start the fire.**
- **Have a fire extinguisher nearby, and make sure it's been inspected within the past six months (see page 10).**
- **Keep a spray bottle filled with water nearby to control flare-ups.**

Although you can cook by placing a cast-iron pan directly on hot coals, using a Tuscan grill (see page 17) is a good idea for three reasons: The frame keeps your pans stable and flat, so there's no tilting of a hot pan when a log shifts. The flat pan that makes up the bottom of a Tuscan grill protects your hearth floor from stains, and contains any grease spills. The Tuscan grill has a rack that can be moved closer to the fire or farther away, giving the cook some control over temperature and cooking time.

If you're worried about stains on your hearthstones (not under the fire but in front of it), you can spread damp dish towels over the stones to protect them from grease spatters and droplets.

SHRIMP WRAPPED IN PROSCIUTTO

Serves 4

Really good, fresh shrimp cooked quickly in a hot pan for just a minute or two and then wrapped in prosciutto, these shrimp are my version of "surf and turf." They're light and easy, as well as completely satisfying. You can make these on the stove but I urge you to make them either at the hearth or over a fire pit outdoors. ❖ Serve the shrimp with a clean, citrusy salad.

24 large perfect, peeled fresh Gulf shrimp
Coarse sea salt, preferably gray salt
Freshly ground black pepper
3 tablespoons extra-virgin olive oil, plus more if needed
24 thin slices prosciutto
12 ripe figs
Rosemary sprigs for garnish (optional)

Build a fire in the bottom of a Tuscan grill (see page 17) set in your fireplace, or directly on the floor of your fireplace. Allow the fire to burn until the flames have died down and the glowing wood provides a steady, even heat.

Heat a large cast-iron pan or plancha on the rack of the Tuscan grill or directly over the fire. (You can do this on your stove if you prefer.) Season the shrimp with salt and pepper. Pour in the olive oil, and cook as many shrimp as will fit in the pan but don't crowd them. Cook them in batches if you have to. Cook the shrimp until they're just turning pink, 1 to 2 minutes. Transfer to a platter to cool.

Wipe out the pan or the plancha with paper towels while the shrimp cool. When they're cool enough to handle, wrap each shrimp in a slice of prosciutto. It helps to have a big cutting board on which to work. Just place it on the floor beside the fire. Gently place the shrimp bundles into the hot dry pan, put the pan back on the rack or directly on the fire, and cook until they're warmed through, just a minute or two.

To serve, tear the figs into four pieces each with your fingers (you're at the hearth! Forget about the knife!) and arrange the shrimp bundles and torn figs on a platter. If you like, add a few rosemary sprigs to the plate. Take a bite of shrimp followed by a bite of fig. Enjoy.

SHRIMP AND PROSCIUTTO, FLAMES, STARLIGHT, ONE GIRLFRIEND (WHO ALSO HAPPENS TO BE MY WIFE), A GOOD BOTTLE OF CHAMPAGNE FROM MY GAL'S COLLECTION, AND I AM THE HAPPIEST MAN ALIVE.

CLAMS
IN A
CATAPLANA
WITH
CHICKEN-APPLE SAUSAGES
AND CRISPY SAGE

Serves 4

Go to a trattoria or taverna in any little seaside town where people support themselves by what they catch in the ocean, and you'll find clams and sausages together on the menu. To cook this in the hearth on a cataplana—a hinged copper pan resembling a clam shell—is to give a nod to those fishermen who realized how good fresh clams can be with some chopped sausage. ❖ I set my cataplana right on hot coals in the fireplace. If you are a cataplana fan who prefers to keep their copper bright and shining, don't do this. Personally, I like rustic kitchen utensils and pans that show some battle scars, but I get it when people want to keep their cookware looking new. A big cast-iron pan set on the coals will serve just fine but have something ready to cover it with when it's time for the clams to steam.

6 chicken-apple sausages (such as Aidells)

2 tablespoons extra-virgin olive oil, plus more if needed

4 perfect whole sage leaves

2 garlic cloves, minced

½ cup finely diced red bell pepper

3 long sprigs fresh thyme

2 pounds Manila or cherrystone clams, scrubbed

⅓ cup chopped fresh flat-leaf parsley

1½ cups white wine

1 lemon

Build a fire in a Tuscan grill (see page 17) set in your fireplace or directly on the floor of your fireplace. Allow the fire to burn until the flames have died down and the glowing wood provides a steady, even heat.

On a cast-iron pan or a plancha set on the Tuscan grill rack, directly over the coals, or on the stove, brown the sausages. Transfer to a platter to cool, and set aside.

Line a heat-proof plate with paper towels. Set the cataplana over the coals in the hearth or use a cast-iron pan with a lid. Pour the olive oil into the cataplana or the pan and when it's hot add the sage leaves. When they're crispy, transfer the leaves to the towel-lined plate and set aside.

Add more oil to the cataplana if needed. When it's hot, add the garlic and cook until it begins to turn golden, about 3 minutes.

Add the bell pepper to the pan and cook for 2 to 3 minutes. Add the thyme, clams, parsley, and white wine. With a lemon peeler (the type used for a lemon twist for drinks), peel the whole lemon into several long strips, each about 3 inches long, adding it to the cataplana just as it comes off the fruit. Set the peeled lemon aside for another use.

If using a cataplana, close it. If using a cast-iron pan, cover it. The wine and juices released from the shellfish will begin to simmer inside the cataplana. The shellfish will open in about 5 to 7 minutes.

Carefully remove the pan from the heat and open the top. Discard any clams that haven't opened. Cut the sausages diagonally into ½-inch slices and add them to the pan.

The cataplana can be separated into two pieces. Use the bottom as a serving bowl and the top as a place to put empty clam shells. If using a pan, have a bowl on the table to collect the shells.

PERSONALLY, I LIKE RUSTIC KITCHEN UTENSILS AND PANS THAT SHOW SOME BATTLE SCARS, BUT I GET IT WHEN PEOPLE WANT TO KEEP THEIR COOKWARE LOOKING NEW.

SKEWERED QUAIL

WITH GRAPE SALAD AND CITRUS-ROSEMARY SALT

Serves 6

Hot, smoky, crisp-skinned quail served with a salad of cool, juicy grapes—the contrast is fantastic. ❖ You have two options for holding the quail near the fire. You can use green branches to skewer the quail or use wooden skewers and then stand the skewered quail in heat-proof pots filled with sand placed close to the fire. ❖ If you opt to cook your quail on branches, choose branches at least 2 to 3 feet long. Make sure they're green, *not* dry wood—to be sure, cut them off the tree rather than gathering them from the ground. Use a sharp knife to strip off the bark before placing the birds. You can stand the tree branches upright on your hearth beside the fire or jam the ends of the branches into pots filled with sand. If you want to be more precise, you can do what our photographer, Frankie Frankeny, did, and drill holes in a big log that can hold the branches in place. ❖ Move the tree branches to shift the quail closer or farther from the fire. Check the birds during cooking to make sure they're browning evenly all the way around. If your quail is skewered and set in pots, rotate the pots every once in a while. ❖ Boned quail are called for here. There's a cool machine that removes the quail bones from the inside. If your butcher can find a quail producer that does this, you may as well take advantage of it. But you can make this with bone-in quail too, if that's what you have.

GRAPE SALAD

2 tablespoons extra-virgin olive oil, plus ¼ cup

2 heaping tablespoons fresh rosemary leaves

3 cups halved red grapes

1 teaspoon Citrus-Rosemary Salt (page 211)

¼ teaspoon freshly ground black pepper

1 teaspoon grated lemon zest

1 tablespoon freshly squeezed lemon juice

6 quail, each about 5 ounces (ask the butcher to bone them)

3 tablespoons extra-virgin olive oil for rubbing

Citrus-Rosemary Salt for seasoning

Build a fire in your fireplace. Allow the fire to burn until the flames have died down and the glowing wood provides a steady, even heat.

FOR THE SALAD: In a cast-iron pan or plancha set on the rack of a Tuscan grill (see page 17) or set directly on the fire, heat the 2 tablespoons olive oil. (You can also do this in a sauté pan on your stove.) Line a platter with paper towels. When the oil is hot, add the rosemary leaves and sauté until crisp, about 30 seconds. With a slotted spoon or spatula, transfer the leaves to the paper-lined platter and set aside to cool.

In a medium bowl, toss the grapes with the 1 teaspoon Citrus-Rosemary Salt, black pepper, lemon zest, lemon juice, and the remaining ¼ cup of olive oil. Add the crisp rosemary leaves and toss. Chill until the quail is ready.

If using wooden skewers, soak twelve 12-inch skewers in cool water for 30 minutes while you work on the birds.

Prepare the quail by removing the wing at the first joint (or have your butcher do this for you). Leave the drumstick portion of the wing. If using green branches, skewer the quails using at least two thin sharp branches per bird to hold it firmly above the fire (see photo, facing page). If using skewers, use two skewers per bird, and form a criss-cross with the skewers by inserting one from the quail's right wing to the left leg and the other from the left wing to the right leg. Work so that the skewers are held in place by the legs and wing joints.

Rub each bird with olive oil, about 1 teaspoon per bird, and season with the Citrus-Rosemary Salt. Stand the ends of the skewers in pots of sand next to the fire. Cook for about 3 minutes on each side, or until the juices run clear when you cut into a thigh (just as you'd check chicken). Allow the quail to cool for a few minutes and then take them off the branch or remove the skewers, twisting them slowly so they don't tear the meat.

Place one quail on each plate and spoon some of the grape salad beside it.

LEG of LAMB ON A STRING

Serves about 1 person per pound

I have a hook set beneath my fireplace mantel for the sole purpose of cooking lamb this way. The lamb is suspended by heavy string from the hook and the leg spins slowly while the meat cooks. Every time you pass, give it a gentle twirl so the lamb spins in front of the heat while it roasts. ❖ Here's the cool thing about this method: the lamb will spin until the string is unwound and then, due to the lamb's weight, it will keep spinning in the opposite direction until it reaches full twist and begins unwinding again. People of every age get a kick out of watching it to see how long it spins without a touch. ❖ This method works for any leg of lamb from 6 to 12 pounds. Ask your butcher to remove the pelvic bone but keep the leg intact and scrape down the bone midway if needed so you have a sturdy place on the bone that will hold the weight of the lamb. Take this book along and hold up the photo so your butcher understands what you're planning. ❖ If you don't have a mantel hook, buy the hook and install it before you buy the lamb so the hook has time to set in place. ❖ I fill a spray bottle with a saltwater solution and spray the lamb about every 10 minutes. ❖ Before you begin cooking, allow 2 to 3 hours for the lamb to come to room temperature after it's come out of the fridge.

SALTWATER SOLUTION
3 cups water
⅔ cup kosher salt

1 leg of lamb, 6 to 12 pounds (see headnote)
Mint Pesto (page 32)

When the lamb has been out of the fridge for at least 2 hours, start a fire in your fireplace. Allow the fire to burn until the flames have died down and the glowing wood provides a steady, even heat.

FOR THE SALTWATER SOLUTION: Fill a medium saucepan with the water, add the kosher salt, and bring to a boil on the stove over high heat. Turn off the heat and allow the solution to cool. When it's cool, transfer to a spray bottle and have the bottle handy on the hearth.

Trim any excess fat from the lamb and discard. Tie a 2-foot-long piece of butcher's twine or kitchen string securely around the bone at the end of the lamb leg. Test it to make sure it will hold the lamb's weight. Tie the other end of the twine to the fireplace hook so the lamb is suspended; the bottom of the lamb should be about 8 to 12 inches above the fire. Place a pan at least 9 by 13 inches under the lamb to catch all the drippings.

The leg will begin to spin; give the heel a twist in the direction in which it is turning. Every 10 minutes or so, check to see if the lamb is turning on the string. If it's not, give it a gentle push so it spins.

After about 15 minutes, begin to baste with the saltwater solution every 5 to 10 minutes, spraying the lamb all the way around.

Feed the fire from both sides (but not from the front), pushing the wood to the center as it burns. At this point don't add any more wood but let the flames die down so the embers are cooking the lamb.

After 90 minutes, begin basting the lamb with the pesto. (Set aside about ½ cup of the pesto for basting; save the remaining pesto to serve as a condiment at the table.)

The lamb will roast for between 1 and 2 hours for a 6-pound leg and up to 2½ hours for a 12-pound leg. Check for doneness by inserting an instant-read thermometer in the thickest part of the leg, but don't let it touch bone. For medium-rare meat, the temperature should be 130°F. Transfer the lamb to a sheet pan, cover lightly with a sheet of aluminum foil, and let it rest for at least 15 minutes.

By the time the lamb is done, everyone who's given it a push feels invested, so I like to carve the lamb at the table, where everyone can see. Use a napkin to hold the leg by the heel, at an angle, with the butt end resting on the platter. Slice away from yourself, at a sharp angle, with the knife blade almost parallel to the bone. Carve slices first from the thick, meaty section of the leg, then, turning the leg over, from the smaller muscle on the other side. Holding the knife at a slight angle with the edge pointing upward, remove small slices from the shank.

Serve a slice of each cut onto every plate, tip the platter, and spoon carving juices over each serving. Add a generous spoonful of pesto to each plate.

SALT-BAKED POTATOES
WITH
MASCARPONE AND PROSCIUTTO BITS

Serves 6 to 8

Imagine the best bar food you've ever had, eaten in front of your own fireplace at home. That's what these salt-baked potatoes are. Serve them in front of the fireplace with ice-cold beer (or root beer for the kids) and maybe a game of checkers. Watch the evening take on a whole different tone. ❖ If you've ever salt-roasted beets or potatoes in your oven, this is the same technique used over a fire. Salt-roasting is a great method because it holds in the flavor and moisture of whatever you're roasting. You'd expect potatoes cooked in a salt bed to taste too salty, but they're not. They come off the heat perfectly cooked, moist inside, and well-seasoned but not salty. Use very small potatoes if you can find them; if not, slice larger potatoes in half. ❖ Forget bacon bits. Back in my Tra Vigne days, I came up with prosciutto bits as a way to use the "heel," the end of the shank that's left when you've shaved every last slice you can from the prosciutto. These were an accident—I left them in the skillet a little too long—but I found I liked how crunchy they were. These add a good meaty flavor to baked potatoes, scrambled eggs, and even pasta sauce. ❖ Save yourself some time: instead of mincing the prosciutto, ask your butcher to grind it for you.

20 to 24 tiny whole Yukon gold potatoes (about 3 pounds total), peel left on

3 to 5 cups kosher salt

2 tablespoons olive oil

6 tablespoons finely minced prosciutto (from the "heel")

½ cup mascarpone or crème fraîche (page 217)

4 tablespoons chopped fresh chives (optional)

⅛ teaspoon freshly ground black pepper

Build a fire in a Tuscan grill (see page 17) set in your fireplace or directly on the floor of your fireplace. Allow the fire to burn until the flames have died down and the glowing wood provides a steady, even heat.

Wash the potatoes and pat them dry. Spread a ¼-inch bed of salt in a large flame-proof pan or Dutch oven and place the potatoes on top of the salt. Set the pan on the grill rack of a Tuscan grill or directly on the fire. You can also bake the potatoes in a 425°F oven until the potatoes are fork tender, about 40 minutes.

While the potatoes cook, make the prosciutto bits. Heat a cast-iron skillet either on top of the stove over medium-high heat or over the coals. When the skillet is hot, pour in the olive oil. When it's hot, add the prosciutto. The prosciutto will give off steam for about 5 minutes while it releases its moisture. When the hiss of steam turns to a sizzle, decrease the heat to medium-low or raise the pan a little above the coals. Cook, stirring occasionally, until the prosciutto bits are crisp, about 30 minutes. While they cook, line a platter with several thicknesses of paper towel.

Using a slotted spoon, transfer the bits to the platter. (You can freeze these for up to 6 months and warm in a skillet as needed.)

Take the pan holding the potatoes off the fire (or out of the oven) and let them cool on their salt bed in the pan for at least 20 minutes.

Spoon the mascarpone into a ramekin or small serving dish and the prosciutto bits into another dish. If serving chives, you can either place them in another ramekin or have the prosciutto and chives share a single bowl. Set out the potatoes, still on their bed of salt, and treat them as finger food. Let everyone spoon as much mascarpone, prosciutto bits, and chives onto their potatoes as they like.

CHEF'S NOTE: The advantage to this method is the salt acts as an insulating layer so the potatoes don't develop an ultra-firm patch from resting directly on a hot pan. For baked potatoes with super-crispy skin, try wetting the salt. With your hands, slush the salt with a little water in a large bowl until it's the consistency of snow. Put down a bed of salt in a baking dish using half of the salt, add the potatoes, and then cover the potatoes entirely using the rest of the salt, and cook on a fire or in the oven as directed above.

ROASTED STRAWBERRIES WITH PANNA COTTA

Makes six ½-cup servings

This is my fired-up version of strawberries and cream. Summer berries, intensified under heat, are spooned over a silken panna cotta. ❖ Gelatin sheets (also called leaves) make a more refined panna cotta, without the rubbery texture that gelatin powder can sometimes add. It's worth the trouble of ordering gelatin in sheets (see Resources, page 218). ❖ Lemon peel brightens the panna cotta's flavor. Use a vegetable peeler to remove the lemon peel—only the yellow part, not the white pith. ❖ Make the panna cotta the night before; roast the berries right on the hearth, and then bring out the panna cotta when the berries are ready. You get to choose whether you want to serve your panna cotta in the ramekins or take the extra step to unmold them. With this recipe, the vanilla sinks to the bottom, leaving flecks of dark across the panna cotta's creamy white surface; you don't get the full effect unless you unmold onto a plate.

PANNA COTTA

2 silver gelatin leaves or 2 teaspoons gelatin powder
2 cups heavy cream
1 cup whole milk
⅓ cup sugar
Pinch of salt
1 whole vanilla bean
Peel from 1 lemon, cut in wide strips

ROASTED STRAWBERRIES

1½ pounds firm strawberries, hulled and quartered
Pinch of coarse sea salt, preferably gray salt
1½ tablespoons freshly squeezed lemon juice
½ cup sugar

FOR THE PANNA COTTA: Soak the gelatin leaves in a large bowl of ice water until soft, 4 to 5 minutes. (If using gelatin powder, mix it with ¼ cup cold water and set it aside.)

While the gelatin soaks, heat the cream, milk, the ⅓ cup sugar, and salt in a large saucepan over medium-high heat. Halve the vanilla bean lengthwise with a small knife. Scrape out the filling and add the filling and the bean to the pot along with the lemon peel. Decrease the heat to medium-low to bring the liquid to a simmer. When you see small bubbles all the way around the rim, take the pan off the heat and set it aside to cool for at least 5 minutes.

Squeeze the gelatin leaves gently to remove excess water. Add the gelatin leaves (or the gelatin powder–water mixture) to the milk mixture. Stir until the gelatin melts, about 30 seconds. Strain the mixture through a fine-mesh strainer.

Ladle into six 4- to 5-ounce ramekins, molds, or martini glasses. Cover and refrigerate at least 4 hours or overnight.

FOR THE STRAWBERRIES: Toss the strawberries with the salt, lemon juice, and sugar. Pour into a cast-iron skillet 10 inches wide or larger and set the skillet on the hearth grate or nestle the skillet right in the embers as long as the fire is not too hot. You can also put the skillet over the grate in your fire pit. After 3 minutes, toss the berries in the pan, and then return the pan to the grate or embers. The berries are done when they are soft and syrupy, after about 5 minutes.

About 30 minutes before serving, put serving plates into the refrigerator to chill. When ready to serve, unmold each panna cotta by dipping the bottom of the ramekin in warm water for just a second or two, and then running a paring knife around the panna cotta gently inside the rim. Tip the mold upside down onto a chilled plate, and then spoon some of the strawberries and their syrup on the plate beside the panna cotta.

PIZZAS ON THE GRILL

I must have worked a thousand days at Tra Vigne's pizza oven. We always had one person making the dough, and one person doing the cooking. On a busy day, making pizza dough was one of my favorite tasks. It's meditative to work flour and water together into a dough, and then to watch it transform again when exposed to heat. I can't help thinking about all the people, over hundreds of years, who've done this task using the same motions.

My wife, Eileen, has become the resident pizza maker at our house. Lately she's been showing our son how to make dough. I watch them in our kitchen and it strikes me what a nice task this is for small hands to learn. And when I think of making pizza with my kids—Roux, Felicia, Giana, and now Aidan—my next thought is, "one more generation of pizza makers." It seems wondrous and a little strange to me that I'm no longer at the end of the line but am one step forward in a very long chain.

PIZZA DOUGH

Makes ten 6-ounce balls of dough
(each about 4 inches in diameter)

PIZZA-MAKING TIPS

- Allow time for the dough to rise twice. I like to start the dough the day before I'll grill the pizzas.

- Don't try to cook pizzas in your grill or in an oven without a pizza stone (see page 14, and Resources, page 218).

- Make sure the grill is very hot first, before you cook the dough.

- If you prefer not to grill, you can make any of these pizzas in a very hot oven, but they won't have the same authentic pizzeria crust, which is blistered outside, and tender inside.

- If you have a wood-burning oven, by all means use it for any of these pizzas.

- You can crack a pizza stone if you put a cold stone on a hot grill rack or a hot stone on a cold surface. Take some care so your stone lasts longer.

SAME DOUGH, DIFFERENT OUTCOME

You only need to make one kind of dough for foccaccia, piadine, pizza, and flatbread, in that order. If you just shape the dough lightly with your fingers, that's focaccia. A thinner, but still soft and doughy version is a piadine, which I usually top with a highly flavored paste or spread, some shavings of a hard cheese, and a salad. Make the dough thinner yet for pizzas (I like them crisp), and then make flatbread (see page 33) by rolling this dough just about as thin as it can go.

Good pizza dough starts with a sponge—a sort of pre-dough mix of yeast, flour, sugar, and water. You let the sponge ferment for about 4 hours, and then you add the rest of the ingredients to make the actual dough. This gives your pizza crust better flavor and the tiny air pockets that make the crust chewy but still even in texture, without big holes formed by air bubbles.

The type of yeast you use matters. I use fresh beer yeast for my pizza dough. Look for this in the dairy section of your market or ask your grocer to order it for you.

Make the dough ahead of time and refrigerate overnight or freeze for up to 6 months. Let it come back to room temperature before you begin to work it.

SPONGE

1 ounce fresh beer yeast or 1 package (2¼ teaspoons) active dry yeast (not fast-acting)
2 cups warm water (105°F to 115°F)
1 tablespoon sugar
2 cups high-gluten (bread) flour

DOUGH

One batch Sponge
1 cup warm water (105°F to 115°F)
1 cup all-purpose unbleached white flour
4 cups high-gluten (bread) flour
2 tablespoons coarse sea salt, preferably gray salt

FOR THE SPONGE: In a large bowl, mix the yeast, warm water, sugar, and high-gluten flour with a wooden spoon until there are no lumps. The sponge will be very wet and sticky. Cover the bowl with plastic wrap and let it rest in a warm (but not too hot) area for 4 hours or overnight.

FOR THE DOUGH: Lightly oil a large bowl and set aside.

In a stand mixer fitted with the dough hook, combine the sponge, warm water, the all-purpose flour, 3 cups of the high-gluten flour, and salt. Mix at low speed until the dough comes together to form a ball that is soft and sticky, but smooth, 5 to 6 minutes. Increase the machine's speed to medium and gradually add the remaining 1 cup of high-gluten flour.

Transfer the dough to a floured work surface. Gently knead by hand until smooth. If you slam the dough hard onto your surface several times this will help gluten develop, making the dough smoother and more elastic.

Transfer the dough to the lightly oiled bowl, cover tightly with plastic wrap, and let rise at room temperature until it doubles in volume, 2 to 4 hours. Divide into 10 equal portions, each about 6 ounces. Roll each section into a ball.

You can begin working with the dough right away; if you want to store it, use a lightly oiled 9-by-11-by-2-inch container with a lid. Place the dough balls side by side and drizzle the tops with olive oil to keep a skin from forming. They will keep, refrigerated, for 24 hours, or freeze for up to 6 months.

IF YOU SLAM THE DOUGH HARD ONTO YOUR SURFACE SEVERAL TIMES THIS WILL HELP GLUTEN DEVELOP, MAKING THE DOUGH SMOOTHER AND MORE ELASTIC.

BUILDING A PIADINE

A piadine is made of four components: a highly flavored spread or paste, a protein or vegetable, hard cheese either grated or crumbled, and crisp greens or a salad. Within that framework, there are a thousand different ways you can go.

A piadine isn't something you measure very seriously. Jump in and make one to get a feel for how much garlic paste or red pepper butter you want spread on the pizza, and how much cheese and greens. Look at the blueprint, then try any of the options following or come up with your own master plan.

PIADINE BLUEPRINT = 1 TO 2 TABLESPOONS HIGHLY FLAVORED PASTE OR SPREAD + 1/4 CUP PROTEIN OR VEG + GRATING OF HARD CHEESE + 1/2 CUP GREENS OR SALAD

PIADINE, FOUR WAYS

GREEK PIADINE WITH KALAMATA TAPENADE, GRILLED PEPPERS, AND FETA

1 pizza serves 4 to 6 as an appetizer

1 ball of dough (Pizza Dough, page 94)
2 tablespoons Kalamata Tapenade (page 58)
2 tablespoons crumbled feta cheese
2 tablespoons chopped roasted red bell peppers (page 135)
½ peeled cucumber, cut into slices
½ very ripe tomato, chopped
2 tablespoons Red Wine Vinaigrette (page 212)
Sprinkle of cornmeal for the pizza peel

Turn a gas grill to high or ignite charcoal and set pizza stone on the grill rack. Let it heat for at least 10 minutes while you roll out dough on a floured surface with a rolling pin until 9 to 10 inches across.

Place the dough on a pizza peel and slide the dough onto the preheated pizza stone. Close the lid on the grill. Cook for 2 to 3 minutes and then slide the peel under the piadine to remove it from the stone.

Smooth on the tapenade with a spoon or spatula, top with the feta, and sprinkle with the red peppers. With the peel, slide it back onto the pizza stone, close the grill lid, and cook for no more than 2 minutes.

Take the piadine off the heat and top with the cucumbers and tomatoes. Drizzle with vinaigrette. You can fold up a piadine if it's meant for one person or treat it like a pizza and cut it into small portions to share.

To prepare any of the versions below, follow instructions for Greek Piadine with Kalamata Tapenade, Grilled Peppers, and Feta, and just switch out the toppings.

CAESAR PIADINE—ROMAINE, ANCHOVIES, GARLIC, AND PARMESAN:

Roasted Garlic Paste (page 212) + grilled Caesar salad + fresh thyme + grated Parmesan

HEARTLAND PIADINE—RED PEPPERS, CHICKEN, AND SPINACH:

Roasted Red Pepper Butter (page 159) + julienned roasted red bell peppers + diced or sliced grilled chicken + baby spinach + tiny tomatoes cut in half + shaved pecorino

GEORGIA PIADINE—SHALLOTS, PEACHES, AND BLUE CHEESE:

Thin-sliced and caramelized shallots or onions (see page 186) + grilled peaches (see page 132) + grated blue cheese + arugula + Honey–Apple Cider Vinegar Dressing (page 213)

PIZZA WITH SHALLOTS, WILD MUSHROOMS, SMOKED OLIVE OIL, AND FONTINA

Makes three 10-inch pizzas; serves 6

While making this pizza, I was thinking about my oldest daughter, Margaux (I call her Roux, which is short for her nickname Margaroux, the culinary version of "kangaroo"). My best book-writing days start with a long bike ride up Spring Mountain. I wear my ear phone but reception is spotty; the only person who has an uncanny ability to call when reception is perfect is Roux. She called a few weeks ago just as I was going around a bend on the road. I pulled over to talk to her and ten seconds later I saw a cheese delivery truck swinging wildly by, going about 70 mph where my bike would have been if Roux hadn't called me. (Months later, I still think about this, that my last moments could have been spent facing a *cheese* truck. A *cheese* truck? Seriously?!)

I thought about Roux for the rest of that day, and the pizza parties she'd enjoyed for childhood birthdays. Roux is grown now, and newly married, but those pizza parties when she was small live on in my heart. Roux reminds me all the time how lucky I am that she is my daughter.

I like to pull out my plancha to cook the mushrooms and shallots for this pizza, but a cast-iron pan on the grill or your stove works just as well. Cremini mushrooms are good here but feel free to use any mushrooms you like. The best mushroom pizzas start with mushrooms that you hunted down yourself with some of your best friends.

½ cup extra-virgin olive oil

7 cups quartered mushrooms

6 to 8 medium shallots, julienned
   (about 1 cup julienne)

1½ teaspoons chopped fresh thyme

2 teaspoons coarse sea salt,
   preferably gray salt

¾ teaspoon freshly ground black pepper

3 balls pizza dough (Pizza Dough, page 94)

1½ cups grated Fontina cheese

1½ tablespoons Smoked Olive Oil
   (page 210)

Turn a gas grill to high or ignite charcoal. If using a gas grill, once it's hot, decrease the temperature to medium-high. Set a plancha or two large cast-iron pans on the grill rack to heat.

Pour about 2 tablespoons of the oil onto the plancha or into each pan. Let the oil heat, then add the mushrooms in a single layer. Drizzle the remaining olive oil over the mushrooms. Cook without stirring until they're brown on the bottom, about 7 minutes. Add the shallots and stir with the mushrooms. Sprinkle on the thyme, salt, and pepper, and cook until lightly caramelized, another 4 minutes. Take the pan off the fire and put the pizza stone on your grill rack to heat.

On a floured surface, roll out each ball of dough until 10 to 12 inches across. Grill the naked rounds of dough on the preheated pizza stone until the dough puffs up and the bottom shows some brown, about 1½ minutes. Either using a peel or long tongs, flip the pizza and grill for another 90 seconds. With a pizza peel, take the pizza off the heat. If you like, you can grill all three naked pizzas and then set them aside to be ready for the toppings.

Top each pizza with ½ cup of the mushroom mixture and ½ cup of the Fontina. With a pizza peel, transfer the pizza back to the pizza stone, close the lid of the grill, and cook for about 1 minute.

Transfer the pizza to a cutting board, drizzle each pizza with about 1½ teaspoons of Smoked Olive Oil, cut into slices, and serve.

PIZZA WITH ASPARAGUS PESTO, CAMBOZOLA, AND INSALATINA

Makes three 10-inch pizzas; serves 6

Asparagus pairs so well with fresh basil in this pesto blend. This pesto rocks on pasta or fish, but I love it best on grilled pizza finished with Cambozola. The intensely flavorful but still light pesto and the over-the-top flavor and texture of the melted cheese turn a humble pizza into something luxurious.

ASPARAGUS PESTO

1½ pounds asparagus, each spear about pencil-size

3 tablespoons pine nuts

2 tablespoons kosher salt

¾ cup loosely packed chopped fresh basil

1½ tablespoons minced garlic (see Chef's Note)

¼ teaspoon coarse sea salt, preferably gray salt, plus more if needed

Freshly ground black pepper

About 1¼ cups olive oil, plus more if needed

¾ cup freshly grated Parmesan cheese

INSALATINA

2½ tablespoons extra-virgin olive oil

2 teaspoons sherry vinegar

¼ teaspoon coarse sea salt, preferably gray salt

⅛ teaspoon freshly ground black pepper

3 cups arugula

3 balls pizza dough (Pizza Dough, page 94)

12 ounces Cambozola cheese

Turn a gas grill to high or ignite the charcoal in a chimney (see page 42). When the charcoal is glowing, pour it into the bottom of the grill and replace the grill rack.

At the stove, heat a large pot of water to boiling. While the water heats, snap the ends off the asparagus and set spears aside. Toast the pine nuts in a small dry pan over medium heat, tossing to heat evenly. Keep an eye on them; they burn easily. As soon as they begin to show color and you can smell them, pour them out of the pan and onto a plate to cool.

Add the kosher salt to the water and cook the asparagus until it just begins to show signs of tenderness, about 5 minutes. Take it out of the water, and pat dry with paper towels.

Grill the asparagus just until the spears show some grill marks, 3 to 4 minutes. (Grilling asparagus is easier if they're in a grill basket, but if grilling directly on the grill rack, place the asparagus so the spears are perpendicular to the grill rack's grating.) When you take the asparagus off the fire, keep the fire going and place the pizza stone on the grill rack to heat while you make the pesto.

FOR THE PESTO: Cut the grilled asparagus into thirds. In a food processor, combine the asparagus, pine nuts, basil, garlic, sea salt, and pepper. Don't oversalt at this point because the Parmesan will add saltiness. Pulse to combine and then, with the machine running, slowly pour in the olive oil. When the blend has the consistency of mayonnaise, stop adding oil. Add the Parmesan in three batches, pulsing after each batch. If the sauce becomes too thick so that the cheese begins to clump, add water a teaspoon at a time. Cover with plastic wrap, pressing the wrap to touch the surface of the pesto, and refrigerate. This keeps in the fridge for 2 days or you can freeze it for 2 weeks but I think it tastes best the day it's made.

FOR THE INSALATINA: In a small bowl, whisk together the oil, vinegar, sea salt, and pepper, and set aside. Don't dress the greens until the pizza comes off the grill.

On a floured surface, roll out each ball of dough until it's 10 to 12 inches across. (I actually like my crusts sort of free-form—*deformata*—so don't worry if they're not pizza-shop round.)

Sprinkle the pizza stone with just a little cornmeal. Transfer the rolled-out dough onto a pizza peel that you've dusted with some cornmeal or use spatulas to transfer the pizza dough to the stone.

Grill the naked pizza on the preheated pizza stone until the dough puffs up and the bottom shows some brown, about 1½ minutes. Either using a peel or long tongs, flip the pizza and grill for another 90 seconds. Take the pizza off the heat with the pizza peel. If you like, you can grill all three naked pizza rounds, and have them ready to be topped and then heated.

Top each pizza with about 4 tablespoons of pesto, smoothing it to edges. Add about 4 ounces of Cambozola per pizza. Return the pizzas to the grill. Close the grill's lid and cook for about 1 minute. Transfer the pizzas to a cutting board with a pizza peel or a spatula. Toss the greens with the dressing, use tongs to divide the greens between the three pizzas, cut into slices, and serve.

CHEF'S NOTE: If you're sensitive to raw garlic, blanch the garlic by boiling the whole cloves in water for a few seconds and then dunking them in ice water.

ROASTED GARLIC PIZZA WITH GRILLED TOMATO VINAIGRETTE AND ARUGULA

Makes three 10-inch pizzas; serves 6

This year I made my own tomato vinegar to toss with our fresh tomatoes. It's been a big hit at my house. This vinegar is also good on a caprese salad when you feel like a double hit of tomato.

You can buy tomato vinegar but it's expensive and to me doesn't taste as good as the homemade stuff, especially in this vinaigrette.

GRILLED TOMATO VINAIGRETTE

2 tablespoons Tomato Vinegar (page 214, or see Resources, page 218)

⅞ cup extra-virgin olive oil

3 balls pizza dough (Pizza Dough, page 94)

6 tablespoons Roasted Garlic Paste (page 212)

1 cup Griddled Onions (page 75)

6 cups arugula

1½ teaspoons coarse sea salt, preferably gray salt

Pinch of freshly ground black pepper

¾ cup grated Parmesan cheese

For a gas grill, put the pizza stone in first and then turn the gas grill to high. For a charcoal fire, ignite the charcoal in a chimney (see page 42). When the charcoal is glowing, pour it into the bottom of the grill, replace the grill rack and set the pizza stone on top of it.

FOR THE VINAIGRETTE: With the Tomato Vinegar in the blender and the machine running, slowly drizzle in the olive oil. Set aside.

On a floured surface, roll out each ball of dough until 10 to 12 inches across. (I actually like my crusts sort of free-form—*deformata*—so don't worry if they're not pizza-shop round.)

Grill the naked round of dough on the pizza stone until the dough puffs up and the bottom shows some brown, about 1½ minutes. Either using a peel or long tongs, flip the pizza and grill for another 90 seconds. Take the pizza off the heat. If you like, you can grill several pizza rounds, and then set them aside until you're ready for the toppings.

Spread garlic paste on the grilled pizza and top with Griddled Onions. With a pizza peel, transfer the pizza back to the pizza stone, close the lid of the grill, and cook for about 1 minute.

Transfer the pizza to a cutting board. Toss the arugula with 2 tablespoons of the vinaigrette. Season with salt and pepper. Mound one-third of the dressed arugula on top each pizza. Top with Parmesan, cut into slices, and serve.

DARK CHOCOLATE-CHERRY CALZONES

Makes 12 calzones

Amarena cherries and dark chocolate fill these miniature calzones, each the perfect size for one person. The contrast of rich dark chocolate and the sweet, distinctive cherries is just right when baked inside a pocket of barely sweetened dough.

Amarena cherries have a unique flavor because they start as wild Italian cherries, which are firmer and tangier than the cherries we know here in the States. The Fabbri family has made these cherries for more than a hundred years. An unopened jar of amarena cherries will keep for years (according to the Fabbri family) but I haven't been able to test that because the jars vanish from my pantry. The ganache can be made up to 2 days in advance and stored in your freezer.

DOUGH

1 package (2¼ teaspoons) active
    dry yeast (not fast-acting)
1 teaspoon sugar
1 cup warm water (105°F to 115°F)
¼ cup extra-virgin olive oil, plus more
    for oiling the bowl
2½ cups high-gluten (bread) flour,
    plus more for sprinkling
½ teaspoon coarse sea salt, preferably
    gray salt

GANACHE

⅝ cup heavy cream
5 ounces dark chocolate (preferably
    72 percent cacao), finely chopped
    (see Chef's Note, page 183)

1 egg
1 tablespoon cold water
36 amarena cherries
3 tablespoons turbinado sugar

FOR THE DOUGH: Oil a large bowl and set aside.

Whisk together the yeast, sugar, and water in the bowl of a stand mixer fitted with the paddle attachment. Add in the ¼ cup olive oil and whisk to combine.

Sprinkle the 2½ cups of flour over the yeast-sugar mixture and then add the salt on top of the flour. This is important; adding the salt before the flour can slow the yeast's action.

Set aside so the yeast can ferment, until bubbles begin to form around the outer ring of the flour, 20 to 25 minutes.

Replace the paddle with the dough hook and knead the dough at low speed for about 10 minutes. The dough will be slightly tacky.

Transfer the dough to a floured work surface. Knead by hand for 1 minute until the dough is no longer sticky. Transfer the dough to the oiled bowl and cover with plastic wrap. Set in a warm spot and let rise until doubled in size, about 1½ hours. The dough can be made the day ahead, covered with plastic wrap, and refrigerated overnight.

Place the dough on a clean (not floured) work surface and divide into 12 equal portions (each about 2 ounces). Let them rest at room temperature for 10 minutes.

While the dough is resting, turn a gas grill to high or ignite charcoal. If using charcoal, wait for the fire to die down before putting the pizza stone in the grill. If using a gas grill, put the pizza stone on the grill rack as soon as you turn on the grill so it can warm up gradually.

FOR THE GANACHE: Heat the cream in a saucepan over medium heat but don't allow it to boil. Add the chocolate to the cream, take the pan off the heat, and let it stand for 1 minute. Gently stir the cream and chocolate together. Set aside to cool. While it's cooling make an egg wash by mixing the egg and the 1 tablespoon cold water.

Roll each dough ball into a disk about 5½ inches in diameter. Spread some of the ganache in the center of each dough round and top with 3 cherries. With a brush, apply egg wash around the edge of each dough round.

Fold over and securely seal the edges by gently pinching them together. Cut three shallow slashes in the top of each calzone with the tip of a knife to allow steam to escape. Brush the top of each calzone with egg wash and sprinkle with turbinado sugar. Set a pizza stone on the grill to heat.

TO BAKE IN A GRILL: Sprinkle flour on a pizza peel and then use it to transfer the calzones onto the hot pizza stone. Close the grill lid. If the grill is hotter than 550°F, the calzones will start to brown in 2 minutes. Rotate the pizza stone (don't turn the calzones over). Let them bake for another 2 to 3 minutes. If your grill is cooler than 550°F, baking will take a little longer.

TO BAKE IN AN OVEN: Preheat the oven to 400°F, and set a pizza stone inside to heat. Transfer the calzones to the hot pizza stone with a pizza peel or spatula, and bake until golden brown, 10 to 12 minutes.

CHAPTER FOUR

IRON AND FIRE: THE PLANCHA

A plancha seems so elemental to me. It's a simple slab of iron, and for centuries, people on every continent have cooked and still cook on some variation of a plancha. Whenever I cook on a plancha (also called a chapa), I think about the wood-burning stove that my grandparents cooked on because the top of their stove offered the same kind of surface as the plancha I cook on at home. It took me years to realize that one of the reasons I liked cooking on a plancha so much was because I was copying how my grandmother had cooked on her old stovetop.

Part of the plancha's appeal is that it's not a polished gourmet cookshop item but just a straightforward slab of iron. Yet the food that comes off the plancha is as beautiful as anything that comes from a 400-dollar pan. I love that with a plancha, there's nothing to figure out or assemble. You just put the plancha over the fire and cook.

INSPIRED
BY
TRADITION

When I visited my grandparents, back in the 1960s, I got to walk with my cattle-ranching grandfather to the wood shed before dawn to help him carry back wood for the stove. I laugh at the image we must have made, my grandfather's arms loaded with big chunks of wood, me beside him holding skinny wood pieces in my skinny arms. ❖ I'd help him fire up the stove while everyone else in the house was still sleeping. At dinner time, my grandmother would reach up behind the stove to where the oregano was drying. She'd cut off a bunch and rub it between her hands over the meat. All my college-age cousins would snicker because the aroma smelled just like marijuana; while she would cook on top of her stove, my nonna would glance over at my cousins, puzzled, never knowing what all the cackling was about. ❖ The plancha connects me to my grandparents' cooking and also to the many people who still cook on a plancha. Throughout South America and Africa, and anywhere people cook over fire, this tool has a long history and is still in use. ❖ My plancha sits on my grill most of the time, and I use it for everything from steaks to griddling onions for burgers to making pancakes and French toast in the morning when I have a group to feed. I think I'm happiest when I get to make something that calls for dried oregano, when I remember my nonna and nonno and how they would cook on top of their old wood stove.

USING A PLANCHA

A plancha, which means "metal plate" in Spanish, is just that: a thick slab of metal made to rest over a flame. There's something about a large flat slab of iron that inspires my cooking but if you don't own a plancha, you can make any of the plancha recipes in this book using one or two large cast-iron pans placed right on your grill rack or over a fire.

Beyond its rustic appeal, the plancha makes my work easier because the cooking surface offers ample space. I've cooked pancakes and French toast for ten people (see page 180) on my plancha, and it was much easier than doing the same amount of cooking inside at the stove. Cleanup is easier, too.

I love that a plancha is so simple. There's nothing to figure out; you just put it over a fire or on a grill. I own a few of them, and use them every time I make a fire or head out on a camping trip. Measure your grill before buying a plancha so you know you're ordering the right size.

Care for your plancha as you would a cast-iron pan. Follow the manufacturer's directions to season it with vegetable oil before cooking on it the first time. Clean your plancha with hot water (don't use soap), towel dry, and reseason if needed. Obviously you want to let a hot piece of metal cool to room temperature before trying to clean it—for your own sake as well as the plancha's.

See Resources, page 218, for where to buy them.

THERE'S SOMETHING ABOUT A LARGE FLAT SLAB OF IRON THAT INSPIRES MY COOKING.

GRILLED AHI TUNA
WITH CARROT CAPONATA AND "BROKEN" CARROT VINAIGRETTE

Serves 6

In the Old World, on sailing ships, a caponata made of sliced vegetables was cooked with vinegar and sugar so the veggies would keep a little longer when sailors left for ocean voyages. ❖ For my caponata, I cook each diced vegetable individually so it is perfectly done and dress it with a carrot vinaigrette made from fresh carrot juice. The vinaigrette is made to be "broken" with the olive oil and carrot juice reduction not quite emulsifying because I like how this looks on the plate. ❖ Sauté all vegetables separately, either using the same pan to sauté one vegetable at a time or using a plancha or several cast-iron pans to cook two vegetables at once.

CAPONATA

½ cup olive oil, plus more if needed

3 cups diced carrots (small dice)

1½ cups diced peeled potatoes (small dice)

1½ cups diced red onion (small dice)

1½ cups diced eggplant (small dice)

2 teaspoons coarse sea salt, preferably gray salt

1 teaspoon freshly ground black pepper

2 cups water

¾ cup golden raisins

½ cup Champagne vinegar

1 tablespoon sugar

¼ cup pine nuts, toasted (see page 58)

1½ teaspoons grated orange zest

½ cup chopped fresh basil

¼ teaspoon Calabrian chile paste

"BROKEN" CARROT DRESSING

2 cups fresh carrot juice (see Chef's Note)

1 teaspoon freshly squeezed lemon juice

¼ teaspoon coarse sea salt, preferably gray salt

Pinch of freshly ground black pepper

¼ cup extra-virgin olive oil

One 2-inch-thick slab fresh ahi tuna (2 to 2½ pounds)

2 tablespoons Cocoa Spice Rub (page 209)

1 tablespoon extra-virgin olive oil

Turn a gas grill to high or ignite charcoal. When the grill is hot or the coals have turned gray, place the plancha or a cast-iron skillet on the grill rack and heat for at least 10 minutes.

FOR THE CAPONATA: Pour 2 tablespoons of olive oil into each pan or on either end of the plancha. When the oil is hot, add each diced vegetables to its own pan (or half of the plancha) and season with ½ teaspoon salt and ¼ teaspoon black pepper. Cook the carrots for 12 minutes, potatoes for 10 minutes, onions for approximately 8 minutes, and eggplant for 8 minutes. Transfer the vegetables to a baking sheet to cool.

Indoors, at the stove, pour the water into a small pan and bring it to a boil. Add the raisins and take the pan off the heat. Set it aside, keeping the raisins in the water to plump for at least 5 minutes.

Still at the stove, pour the vinegar and sugar into a small saucepan over high heat. Bring to a boil and cook until the mixture is reduced to ½ cup, 6 to 8 minutes.

Strain the raisins, reserving the soaking liquid. If the finished caponata could use some moisture, this liquid works well. Combine all the ingredients including remaining olive oil, salt, and pepper, in a large bowl.

Caponata can be served warm or at room temperature, and it keeps for 3 days covered in your refrigerator.

FOR THE DRESSING: Indoors at the stove, in a nonreactive pan, bring the carrot juice to a boil, then decrease the heat. Simmer until the juice is reduced to about ½ cup. Strain the juice and wipe the pan clean, then pour the reduction back into the pan. Reduce over medium heat until the juice has the consistency of molasses, 3 to 5 minutes. Take the pan off the heat. Whisk in the lemon juice, season with salt and pepper, and slowly add the olive oil. I like to store this in a glass bottle and shake it up before using although it will still separate. This keeps in the refrigerator for 1 week.

Generously rub the tuna with Cocoa Spice Rub. Lightly drizzle with olive oil. Place on the hot plancha, searing all sides until a rich brown color, about 1½ minutes per side for medium-rare tuna. Remove the tuna from heat and let it rest for 5 minutes. Then cut the tuna into 2-inch cubes.

To serve, spoon about 1 cup of caponata on each plate, and top with 2 to 3 cubes of tuna. Drizzle each plate with the carrot vinaigrette.

CHEF'S NOTE: I prefer carrot juice that I get myself from a juice extractor (such as Magimix). If you don't have a juicer, you can use store-bought carrot juice but strain it three times through a fine-mesh strainer before you reduce it.

CAULIFLOWER "STEAKS"
WITH
PARSLEY BUTTER SAUCE

Serves 6 as side dish

My friend Claudia Sansone says that this way of cooking cauliflower is "shockingly good." There is something very satisfying about slicing a whole head of cauliflower into slabs, or "steaks" as I call them. It's a little tricky to cook these on a standard grill because the cauliflower tends to break apart and the flame burns the butter. When cooked on a plancha, the slices stay intact and develop a gorgeous golden crust. ❖ Smaller heads of cauliflower can be sliced more easily; larger heads tend to crumble, so seek out really fresh cauliflower with small heads for this dish. Look in farmers' markets, and try making this with purple and gold cauliflower too. ❖ This is a welcome dish for vegetarians. I also like to serve a piece of grilled salmon on top of a cauliflower steak. For a great sandwich, use any leftover cauliflower with grilled portobello mushrooms and roasted peppers.

2 small or 1 large head cauliflower (about 2 to 2¾ pounds)

Approximately ½ cup unsalted butter, at room temperature

2 tablespoons coarse sea salt, preferably gray salt

1 tablespoon freshly ground black pepper

2 lemons

1 tablespoon minced fresh flat-leaf parsley

Freshly grated Parmesan cheese (optional)

1 to 2 tablespoons extra-virgin olive oil for drizzling

Turn a gas grill to high or ignite charcoal. When your gas grill is hot or the coals have begun to turn gray, place the plancha on the grill rack and heat for at least 10 minutes.

Keep the core and stalk in place until after you've sliced the cauliflower. With a large sharp knife, cut the cauliflower head into slices, each about ½ inch thick. Cut away the stalk (just the base of it) from the bottom of each slice. With a knife or your fingers, give each cauliflower slab a good smear of softened butter on each side. Sprinkle each side with salt and pepper.

Place the cauliflower slabs on the hot plancha and cook until they show a nice caramelized crust, 5 to 6 minutes. While the cauliflower cooks, halve the lemons and place them cut-side down on the hot plancha for about 2 minutes. Remove from the grill and set the lemons aside. With a spatula, gently turn each cauliflower slab, and grill the other side until caramelized, another 5 minutes.

When both sides are golden brown, transfer the cauliflower slices to a serving platter, drizzle with juice from the grilled lemon, and garnish with parsley and, if you like, with a sprinkle of Parmesan. Drizzle with olive oil and serve while hot.

GRILLED
BEEF CHILI

FOR THOSE OF YOU WHO ARE THINKING, "LARD, NO WAY," HOLD ON A MINUTE.

Serves 10 to 12

This spicy chili has its game on, in part because I cook it with lard. For those of you who are thinking, "lard, no way," hold on a minute. Lard has less saturated fat than butter and more flavor. You can always substitute olive oil if you're not up for lard, but try it my way and see if you don't like what lard contributes. ❖ Masa harina makes the chili a little thicker while adding a complex flavor note. You can find it in Mexican markets, supermarkets, or see Resources, page 218. ❖ Cutting a chuck roast into cubes takes time. Ask your butcher to cut the beef for you, and save yourself the effort. ❖ I like this dish spicy. If you like a milder chili, halve the amount of chili powder.

3 pounds beef chuck roast, cut into ¾-inch cubes

2 teaspoons coarse sea salt, preferably gray salt

2 teaspoons freshly ground black pepper

1½ teaspoons ground cinnamon

3 teaspoons ground cumin

¼ cup chili powder

¼ cup masa harina (see headnote)

½ cup plus 2 teaspoons extra-virgin olive oil

4 jalapeño chiles

4 large red onions, peeled

¼ cup lard (or another ¼ cup olive oil)

2 tablespoons minced garlic (about 6 cloves)

¼ cup tomato paste

2 teaspoons dried oregano

Two 12-ounce bottles beer, either dark or light beer

One 12-ounce can diced tomato, juices reserved

1 quart Chicken Broth (page 217) or low-sodium store-bought stock

Three 12-ounce cans black beans, drained

Turn a gas grill to high or ignite charcoal. When your gas grill is hot or the coals have begun to turn gray, place the plancha or cast-iron pan on the grill rack and heat for at least 10 minutes. While the plancha is heating, season the beef cubes with salt and pepper on all sides.

Place about half of the beef chunks on the hot plancha, and cook until the beef has browned on every side, 4 to 5 minutes total, turning the cubes with tongs or a spatula to brown each side. Transfer the cooked beef to a baking sheet, and add the remaining beef cubes to the plancha. Cook, browning the meat on all sides. Transfer the cooked beef to the baking sheet with the first batch and save all the juices from the plancha. Take the plancha off the heat (place it somewhere safe where kids can't touch it), but leave the grill on.

In a large bowl, season the cooked beef with ½ teaspoon of the cinnamon, 1 teaspoon of the cumin, and 2 tablespoons of the chili powder. Mix the spices and beef cubes with your hands or a wooden spoon. When all the beef has been coated with spices, add the masa harina to the bowl, and mix again. Set the beef aside while you grill the vegetables.

Oil the whole chiles and onions with 2 teaspoons of the olive oil and grill, turning with tongs to cook all sides. When the skin has blistered and blackened on the chiles, transfer to a brown paper bag, seal up the bag, move them away from the heat, and let them steam for about 10 minutes. Take the onions off the grill when they show some char, and let them cool. Keep the grill on.

When cool enough to handle, dice the onions. Peel the skin from the chiles, and discard the skin and seeds. Mince the chiles. Keep the onions and garlic separate from the minced chiles.

Preheat a cast-iron Dutch oven on the grill over medium-high heat. Add ¼ cup of the olive oil to the pan. When the oil is hot, add half of the seasoned beef to the pan. Turn the beef with tongs so every side gets the heat. After about 4 minutes, transfer the beef from the pan to a baking sheet. Add the remaining ¼ cup of olive oil to the pan. Let it heat, then cook the remaining beef for an additional 4 minutes. Transfer the meat to the baking sheet with the first batch, leaving the juices in the Dutch oven to sauté the vegetables.

Add the lard to the hot Dutch oven (or add another ¼ cup of olive oil). When the lard is melted, add the onions and garlic and sauté until the onions start to caramelize, 1 to 2 minutes. Add the minced chiles and cook for another minute. Stir in the tomato paste. Add the remaining 1 teaspoon of the cinnamon, 2 teaspoons of cumin, and 2 tablespoons of chili powder (make these heaping tablespoons if you want a real kick of spice). Stir in the oregano and the beer. Stir in the diced tomatoes, with any juice reserved from the can, and then add the beef cubes. Pour in the chicken broth. Simmer, covered, on a medium grill or over a medium fire until the meat is tender, about 1½ hours. Stir in the beans. Cook until the beans are heated through, 5 to 10 minutes.

Ladle the chili into mugs or bowls and serve with slices of Polenta Bread slathered with Balsamic Honey Butter.

POLENTA BREAD
AND
BALSAMIC HONEY BUTTER

Serves 10 to 12

This bread is so good, you'll want to serve it often. You can bake it in your oven, but I like to cook it on the grill so I don't have to go into the kitchen to check on it. This works if you have a large, very stable grill.

 Under no circumstances should you place a large heavy pot on a grill that's not sturdy enough to hold it. If you have any doubts, cook this bread in your oven (see Chef's Note).

BALSAMIC HONEY BUTTER

1 cup (2 sticks) unsalted butter, at room temperature

6 tablespoons honey

1 teaspoon balsamic vinegar

POLENTA BREAD

1 cup (2 sticks) unsalted butter, plus more
  for greasing the pan

2 cups all-purpose flour

1½ cups finely ground polenta

¼ cup sugar

2 tablespoons baking powder

2 teaspoons baking soda

1½ teaspoons coarse sea salt, preferably gray salt

1 cup grated Asiago cheese

⅓ cup finely sliced green onions (green part only)

4 eggs

2 cups buttermilk

FOR THE BALSAMIC HONEY BUTTER: With a stand mixer fitted with the paddle attachment or in a food processor, cream together the softened butter, honey, and vinegar until the vinegar is completely stirred in and the butter is smooth in color and texture. Spoon the flavored butter into a crock or serving bowl and refrigerate for at least 1 hour. You can make this several days ahead if you like. Keep it tightly covered in the fridge until you're ready to serve the bread.

FOR THE POLENTA BREAD: Turn on the grill to low (375°F is an ideal temperature), or ignite charcoal. Spread the coals when they're glowing, and don't begin cooking until the coals have burned down a little.

Butter a 5-quart Dutch oven. Melt the butter in a small, heat-proof bowl in the microwave, and set it aside to cool.

In the bowl of a stand mixer fitted with the paddle attachment or with a hand mixer, combine the flour, polenta, sugar, baking powder, baking soda, salt, cheese, and green onions just until the green onions and cheese are evenly distributed.

In a separate bowl, whisk together the eggs, buttermilk, and melted butter. With the mixer on medium speed, pour the egg mixture into the bowl with the polenta mixture in a slow, steady stream. When all the liquid has been added, mix for 1 minute on medium speed to activate the baking powder.

Spread the batter in the Dutch oven and top with the lid. Place the covered Dutch oven on the grill rack, close the grill lid, and let the bread bake until the top is golden brown and gives some resistance when touched at the center, about 1 hour.

Remove the lid and transfer to a rack or a heat-proof counter to cool for 10 minutes. With mitts (the Dutch oven will be hot and heavy), tilt and rotate the pan, and gently tap it to see if the bread releases from the sides. If not, run the blade of a small metal spatula along the sides of the pan. Tip the Dutch oven on its side and use a metal spatula to remove the bread.

Place the bread on a cutting board, slice into wedges, and serve with the Balsamic Honey Butter.

CHEF'S NOTE: To bake in the oven, preheat the oven to 350°F. Bake the bread in the pan with the lid on for 50 to 60 minutes. Begin checking the bread after 50 minutes. The bread is done when it's golden brown and gives some resistance when pressed lightly in the center.

GRILLED CEVICHE-MARINATED CALAMARI AND SHRIMP WITH CANCHA POPCORN

Serves 6

In Ecuador, ceviche is served with *cancha* or *maiz chulpe* (the name changes according to the region)—dried kernels of corn tossed in oil and then toasted in a skillet until they puff. You and I know *cancha* as "Corn Nuts." I loved the flavor of *cancha* with ceviche but wanted something that soaked up the marinade a little better. I came up with popcorn tossed with ground-up Corn Nuts. You can laugh, but it works very well and if you hide the Corn Nuts package, your guests will have a hard time figuring out that elusive, exotic flavor. ❖ My version of ceviche is "grill and chill." It's not done in the order you'd expect. You grill the seafood very briefly and then refrigerate. While it's chilling, make the marinade, and toss it all together 30 minutes before serving. Make the marinade and grill the seafood the day before, if you like, but don't combine them until you're ready to serve. ❖ This recipe is a good one for people who are a little uneasy about true ceviche, in which the seafood is never touched by heat.

3 tablespoons extra-virgin olive oil

1 pound calamari, cleaned and split (ask your fishmonger to do this for you)

1 pound large (about 16 per pound) shrimp, peeled and deveined

1 teaspoon coarse sea salt, preferably gray salt

½ teaspoon freshly ground black pepper

3 whole tomatoes

2 medium red bell peppers

1 serrano chile

1 large yellow onion, peeled and sliced into ½-inch-thick whole rounds

¼ teaspoon grated lemon zest

2 tablespoons freshly squeezed lemon juice

¼ teaspoon grated orange zest

3 tablespoons freshly squeezed orange juice

¼ cup extra-virgin olive oil

½ teaspoon coarse sea salt, preferably gray salt

⅛ teaspoon freshly ground black pepper

CANCHA POPCORN

¼ cup Corn Nuts

¼ cup peanut oil

⅓ cup uncooked popcorn kernels

¼ teaspoon coarse sea salt, preferably gray salt

2 teaspoons finely chopped fresh cilantro, optional

Turn a gas grill to high or ignite charcoal. When your gas grill is hot or the coals have begun to turn gray, place the plancha or a large cast-iron pan on the grill rack and heat for at least 10 minutes.

While the plancha heats, drizzle the olive oil over the calamari and shrimp and season with the salt and pepper. On the hot plancha, grill the calamari first. It's done when it gets just a little color and begins to curl, about 1½ minutes for the main pieces and 2 minutes for the tentacles. Take it off the heat with tongs, let cool, and then refrigerate.

Cook the shrimp on the plancha or in a pan just until they begin to turn pink, 1½ to 2 minutes on each side. Remove from heat, let cool, and refrigerate.

Take the plancha off the heat (place it somewhere safe where kids can't touch it) but leave the grill on.

RECIPE CONTINUES

If using a gas grill, decrease the heat to medium. Cut an X in the bottom of each tomato and place them on the grill away from direct heat, with the X-side up. Turn them after 2 minutes using tongs or a spatula. Add the bell peppers, the serrano chile, and the onion slices to the grill and cover the grill. After 3 to 4 minutes, turn the tomatoes, onions, and chile and close the lid again.

Take the tomatoes off the grill when they are blistered but still hold their shape, about 8 minutes. Take the chile off the grill when it's blistered all over, after about 10 minutes. Put it in a paper bag that's large enough to hold it and all the peppers, and fold up the top of the bag. Keep cooking the bell peppers until they're blackened all the way around, 15 to 18 minutes, then add them to the bag with the chile and let them steam. Grill the onion slices until they show dark color on each side, about 18 minutes total.

When the tomatoes have cooled enough to handle, peel away the skin and discard. Halve the tomatoes horizontally and squeeze out the seeds into a sieve suspended over a bowl to catch the juices. Peel the peppers and chile and discard the skins.

Coarsely chop about half of the tomatoes, peppers, chile, and onions and place into a blender. Add any liquid saved from the tomatoes. Add the lemon and orange juices and zests, olive oil, salt, and pepper, and blend until smooth. The liquid in the blender will be the marinade for the seafood. Finely chop the remaining tomatoes, peppers, chile, and onions, and refrigerate. The diced vegetables will garnish the platter when you're ready to serve.

Thirty minutes before serving, toss the calamari and shrimp in the marinade with all the reserved diced vegetables in a serving bowl. Refrigerate to chill, while you make the popcorn. (This is best with fresh, hot popcorn, so don't pop the corn until you're almost ready to serve.)

FOR THE POPCORN: First, grind the Corn Nuts in a clean coffee grinder or spice grinder and set aside.

Pour the peanut oil into a large pot with a cover and place over high heat. When the oil is hot, add the popcorn and cover the pot. Take the pot off the heat when the popping slows down.

In a bowl, toss the fresh popcorn, the ground Corn Nuts, salt, and the cilantro, if using.

Pour the cancha popcorn over the seafood, and serve right away while the ceviche is cold and the popcorn is warm.

GRILLED MUSHROOMS WITH SAUSAGES, ONIONS, AND PEPPERS

Serves 6 to 8

This dish has a lot of meaning for me because it speaks about my ancestors in Italy as well as the mushroom hunting I've done here in California. This food connects those two points in time and those two groups of people, the Calabrians and their American descendants. ❖ When I make this, I think of my daughter Felicia, who, like me, keeps many of these food memories. Felicia leads with her heart, and has the soul of an artist. Having an artist's soul doesn't always make for a calm life, but Felicia experiences every day with all her being, and inspires me to see old things in new ways. Having Felicia as a daughter brings me much joy.

3 tablespoons extra-virgin olive oil, plus more as needed

8 links hot or sweet sausage, preferably Calabrese

1 pound mushrooms, stemmed and cut into ½-inch julienne (julienne the stems too)

Coarse sea salt, preferably gray salt

Freshly ground black pepper

3 sweet onions, cut into ½-inch-thick slices

3 red bell peppers, cored, seeded, and cut into ½-inch julienne

2 teaspoons dried oregano

1 tablespoon chopped fresh flat-leaf parsley

Turn a gas grill to high or ignite charcoal. When your gas grill is hot or the coals have turned gray, place the plancha or a big cast-iron skillet on the grill rack and heat until smoking hot, at least 10 minutes. Pour in the olive oil.

Brown the sausages on the plancha or in the pan; remove them from the pan and set aside. Add more oil to the pan if needed. Add the mushrooms, and sprinkle on some salt and pepper. Let them cook without moving them for about 7 minutes. When they've caramelized, stir the mushrooms and add the onions and bell peppers and a little more salt and black pepper. Let them cook until all the vegetables are gorgeously caramelized. Sprinkle on the oregano and parsley, and put the sausages back on top of the vegetables on the plancha or in the pan.

This dish is very flexible; after a long day of mushroom hunting you have to be flexible. Serve when ready.

POTATO POLPETTE, TWO WAYS

Makes 8 polpette

What do you do with leftover mashed potatoes? I make polpette. ❖ For my money, a polpetta—a croquette of mashed potatoes with a savory filling—trumps any other kind of potato dish hands down. The beauty of a polpetta is that it's versatile: you can make these from just about any leftovers in your fridge. It's especially good with leftovers from the grill. I'll show you two ways to fill a polpetta—but don't stop with these fillings. Try grilled squash, sweet potatoes, or thinly sliced grilled asparagus. ❖ You can use a mold such as a round ramekin or the lid of a wide-mouthed canning jar to help shape consistent patties (see Shaping Burgers, page 66). ❖ Halve this recipe if you're cooking for two or three people. At my house, kids from ages six to twenty-eight stay close to the kitchen when they know I'm cooking polpette. ❖ I like the smoky flavor that they get by cooking them outdoors, but polpette can be cooked just as easily inside at the stove.

3 pounds russet potatoes

5 quarts water, plus more if needed

5 tablespoons kosher salt

½ teaspoon coarse sea salt, preferably gray salt, if needed

¼ teaspoon freshly ground black pepper

Wild Mushroom Filling (facing page) or
Prosciutto and Dried Fruit Filling (facing page)

6 tablespoons sesame seeds, toasted
(if using mushroom filling; see Chef's Note), or
6 tablespoons poppy seeds (if using prosciutto filling)

Extra-virgin olive oil

2 to 3 tablespoons butter (if cooking at the stove)

Peel the potatoes, and cut them into large chunks. Put the potatoes in a large pot and cover them with the water. Add the kosher salt to the water, and bring to a boil over high heat. Decrease the heat to medium and boil gently until the potatoes are tender, about 10 minutes.

Preheat the oven to 325°F.

When the potatoes can be pierced easily with a fork, drain them. Transfer with a slotted spoon to a large sturdy baking sheet (two baking sheets if they won't fit easily on one). Place the sheets in the oven and bake until the potatoes have lost most of their moisture, about 5 minutes. Let the potatoes cool and then press through a ricer. If you don't have a ricer, push the potatoes through the large holes of a box grater (watch your fingers) or a colander. Taste the potatoes to see how salty they are; if you taste salt, decrease the amount of salt used in the fillings. Shape the potatoes into 16 patties, each 3½ to 4 inches in diameter. Each patty will contain about ¼ cup of mashed potatoes.

Spoon about 2 tablespoons of the filling onto one of the potato patties. Top with another patty and gently pat the edges to seal. Repeat until all 16 patties have been formed into 8 polpette. Sprinkle with pepper but don't add more salt at this point unless the potatoes taste bland.

Pour some seeds onto a piece of plastic wrap or parchment paper and spread it with your fingers. Place the polpetta onto the seeds, sprinkle more of the seeds on the top, and lightly press the seeds with your fingers to help them adhere to both sides.

TO COOK THE POLPETTE ON THE PLANCHA: Turn a gas grill to high or ignite charcoal. When your gas grill is hot or the coals have begun to turn gray, place the plancha on the grill rack and heat for at least 10 minutes.

Pour a little olive oil on a paper towel and rub down the plancha, using tongs to hold the towel. Place as many polpette on the plancha as can fit.

Cook until a crust forms on the potatoes, about 4 minutes. Gently turn with a spatula and cook until a crust forms on the other side.

TO COOK THE POLPETTE AT THE STOVE: Heat a griddle, large cast-iron skillet, or saucepan over high heat. Add 1 tablespoon of extra-virgin olive oil and 1 tablespoon of butter to the pan. When the oil is hot, add three or four polpette. Cook until a crust forms on the potatoes, 5 to 8 minutes. Gently turn with a spatula and cook until a crust forms on the other side.

When a batch of polpette is done and transferred to a serving platter, clean out the pan with a paper towel and add another 1 tablespoon of olive oil and 1 tablespoon of butter before cooking another batch.

GRILLING ISN'T JUST FOR BIG EXPENSIVE CUTS OF MEAT. WITH A LITTLE CREATIVITY, LEFTOVERS CAN BENEFIT FROM SOME TIME ON THE FIRE.

WILD MUSHROOM FILLING

The Chiarellos are a family of mushroom hunters. If we come home with a lot of wild mushrooms, you can bet that polpette will put in an appearance that week.

¼ pound shiitake or other mushrooms
1½ tablespoons extra-virgin olive oil
½ teaspoon coarse sea salt, preferably gray salt
¼ teaspoon freshly ground black pepper
½ teaspoon finely chopped fresh thyme

Trim off the mushroom stems. (Shiitake stems are too woody to use in this filling; if you're using other mushroom varieties, dice and use the trimmed stems after cutting off the tough stem bottom.) Dice the mushroom caps.

Heat a saucepan over high heat until it's hot. Add the olive oil, and heat until the oil is hot but not smoking. Add the mushrooms to the hot oil and don't move them until they are caramelized, 8 to 10 minutes. Once the bottoms of the mushrooms show some good dark brown color, then you can stir them.

Add the salt, pepper, and thyme. Cook for 1 more minute and then take off the heat. Let cool slightly before you fill the polpette.

CHEF'S NOTE: In a dry saucepan over medium-high heat, toast the sesame seeds. When you begin to smell their fragrance, take the pan off the heat and pour the sesame seeds onto a plate or piece of parchment paper to cool.

PROSCIUTTO AND DRIED FRUIT FILLING

Use prosciutto bits for this recipe, not paper-thin prosciutto slices. Ask your butcher or the deli person if you can buy the whole "heel" of the prosciutto, and then chop it into ⅛-inch pieces or ask the butcher to coarsely grind it for you.

½ cup dried fruit, preferably apricot, pear, peach, or a combination
1 cup water
2 tablespoons unsalted butter
¼ pound chunk prosciutto, cut into ⅛-inch bits (see headnote)
¼ teaspoon minced fresh rosemary
¼ teaspoon coarse sea salt, preferably gray salt
¼ teaspoon freshly ground black pepper
2 teaspoons white balsamic vinegar

Soak the dried fruit in the 1 cup water to soften, 30 to 60 minutes. Drain the fruit and pat dry with paper towels. Dice the fruit and set aside.

Heat the butter in a saucepan over medium-high heat. When it's melted, add the prosciutto bits and cook until they begin to brown, about 5 minutes. Add the minced rosemary, dried fruit, salt, and pepper and cook for 1 minute. Deglaze the pan with the vinegar, and turn off the heat. Taste and add more salt and pepper if needed. Let cool slightly before you fill the polpette.

ROASTED
LEMON
GRANITA

Makes 2 cups

When you roast lemons, the juice tastes completely different from the juice of raw lemons. The more complex and layered flavor means the juice of roasted lemons works well in a granita. Compared to the tiny crystals of a sorbet or gelato, the larger crystals of a granita last longer on your tongue, so you get a more concentrated roasted lemon-sugar flavor. If you're more a fan of ice cream than granita, pour the roasted lemon juice into your favorite ice cream base.

12 lemons

¼ teaspoon coarse sea salt, preferably gray salt,
  or kosher salt

2 tablespoons honey

¾ cup sugar

¾ cup water

2 star anise

1 teaspoon anise seed

Pinch of freshly ground black pepper

GRILLING OR ROASTING LEMONS

Because the acidity in lemons can clash with a good wine, I'm a big fan of roasting lemons to bring down their acidity.

Roasting is easy. Just halve the lemons crosswise at their midsection and put them on the hot grill rack or plancha, cut-side down. Let them roast until they show a good amount of char, 3 to 5 minutes depending on the heat of the coals, then take them off the heat using tongs. You can also use the tongs to squeeze the hot lemons over a strainer, capturing all the juice you can.

The juice of roasted lemons is especially good over vegetables: drizzle it over broccoli rabe or steamed cauliflower as well as over a roasted chicken, fresh crab, or any fresh fish.

Turn a gas grill to high or ignite charcoal. When your gas grill is hot or the coals have begun to turn gray, place the plancha on the grill rack and heat for at least 10 minutes.

Slice a thin section from the base and top of each lemon (so they can stand without wobbling) and halve each lemon crosswise at its midsection.

Place the lemons cut-side down on the hot plancha. (You can also put them right on the grill rack or in a cast-iron pan set over the grill or campfire.)

Grill until the cut side shows some char and the lemons look plumper, about 3 to 5 minutes depending on the heat of your fire. (If I want a smokier flavor, I'll turn the lemons over to get some heat on their stem ends as well.) Take them off the heat and use tongs to press the hot lemons against a fine-mesh sieve held over a bowl, capturing all the juice. The juice will contain tiny flecks of char, but that's fine. Stir in the salt.

In a small saucepan, heat 1⅓ cups of the roasted lemon juice (save any leftover juice for another use) over medium heat. Increase the heat to high and stir in the honey, sugar, the ¾ cup water, star anise, anise seed, and black pepper. When it comes to a boil, pour through a fine-mesh strainer into a large bowl.

Freeze the liquid in a 13- by 9-inch metal baking pan, stirring with a fork and breaking apart any lumps of ice every 30 minutes. It will take at least 3 to 4 hours for the mixture to solidify. Don't let it freeze solid: each time you stir the granita, set a timer for 30 minutes so you don't forget about it. Once it's frozen to the consistency of a slushie, cover the pan with plastic wrap. It can stay in your freezer for up to 3 days. Just slush it up with a fork when you're ready to serve.

CHEF'S NOTE: When serving, drizzle on a little lemon vodka for a more intense lemon flavor. I recommend Charbay Meyer Lemon Vodka; see Resources, page 218.

DINNER AT THE LAKE

When I was a kid, trout fishing was a treat I got to do with my big brother Ron. He taught me how to fish and how to cook fish over a campfire. Ron called it cooking hobo-style (see following note) because no special equipment was needed. He would pack foil and seasonings in his backpack with a few potatoes and apples. You had to catch your own dinner. The whole meal came together out of one pack and what we caught.

I can recall every detail of the last time we did this: a moon so bright it lit the hiking trail, pulling the fish out of the lake early in the morning, setting up our fire. These days, when I cook trout, I think of Ron, and those memories give the fish extra flavor.

When you take your kids—or your younger brother—camping, or you cook for friends around a campfire, you are giving them flavors that they will be able to recall decades later. Their fish will taste a little better from that day forward, and so will yours.

Back in the early part of the nineteenth century, hobos were not homeless people but migrants—workers who jumped on board freight trains in search of any work that paid. Some people believe the word *hobo* was first used to refer to soldiers trying to make their way home on trains after the Civil War, but *hobo* was most often used in the United States after the Great Depression. ❖ *Hobo* and *homeless* are not the same thing. A hobo's life was hard but nowhere near as hard as life is for the homeless in our country today. I'm a big supporter of Meals on Wheels and Clinic Olé. For more information on these great organizations, go to www.mowaa.org or www.clinicole.org.

NONNA'S ROASTED GARLIC BREAD

Serves 8 to 10

You probably expect a loaf of homemade bread here, but no. My nonna knew a good baker and she bought his bread and then coal-roasted her own garlic for her garlic bread. You don't need to reinvent the wheel.

This is great for a camping trip as long as you make it your first night out. Before you leave home, make a compound butter from the garlic paste, thyme, and softened butter, roll it into a log, wrap in aluminum foil, and freeze it. Take it out of the freezer and store in a cooler for the camping trip. Remember to take the butter out of the cooler when you start the fire, so it's soft enough to spread.

½ cup Roasted Garlic Paste (page 212)
½ cup (1 stick) unsalted butter, at
    room temperature
1 tablespoon finely chopped fresh thyme
One 2-pound loaf ciabatta or bâtard,
    halved lengthwise

Stir together the garlic paste, softened butter, and fresh thyme. Either roll it into a log and freeze it or set it aside to use right away. A compound butter will keep in your freezer for up to 1 month.

Have ready a campfire or a charcoal fire that is turning to ash or turn your gas grill to high. When the fire is hot, clean the grill rack. Decrease the temperature to medium-high, and brush or wipe a little olive oil on the grill rack.

Toast both crust and cut sides of the bread on a grill pan set over a campfire, a hot grill rack, a grill pan on the stove, or under your broiler. Toast until grill marks show or until the bread is golden brown and toasty, about 4 minutes per side. Spread the butter mixture onto the cut side of the toasted bread. Put it back on the grill rack or grill pan with the buttered side up for just 1 to 2 minutes. (If using a grill, close the lid for the last minute.) Slice and serve.

FRESH-CAUGHT TROUT COOKED IN FOIL

Serves 4

Optimally, your trout will weigh about ¾ pound each, but this recipe works no matter how big or small your fish ends up being. Just remember to add a few inches when you tell people how big the fish were.

If you are buying fish, ask your fishmonger to clean and debone them for you.

4 trout, about ¾ pound each
    (see headnote)
About 3 tablespoons extra-virgin olive oil
2 lemons, thinly sliced
4 tablespoons fresh flat-leaf parsley
    leaves, stemmed
4 teaspoons fresh tarragon
Coarse sea salt, preferably gray salt
Freshly ground black pepper

Start a campfire, ignite charcoal, or turn the gas grill to high.

Scale the fish and lift out the bones. Leave the tail intact but cut off the fins. Rinse the fish inside and out with cool water and pat dry with paper towels.

Have ready 12 sheets of aluminum foil, each 16 inches long. For each fish, stack two sheets of aluminum foil and have a third sheet of foil ready for the top. Drizzle about 1 teaspoon olive oil on the top sheet of foil and place the fish on top skin-side down. Open the fish and arrange three to five thin lemon slices inside—enough so the trout has lemon from end to end. Drizzle on another 1 teaspoon olive oil and sprinkle with 1 table-spoon parsley leaves and 1 teaspoon fresh tarragon. Sprinkle with sea salt and pepper. Place the third sheet of foil on top of the fish, then neatly fold each side into a foil packet, using the bottom layers of foil to close and seal the top sheet of foil in place.

When the coals are more gray than red, put the foil packets right on top the coals (or cook on a gas grill set to medium). Shovel some coals from the edge of the fire over the packets to cover them or fill a grill basket with hot coals and rest the grill basket on top of the fish packets. Roast the fish for about 4 minutes. Take one packet out of the fire and open it to see if the fish looks done—when it's opaque and more white than pink. If it's still pink inside, rewrap the fish and put it back on the coals for another 2 to 3 minutes.

Take the packets out of the coals, let them cool for at least 2 minutes, and then let each person unwrap their own fish.

FOIL-WRAPPED EMBER-ROASTED BEETS WITH GOAT CHEESE

Serves 4

For a camping trip, scrub and package the beets in two large aluminum foil packets before you leave home, so they're ready for the fire. I triple-wrap the beets in foil so there's less chance of beet-to-ash contact. You can form packets as we did with the trout (see page 120) or you can wrap the foil into a shape like a beggar's purse.

If you're cooking these at home on a gas grill, set the heat to medium, and put the packets in the center of the grill rack until the beets are tender, about 45 minutes.

VINAIGRETTE

1 tablespoon Champagne vinegar

2 tablespoons extra-virgin olive oil

½ teaspoon coarse sea salt,
    preferably gray salt

¼ teaspoon freshly ground black pepper

MARINATED GOAT CHEESE

3 tablespoons extra-virgin olive oil

3 teaspoons chopped fresh rosemary

3 tablespoons grated lemon zest
    (from about 3 lemons)

½ teaspoon coarse sea salt, preferably
    gray salt

¼ teaspoon freshly ground black pepper

Four 2-ounce rounds soft chèvre
    goat cheese

1½ pounds baby beets, preferably
    a mix of red and yellow

5 tablespoons extra-virgin olive oil

2 teaspoons coarse sea salt, preferably
    gray salt

½ teaspoon freshly ground black pepper

FOR THE VINAIGRETTE: Whisk together the vinegar, olive oil, salt, and pepper. Set aside.

FOR THE GOAT CHEESE: Whisk together the olive oil, rosemary, lemon zest, salt, and pepper. Spoon half of the marinade into a baking dish with a cover or any

container with a tight-fitting lid. Place the goat cheese rounds on top of the marinade and spoon the remaining marinade over the top. Cover and refrigerate for at least 1 hour or overnight. If you're taking this on a camping trip, mix the cheese and marinade just before you leave home, and pack it in your cooler.

Clean and trim the top of each beet, leaving about 1 inch of green stem. In a large bowl, toss the beets with olive oil and a generous amount of salt and pepper. Divide the beets into two batches; you'll make two foil packets in all.

Have ready six sheets of aluminum foil, each about 20 inches long. Arrange the foil sheets into two 3-sheet stacks. Divide the seasoned beets into two batches and place one batch on each foil stack. Pull up the sides of the foil and twist at the top.

Place the packets in the embers of the campfire after the fire has died down. Let them cook until the beets are tender but not too soft, about 45 minutes. Carefully open a packet and pierce a beet with a knife to test if beets are done. Let them cool for at least 10 minutes in their packets before you unwrap them. If you like you can pop the beets out of their skins before cutting them into quarters.

Place a round of goat cheese on each of four plates. Divide the beets among the plates next to the cheese and and drizzle with vinaigrette before serving.

ROSEMARY-LEMON BARS

Serves 16

A cross between standard lemon bars and lemon cake, this dessert travels well, so it's a good addition to camping trips or a day at the beach. Finely minced rosemary gives it an herbal note that complements the lemon. For more subtle rosemary flavor use 2 teaspoons. I use a full 1 tablespoon for a bigger herbal punch. When the cake is warm you'll taste more of the rosemary than when it's cooled. It's good either way.

1½ cups all-purpose flour

½ teaspoon coarse sea salt, preferably gray salt

1 cup (2 sticks) unsalted butter, at room temperature, plus more for greasing the pan

2 cups granulated sugar

4 eggs

2 teaspoons pure lemon extract (optional)

2 teaspoons grated lemon zest

1 tablespoon minced fresh rosemary (see headnote)

LEMON GLAZE

1 cup confectioners' sugar

3 tablespoons freshly squeezed lemon juice

2 teaspoons grated lemon zest

Preheat the oven to 350°F. Butter a 13- by 9-by-2-inch baking pan and set aside.

Sift together the flour and the salt and set aside.

In the bowl of a stand mixer fitted with the paddle attachment or with a hand mixer, cream the butter and granulated sugar on medium speed until the mixture looks pale yellow and creamy, about 3 minutes. Add the eggs, one at a time, beating for 30 seconds after each egg. Add the lemon extract, zest, and the rosemary. Gradually add the flour mixture, while continuing to beat at medium speed. Mix for 30 seconds after the mixture is blended.

Pour the batter into the buttered pan and bake until the cake is a light golden brown on top and a skewer comes out clean when tested in the center of the cake, 30 to 40 minutes.

FOR THE GLAZE: Combine the confectioners' sugar, lemon juice, and zest in a medium bowl, stirring with a wooden spoon until smooth.

When the cake comes out of the oven, pierce the entire top with the tines of a fork in even rows, then pour on the glaze while the cake is still hot.

Cut into 16 squares and serve warm or at room temperature.

ONE PERFECT COCKTAIL
FOR FIRST NIGHT

I went on a fishing trip to Montana with a group of friends that included renowned vintner Dan Duckhorn. Dan carried a cooler onboard the plane but wouldn't tell us what was inside. That night, when our fish was over the fire, Dan opened the cooler and pulled out an ice-cold cocktail shaker, along with ice and the makings for one perfectly chilled, delicious cocktail for each of us.

That made a big impression on me. There's something about having a well-considered cocktail when you're sitting beside a fire, with a tent as your lodging, that makes the drink taste even better than usual. My favorite first-night cocktail is the Highwayman's Mojito (page 203), but I've also made Dan Duckhorn's favorite drink (see page 200) for my fishing buddies. Bring a cocktail like Dan's and you'll be a first-night hero even if your catch isn't as big as you'd hoped.

CHAPTER FIVE

LIVE FIRE: THE FIRE PIT

The fire pit offers a more communal sort of cooking than standing over a grill. I cook entire meals over my fire pit and barbecue is just the start. You can let a pot of chicken stew simmer or bake beans Italian style by hanging the pot from a hook over the fire. The fire pit is also a good place to cook and share a hot appetizer, or to make s'mores under the stars.

When you cook outside, the pace is slower; there's a tendency to relax a little more, and let the fire do the work. If you have guests, it's more comfortable to cook at the fire pit while they enjoy the experience with you. When you cook outside by the fire pit, you don't miss as much. You get to feel a breeze on your face, hear the wind rustling through the leaves—things you miss when you cook indoors.

WHY A FIRE PIT IS MY FAVORITE STOVE

People ask me all the time which stove I prefer. If the best stove is the one that can generate the most heat and give me the most control, then my favorite stove might be my fire pit. The fire pit can reach a very high temperature. I can raise and lower the racks to bring the food closer to the heat for faster cooking or farther away for a low, slow roast. ❖ Best of all, the crowd that hangs around the stove inside my house fits better around the fire pit outside. When I'm inside cooking, I love having people gathered around, but if I find myself tripping over someone's feet, then cooking becomes less fun, more frustration.

HOW TO BUY (OR BUILD) A FIRE PIT

When I say "fire pit" four different people will have four different ideas of what I'm talking about. The original fire pit, a basic hole in the ground, was lined with leaves or rocks and then covered once the food was added so the ground acted as insulation, holding in the heat. We're not cooking over that kind of fire pit; although it's a time-honored way of cooking, I don't feel like digging a pit.

These days you can buy a fire pit, have it shipped to you, and put it together in no time. The high-end fire pit that we're using in this book is custom-made, built with a low circular brick wall and a sturdy metal frame that holds grates as well as a strong metal hook for holding a pot of chili (see page 108) or chicken and dumplings over the fire (see page 141). If you don't have access to this kind of fire pit, flip to page 219 to see our low-end fire pit. I built this fire pit in an hour in my backyard using ordinary bricks. If you have a grate and bricks, then the fire pit is within your reach and affordable, as well as easy to take apart and store.

If you already have a fire pit but don't have a grate for it, you can have grates custom-made. (See Resources, page 218.) Before you do that, check with the manufacturer to see if they sell grates for their fire pit, and even take a trip to your local hardware store to see if they might sell a grate that fits your equipment. Remember that you control heat over a fire pit in two ways: You can raise or lower the food away from the flame, or you can spread out the coals or glowing logs to reduce the heat a bit.

If you don't have a grate, you can still cook over a fire pit. Look at the beef cooked on lances on pages 136 and 138. Flip to page 85 and see how we cooked quail on branches. Thinking about how people cooked hundreds of years ago can spark some creativity. You could spend thousands to re-create your kitchen outdoors but don't do it. There is much more satisfaction to be found in cooking with what's on hand.

THE FIRE PIT FIRE

Build a fire pit fire just as you would a campfire or a fire in your hearth. See How to Start a Fire, page 26. Before burning any wood, see Woods to Never Cook Over, page 19. Check that your wood supply is well stocked before you start the fire.

There's a time lag between when you start the fire pit fire and when it's ready for cooking. Don't cook over flames ever. Let the fire peak and then, when the logs are glowing and there's a steady, even source of heat, that's the time to begin cooking. The one temptation that you want to avoid with a fire pit is to start the fire and then walk away to complete some other task.

 I like to bring my knives, cutting boards, and bowls outside, and work next to the fire. If you can't do this, have another adult sit by the fire and keep an eye on it while you're in the kitchen.

LET THE FIRE PEAK AND THEN, WHEN THE LOGS ARE GLOWING AND THERE'S A STEADY, EVEN SOURCE OF HEAT, THAT'S THE TIME TO BEGIN COOKING.

GRILLED
ITALIAN
PEPPERS STUFFED
WITH
SAUSAGE

Serves 8

I like to cook with a wide variety of peppers; it's the first thing I look for when I hit the farmers' market. When you find peppers that look beautiful, this is a good way to use them. It's hard to go wrong with peppers stuffed with sausage. You can use either hot or sweet sausage, and this recipe will work with just about any pepper, from big red bells to small Gypsy peppers. ❖ Once you've stuffed the peppers, you can finish them at your fire pit, on the grill, on the plancha, at the hearth, in a grill pan on your stove, or in a wood-burning oven.

4 tablespoons kosher salt

16 Italian sweet green peppers or any bell pepper

2 pounds bulk Italian sausage, either sweet or hot

3 tablespoons finely grated Parmesan cheese

1½ teaspoons dried oregano

2 tablespoons chopped fresh flat-leaf parsley

2 tablespoons chopped fresh basil, minced

1½ cups finely diced onion

1½ cups fine dried bread crumbs

1¼ cups cool water

2 eggs

2 cup Grilled Tomato Sauce (page 215)

Start a fire in a fire pit (or start a gas or charcoal grill). Stay nearby (or have another adult stay near), until the flames have died down, and the fire bed provides an even heat source. If cooking on a grill rack, clean it once it's hot. If using a plancha, put it on the rack or directly on the fire about 10 minutes before you're ready to cook.

Inside, on the stove, heat about 4 quarts of water in a large pot over high heat. Add the kosher salt.

Slice off the stem end from each pepper and discard it. Gently scrape out the seeds and cut out the ribs with a small paring knife, taking care not to break the pepper. You want each pepper to be whole for stuffing.

When the water in the pot boils, add all the peppers. Let them cook for 4 minutes, then using tongs, transfer the peppers to a baking sheet to cool.

Form the sausage meat into six to eight sausage patties, each about ¼ inch thick. Either on the grill rack or in a sauté pan, cook the patties until they're brown on both sides, about 5 minutes. Let them cool.

When cool enough to handle, dice the sausage meat. In a large bowl combine the meat, cheese, oregano, parsley, basil, onion, bread crumbs, the 1¼ cups water, and eggs, using your hands or a wooden spoon, until all ingredients are evenly distributed.

With a spoon or your fingers, gently stuff each pepper with the meat mixture. Fill to ½ inch from the top of the pepper. Any leftover meat can be stored in the freezer for up to 1 month.

Place the peppers onto a hot grill rack, grill pan, or plancha. Use tongs to turn them when the skin begins to darken, about every 2 minutes. Cook for about 8 minutes in all. Warm the tomato sauce while the peppers cook.

To serve, take the stuffed peppers off the fire, arrange in a serving dish, and pour on the warm tomato sauce.

SANDWICH VARIATION: Toast a hoagie roll or Italian bun. Top each toasted bun with one or two grilled stuffed peppers. Add a slice of provolone while the peppers are hot so it melts, and finish with a generous drizzle of warm tomato sauce.

SKEWERED
MORTADELLA AND PROVOLONE

Serves 8

If I had to choose just one guilty pleasure for this book, this would be it. This dish reminds me of my mom and the day a friend from church introduced her to fried bologna. She was so excited about frying her own bologna. I have a vivid memory of her snipping the edges of the perfectly round bologna slice so it wouldn't curl up in the pan. This, from a woman who made her own wine, pickles, pasta, and even prosciutto. The thing was, we never ate foods like "boloney." To a kid who grew up on homemade gnocchi and Nonna's sauce, fried bologna seemed exotic. ❖ Years after my mom died, I was in Italy, walking through Bologna, in Emilia-Romagna, when I saw someone eating a mortadella steak that was easily three-quarters of an inch thick, cut into wedges with a creamy cheese over the top. It struck me like a bolt of lightning, the link between Bologna and Italian bologna, which is called mortadella. Even the homogenized supermarket bologna that most Americans know had its roots here, in the Italy of long ago when meats had to be preserved so there was enough to eat in the winter. I stood there feeling as if I'd come full circle from the day my mom first fried bologna in our kitchen when I was a boy. ❖ For this dish, you'll have to go to an authentic Italian deli to buy the mortadella; ask the butcher to slice it into one-inch-thick rounds. ❖ When the skewers come off the heat, I pour myself a cold beer or a glass of unoaked Chardonnay and am completely happy, sitting back with my own version of fried bologna while I spend a few moments thinking about my mom. ❖ Please note: I never waste a fire. To build a fire for just this one dish would break my mother's heart. Instead, I plan a whole meal to be cooked at the fire pit, and start with these. These are great as a snack while you start cooking the chili (see page 108) or chicken and dumplings (see page 141).

1½ pounds mortadella, cut into 1-inch-thick rounds

1½ pounds provolone cheese

¼ cup extra-virgin olive oil

1 tablespoon dried oregano

2 teaspoons Calabrian chile paste,
    or ¼ teaspoon red pepper flakes

2 to 4 garlic cloves, minced

4 teaspoons minced fresh flat-leaf parsley

Grilled Peach-Nectarine Mostarda (page 132)

Soak eight 12-inch wooden skewers in cold water for at least 30 minutes.

Cut off the outside skin from each mortadella slice and discard. Slice the meat and the cheese into neat 1-inch cubes. (For good-looking skewers, cut all the cubes the same size.)

Pour the olive oil into a medium bowl. Add the oregano, chile paste, a little or a lot of the garlic, and parsley. Add the cheese and meat cubes, toss well, and refrigerate. Marinate for 1 hour.

Start a fire in a fire pit. Stay nearby (or have another adult stay near) until the flames have died down, and the fire bed provides an even heat source. Decide how you'd like to cook the skewers: if your fire pit has a grill rack, you can place the skewers across the rack. If your fire pit doesn't have a rack, use a plancha or a large cast iron skillet grill pan on top of your stove.

Skewer the meat and cheese, alternating so you have 4 cheese and 4 meat cubes on each skewer.

Grill the skewers until the meat shows a little brown and the cheese is soft, about 2 minutes per side. Don't leave it on the grill so long that the cheese melts.

Serve it with the mostarda.

GRILLED
PEACH-NECTARINE
MOSTARDA

Makes 6 cups

Grilling the fruit adds a smoky flavor note to this sweet, pungent condiment. Choose fruit that is ripe but still firm so it doesn't break over the fire. You can use any fruit you like for mostarda: grilled apples and pears or grilled figs and berries are great in this recipe. ❖ Mostarda keeps for up to 3 months. When I have good fruit on hand and a fire already going, I grill the fruit, set it aside, and then make mostarda when time allows.

3 large nectarines, peeled, halved, and pitted

3 large peaches, peeled, halved, and pitted

1 serrano chile

2 tablespoons extra-virgin olive oil

3 tablespoons freshly squeezed lemon juice

½ teaspoon sea salt, preferably gray salt

Freshly ground black pepper

2½ cups sugar

⅓ cup water

1 shallot, minced

Pinch of red pepper flakes

⅔ cup dried cherries

½ cup golden raisins

½ cup dry white wine

2 bay leaves

1½ cups Dijon mustard

Have ready a low-to-medium wood or charcoal fire in the fire pit or set a gas grill to medium. When the fire pit rack or the grill rack is hot, clean it, and brush or wipe it with a little olive oil.

In a large bowl, drizzle the fruit halves and the whole serrano chile with the olive oil, 1 tablespoon of the lemon juice, salt, and black pepper. Toss with your hands so the fruit is evenly coated.

Place the fruit on the grill, cut-side down. Grill the fruit until it shows light grill marks, about 3 minutes. Turn the fruit over and cook for another 2 to 3 minutes. Take the fruit off the heat. Let the serrano roast until it's charred all the way around, and then pop it into a small brown bag, seal, and let it steam for 10 minutes.

Scrape the skin from the chile, cut in half, and scrape out the seeds. Discard the seeds and the stem, and mince the chile. Set aside.

Indoors at the stove, in a large, heavy nonreactive pot combine the sugar, the ⅓ cup water, and remaining 2 tablespoons of lemon juice. Cook over high heat until the sugar turns dark amber, 12 to 15 minutes. Decrease the heat to medium-low and stir in the shallots, red pepper flakes, and minced serrano, and then quickly add the grilled fruit, the cherries and the raisins, the wine, and the bay leaves. Cook gently, until the fruit is tender, 10 to 15 minutes. Remove the pot from the heat, and let cool for at least 10 minutes. Gently stir in the mustard and taste for seasoning. When the mostarda has come to room temperature, refrigerate in a covered container. Store, tightly covered, in your freezer for up to 3 months.

3-LITER OO CAN MUSSELS
AND
GYPSY PEPPERS

Serves 4

I like to reuse when I can; here an olive oil tin gets a new life. You can either go to your local food warehouse and buy a big tin of olive oil or go to your favorite pizza place and ask if they have any empty tins you can take. (You may want to order a pizza before you ask.) Grab a tin for every four people you're serving and double or triple this recipe as needed. ♣ Gypsy peppers are sweeter than bell peppers, with a thin skin that makes them cook up nicely. You'll find them at farmers' markets in September or October.

One empty 3-liter olive oil tin

1 pint Gypsy peppers

1 tablespoon extra-virgin olive oil

1 tablespoon minced garlic

**2 tablespoons Pernod, or 2 tablespoons skillet-toasted
   fennel seed**

1 cup dry white wine

2 pounds mussels, scrubbed and debearded

2 cups peeled, seeded, and finely diced tomatoes

1½ tablespoons chopped fresh tarragon

2 tablespoons unsalted butter

Coarse sea salt, preferably gray salt

Freshly ground black pepper

If the top lid of the tin is still attached, use a can opener to completely remove it, staying as close to the rim as you can. Leave the bottom lid intact. Set the tin aside.

Start a camp fire, ignite charcoal, or turn a gas grill to high. When the grill rack is hot, clean it, and wipe with a little olive oil.

Roast the peppers on the hot grill rack for 5 minutes. Place the peppers in a brown paper bag to steam. When the peppers have cooled for 30 minutes, remove the skin and seeds, and discard. Dice the peppers and set aside.

Either inside at the stove or outdoors at the fire, heat a medium sauté pan over high heat. Add the oil to the skillet, and when it's hot, add the garlic. Sauté until the garlic begins to color. Add the diced peppers. Stir. Add the Pernod or the toasted fennel seed. (If using the fennel seed, add the wine right away. If using Pernod, allow it to evaporate until the pan is almost dry before adding the wine.) Add the wine and cook until the liquid is reduced by half, about 5 minutes. While the wine reduces, pour the mussels into the olive tin.

Have ready 2 sheets of aluminum foil, each 16 inches long. When the wine has reduced, pour the hot liquid over the mussels in the can. Fold one sheet of aluminum foil in half crosswise, forming a lid that will sit inside the can above the mixture. Cover the entire top of the tin with the second sheet

of foil to keep the steam in the can. Set the tin on the grill or on a campfire, and sit close so you can hear the sound of the mussels popping open.

Cook until the first mussel opens, 3 to 5 minutes, then take both sheets of foil off the tin and discard them. With tongs, transfer the mussels to a platter as they open. (If you're camping, transfer to a clean sheet of newspaper.) Discard any that fail to open.

If you want to reduce the sauce faster, use a sauté pan, either inside on the stove or right on the grill. Empty all the juices in the can into the sauté pan and then add the diced tomato to the pan. If you want to rough it, add the diced tomato and its juice to the juices left in the tin.

Simmer for about 2 minutes to soften the tomato, then take the tin or sauté pan off the heat and stir in the tarragon and the butter. When the butter melts, return all the mussels to the sauce in the can.

To serve, empty the tin into a big serving bowl with a big flourish and let everyone help themselves.

COSTOLETTA DI BOVARO
(ITALIAN COWBOY STEAKS)
WITH SALSA VERDE

Serves 8 to 10

I love everything about this method of live-fire cooking: spearing tender beef on a lance and jamming the lance into a fire pit so the heat rises and cooks the steak perfectly. I like that moment when you serve the beef, resting the tip of the lance on a plate and carving right off the sword so the succulent beef slices fall onto the plate. I love the meat's aroma, and the feel of a lance in my hand. This meal is basic and elemental—just beef, metal, and fire—and yet there's something almost formal, in the best possible way, in how you honor guests by carving from the lance onto their plates. ❖ Tenderloin is my preferred cut of beef for this method but round steak and flank steak can be cooked this way too. (Think of this method the next time you want to make fajitas.) You can use the lances to cook chicken or game birds, or even a whole fish. ❖ You ribbon the pieces of steak onto two lances. (Think of old-fashioned ribbon candy and you'll know what I mean.) You don't want the steak stretched out; push it together on the lance so it stays juicy during cooking. ❖ See Resources (page 218) for lances like the ones we used in these photographs. ❖ One thing about the salsa verde: I use this sauce at my restaurant, Bottega, every day but sometimes change it in small ways. Compare the version I made here for beef with the version I made for the grilled tuna loin on page 169. This version is bolder due to oregano, which works for the Costoletta but would overpower the tuna. You can do this too. If you have a sauce or a salad dressing recipe that you use often, think about how to change it up in small ways depending on where you're using it.

MARINADE

4 cups red wine

1 large yellow onion, peeled and quartered

20 whole black peppercorns

6 juniper berries

3 bay leaves

Two 6-inch lengths of beef tenderloin
 (about 1½ pounds each), cut from the center

SALSA VERDE

2 teaspoons coarse sea salt, preferably gray salt,
 plus more for seasoning

2 tablespoons minced fresh garlic

½ cup packed fresh (not dried) oregano

½ cup packed fresh mint

¾ cup packed fresh cilantro (see Chef's Note, page 72)

1½ cups packed fresh flat-leaf parsley

2 cups extra-virgin olive oil

½ cup white wine vinegar

2 tablespoons freshly squeezed lemon juice, plus
 more for seasoning

⅓ cup water, plus more if needed

½ teaspoon freshly ground black pepper, plus more
 for seasoning

One large onion, peeled and quartered
 (for tip of lances)

YOU DON'T WANT THE STEAK STRETCHED OUT; PUSH IT TOGETHER ON THE LANCE SO IT STAYS JUICY DURING COOKING.

FOR THE MARINADE: In a large pan, container, or heavy-duty plastic bag, combine the wine, onion, peppercorns, juniper berries, and bay leaves. (For more intense flavor, combine the peppercorns, juniper berries, and bay leaves with a little of the wine in a blender, and then transfer to the bowl with the remaining marinade ingredients and combine.) Add the beef and refrigerate, marinating for at least 4 hours or preferably overnight, turning the beef in the marinade occasionally.

FOR THE SALSA VERDE: Mince the salt and garlic together until it forms a chunky paste. Add the oregano, mint, cilantro, and parsley to the bowl of a food processor, add the salt-garlic, and turn on the machine. With the machine running, slowly pour in the oil and then add the vinegar and lemon juice. Stop to taste. Pour in a little of the water, and see how thick the sauce is. If it's too thick, pour in the remaining water. Add the pepper and taste. Add more salt, pepper, or lemon juice as desired. Cover and refrigerate until ready to serve. If you make this the night before, smooth plastic wrap across the top.

 Start a fire in the fire pit. Stay nearby until the flames have died down, and the fire bed provides an even heat source.

Skewer the tenderloins onto the lances, working the beef over and under the lance to create a kind of ribbon effect. Push 2 onion quarters onto the tip of each lance and slide them up just a little. These protect the beef from ash. Impale one end of each lance into the earth beside the fire, and turn the lances every 10 minutes until the beef is cooked all the way around. You can test doneness using a meat thermometer; the meat is medium-rare at 135°F. A better way to do this is to pull the lances off the fire, and let them rest for 15 minutes. Rest the tip of the lance on a plate and carve a few slices of the meat. (Use a very sharp knife for carving so the beef doesn't slide down the lance.) If you'd like your beef a little more well-done, sprinkle on some sea salt and put the lances back over the fire.

Ladle the salsa verde into several bowls and place them at opposite ends of the table. You can make the table formal with steak knives and forks, or you can spoon on salsa verde, and eat the meat with your fingers.

BEEF, METAL, AND FIRE

Some foods have the power to transport you to other worlds. Beef tenderloin skewered on lances takes me to another time. While the meat is being carved off the lance, I'm dreaming about riding on horseback through wild grasslands, far from restaurant kitchens and produce orders.

In my mind, my posse and I butcher our own beef and start a blazing fire. As the meat cooks, we untie our botas from our saddles, and pour a stream of cool red wine straight into our gullets. As gauchos have done for centuries, we share a drink along with tales of adventures past.

When I cook and serve beef this way, skewered on the lance, it feels so familiar that I think I must have been a gaucho in a past life. My ancestors, I'm sure, were cowboys in Italy, and in my cattle-ranching grandfather, the gaucho gene ran strong. The traditions of meat and fire that go back so many years transcend generations and even cross continents for those of us in touch with our inner cowboy.

This style of cooking is the reason I wrote this book. This is cooking as a mindset, a way to strip down to the basics and forget about all the things you don't need. Give me beef, metal, and fire—and my friends and family—and I will meet the next half century with a grateful heart.

GRILLED
CHICKEN STEW
AND
DUMPLINGS

Serves 6

Plump, tender dumplings floating on a pot of chicken stew over a fire—this is comfort food with some good camping vibes thrown in. ❖ Because you have to grill the chicken, wait for it to cool, then take it apart for the chicken stew, this is a relaxed kind of meal, one that shouldn't be hurried. It's worth taking your time and enjoying the journey.

One 4½-pound chicken, cut into pieces

1 tablespoon coarse sea salt, preferably gray salt

½ teaspoon freshly ground black pepper

½ cup (1 stick) unsalted butter

½ cup all-purpose flour

2 tablespoons extra-virgin olive oil

1 medium yellow onion, cut into 1-inch chunks

2 carrots, cut into 1-inch chunks

2 stalks celery, cut into 1-inch pieces

2 teaspoons minced garlic

1 bay leaf

1 sprig thyme

¼ teaspoon ground turmeric

1 teaspoon coarse sea salt, preferably gray salt

¼ teaspoon freshly ground black pepper

4 cups Chicken Broth (page 217) or store-bought low-sodium stock

DUMPLINGS

1½ cups all-purpose flour

2 teaspoons baking powder

½ cup coarsely ground cornmeal

1 tablespoon sugar

1 teaspoon coarse sea salt, preferably gray salt

1½ cups heavy cream

4 teaspoons chopped fresh flat-leaf parsley, for garnish

 Start a fire in a fire pit. Either move your knives and cutting boards outside so you can prepare the chicken beside the fire or have another adult stay near while the fire burns down a little.

Season the chicken pieces well with salt and pepper on both sides. Lay chicken pieces skin-side down on the rack. Cook until the chicken shows grill marks, about 8 minutes, and then turn all the pieces over using tongs. Cook until an instant-read thermometer inserted into a chicken piece reads 150°F, another 6 to 8 minutes. The chicken doesn't need to be cooked all the way through because it will finish cooking in the stew.

Set the chicken aside until cool enough to handle. Pull the meat from the bones, discard the bones, and cut the meat into 1-inch chunks. Set aside.

In a skillet or sauté pan, either on a grill rack over the fire or inside at your stove, make a roux. Put the butter in a pan and let it melt. Add the flour and cook, stirring until the flour is just beginning to turn an amber color, 3 to 5 minutes. Take it off the heat and set aside.

Heat a 5-quart Dutch oven on a grill rack over the coals. When the pan is hot, add the olive oil. When the oil is hot, add the onion and cook until it starts to show a little color, about 2 minutes. Add the carrots, celery, garlic, bay leaf, thyme, turmeric, salt, and pepper to the pot. Cook for another 2 minutes. Add the roux to the Dutch oven, scraping all of it out of the pan. Pour in about one-fourth of the broth, stir until smooth, and bring to a boil, whisking continuously. Whisk as you add the remaining broth and bring to a simmer, uncovered. If the liquid boils too vigorously, take the pot off the fire and let it cool for a few minutes. When the liquid has thickened to your liking, add the chicken meat and simmer for 15 minutes.

FOR THE DUMPLINGS: While the stew thickens, whisk together the flour, baking powder, cornmeal, sugar, and salt in a large bowl. Add the cream and mix until just combined.

About 15 minutes before you'd like to serve the stew, drop 12 dumplings—each dumpling 1 heaping tablespoon of batter—onto the stew. Once the dumplings have been added, don't stir the stew. Cover and simmer until the dumplings float and are no longer doughy, 12 to 15 minutes.

To serve, ladle one or two dumplings into a bowl, and then top with stew, making sure you spoon a good amount of chicken into each bowl. Garnish each serving with a sprinkle of parsley.

S'MORES
WITH
ESPRESSO MARSHMALLOWS

Serves 8

Regular store-bought marshmallows are great roasted over the fire but homemade marshmallows flavored with espresso make your s'mores more interesting. ❖ Bring out bars of both dark and milk chocolate to keep ready beside the fire.

Espresso Marshmallows (facing page),
   cut into 2-inch squares
2 packages store-bought graham crackers
   (about 36 crackers)
Eight 3-ounce bars of good-quality chocolate (4 dark
   chocolate, 4 milk chocolate), such as Scharffen Berger

Toast one or two marshmallows over a flame until they're roasted exactly the way you like. Have two graham crackers standing by. Break off a piece of chocolate and set it on one graham cracker. Put your roasted marshmallow on top of the chocolate and then sandwich it between the two graham crackers and pull it off the roasting fork.

ESPRESSO MARSHMALLOWS

Makes sixteen 2-inch-square marshmallows

Just-made marshmallows are incredible and you can flavor them any way you like: these espresso marshmallows are great for s'mores and they're good in hot chocolate, too. ❖ Maybe it's possible to make these without a stand mixer, but it would be a challenge to pour in the hot sugar mixture while trying to steer a handheld mixer. I would say if you don't have both a candy thermometer and a stand mixer, skip this recipe and go for store-bought marshmallows. ❖ Cornstarch is the secret for keeping the marshmallows from merging together into one big sticky mass. Don't skimp on the cornstarch; better to put down too much cornstarch than to use too little.

2 to 3 cups cornstarch, for dusting the pan and covering and tossing the marshmallows

2 tablespoons water

1 tablespoon plus 1 teaspoon powdered gelatin

1¼ cups plus 1 tablespoon sugar

3 tablespoons dark rum

3 tablespoons brewed espresso

Pinch of cream of tartar

¾ cup light corn syrup

½ vanilla bean

3 egg whites

Line an 8-by-8-inch baking pan with plastic wrap. Sprinkle enough cornstarch on top of the plastic wrap to form a ⅛-inch-thick layer. Coat a wooden spoon with nonstick cooking spray or coat with canola oil. (Don't skip this step or the marshmallow mixture will stick to the spoon like glue.)

Put the water in a small bowl, and sprinkle the gelatin on top. Set this aside while you heat the sugar.

In a 2-quart or larger saucepan, combine the sugar, dark rum, espresso, cream of tartar, corn syrup, and the half vanilla bean. Bring the mixture to a boil over high heat; when it begins to boil, decrease the heat to medium. Clip a candy thermometer to the pan.

While the espresso mixture heats, begin whipping the egg whites in the bowl of a stand mixer fitted with the whisk attachment on low speed. When the thermometer on the pot registers 120°F, increase the mixer speed to medium. You want the egg whites to be whipped when the sugar syrup is ready.

When the espresso-sugar mixture in the pot registers 240°F, add the gelatin-water mixture, stirring until the gelatin has completely dissolved, 30 to 45 seconds. Use tongs to lift out the vanilla bean and discard it.

Decrease the mixer speed to low. With the machine running, drizzle in the hot espresso-sugar mixture a little at a time. Try to aim so the espresso mixture falls on the egg whites and not on the beaters.

When all the syrup has been added to the egg whites, increase the mixer speed to high. Whip until the mixture becomes cohesive and pulls together in the center of the bowl, forming light, glossy peaks, 10 to 15 minutes.

Carefully (because the mixture is hot), with the oiled wooden spoon, transfer the mixture onto the prepared bed of cornstarch. Sprinkle with more cornstarch (the cornstarch keeps out air), and let the mixture come to room temperature. Refrigerate until the marshmallows have set, 4 to 6 hours. Don't try to cut them into squares before they set. Once they're set, cut into 2-inch squares and arrange them in an airtight container. Spoon on lots of cornstarch, then store in the refrigerator until ready to serve. They'll keep for 2 weeks as long as you have a good amount of cornstarch protecting them from air. Let them come to room temperature before eating.

CHAPTER SIX

FIRE IN A BOX: THE HOT BOX

Midnight lechón breaks when I was a student at Florida International University—that was my introduction to the hot box. *Lechón*, the Cuban-style roasted pig with sautéed onions pushed under the skin, was a revelation, the perfect food for hot, sultry Miami nights. I would head out with my girlfriend toward La Calle Ocho en La Pequeña Habana (Eighth Street in Little Havana) where food vendors pulled their wheeled hot boxes up the street. After a night of clubbing, we'd stroll to the section where the vendors sold lechón. When you stopped at a cart, the guy would open the top of the hot box and break apart some of the meat from the leg, serving the sweet, tender pork with bread or a big plate of black beans.

We'd buy *guarapo de cana*—fresh sugar cane juice—and smuggle it into a flask of rum to make a sort of Highwayman's Mojito (page 203). We'd give the drink a squeeze from a fresh lime, no mint needed. The guarapo with rum, the pork with black beans—it's just as good a meal today as it was in the 1980s.

WHY I COOK WITH A HOT BOX

The hot box, also known as a box roaster, was made for cooking street food. The oldest known brand of hot box is called La Caja China (kah-ha sheen-ah) and has its roots in Cuban-style cooking. While the box was designed to roast a whole pig, it's a smart piece of equipment because it's portable, it's easy to start, you don't need to dig a pit in the ground, and the pig (or rack of ribs or dozen chickens or whole boatload of fish) cooks perfectly, with tender, juicy meat and crisp skin.

Plus you don't need to stand over the fire on a hot day. You close up the box and let it cook. This method is the easiest way to cook a big amount of food for a large party. The hot box is large—it has to be to hold a pig—and can cook a lot of food at one time, but it doesn't take up more room than a standard gas grill.

The hot box I use is made of wood lined with aluminum, and it's set on wheels. This wood-and-metal box does a great job of holding the heat in during cooking, but it's still light enough so I can single-handedly roll it wherever I want it.

The hot box offers a different way of cooking because the fire sits above the food. Once you've put the food inside, you build a fire on top of the box. What's the advantage to this? The air inside stays at a hot, steady temperature; the heat doesn't build and diminish the way it can on a grill or over a fire.

The other nice aspect of a hot box is how predictably it burns fuel. Right on the side of my hot box, it tells me how many pounds of charcoal to start with and how many pounds to add after the first hour and the second hour. I always have the amount of charcoal I need to burn because I know exactly how much the hot box will require until the pig is cooked.

More than any of these advantages, I like the hot box for that one moment—zero hour, when it's time to see inside: your guests have been milling around, drinking sangria, and then, when you give the signal, everyone gathers to watch. The top of the box is lifted off (you and your buddy carrying it to a safe spot) and there is the meal, perfectly cooked. Don't be surprised if you (and the pig) get a big round of applause. Who can resist that?

HOW TO START A FIRE IN THE HOT BOX

Firing up a hot box is a little different from a regular grill because you put the meat, fish, or vegetables in the box first and then light the coals on top of the box. First, follow the directions for each recipe in this chapter; once you put the food in the hot box, here's how you start the fire on top.

Place the ash pan in place on top of the box to protect the food from ash. The grate that holds the charcoal sits on top of the ash pan. You'll need 16 pounds of charcoal to start and an additional 26 pounds of charcoal that you'll add throughout cooking. See page 20 for thoughts about which kind of charcoal is best.

NOTE: This is the standard formula for all hot boxes as I write this, but who's to say that new hot boxes with new charcoal amounts won't appear. Check your hot box to make sure the charcoal amounts we give here are right for your model.

For a pig under 50 pounds (and for ribs, fish, a bunch of chickens, or a few turkeys) pour 16 pounds of charcoal on top of the box and light it. Note the time. After 1 hour, you'll add another 8 pounds. After 2 hours, you'll add another 8 pounds. After 30 more minutes, you'll add the last 10 pounds of charcoal.

 You'll have to lift out both the coal grate and the ash pan that sits under it when you want to turn over the pig or the ribs. This is easy, but have a partner help lift the other end. Don't try to lift out the hot coal pan by yourself. That's a disaster in the making. When you lift the coal pan, rest it on the wide handles on one side of the hot box. Make sure you have at least two pairs of heat-proof gloves ready.

TRIFECTA OF RIBS:
BEEF, PORK, AND LAMB

Serves 30 to 36

Ribs lovers, admit it: you've always wanted to throw three different kinds of ribs on the fire and host a rib bacchanalia. This is definitely the easiest, fastest kind of party to throw for a lot of people; the hot box does the hard part of the job for you. Each type of rib meat—beef, pork, and lamb—calls for a different seasoning. Figure that each rib recipe below serves about a dozen people. If you like you can cook just one kind of rib and still have a good-size rib feast.

BEEF RIBS
WITH COFFEE BBQ SAUCE

Serves 12 to 16 generously

This sauce was inspired by very dark coffee that had been sitting in a pot over a campfire. Reducing the coffee adds an addictive bottom note to this sauce that's hard to identify if you don't know what it is. ❖ A slab of beef ribs weighs about 5 pounds. When ordering ribs for a party, figure on 2 to 3 pounds of beef ribs per person (2 pounds if you're entertaining friends of my petite wife and 3 pounds if your guests are from Texas). ❖ This recipe makes a good amount of the BBQ sauce. Pour it into bowls, and have sauce within easy reach.

COFFEE BBQ SAUCE
1 cup brewed coffee or espresso
¼ cup extra-virgin olive oil
4 tablespoons minced garlic
2 cups ketchup (homemade, see page 75, or store-bought)
2 cups honey
1 cup balsamic vinegar
½ cup soy sauce

4 full slabs of beef ribs, about 20 pounds total
Coarse sea salt, preferably gray salt
Freshly ground black pepper
½ cup extra-virgin olive oil, plus more if needed

FOR THE BBQ SAUCE: In a small saucepan over medium-high heat, reduce the coffee to ½ cup, 3 to 4 minutes.

Heat the ¼ cup olive oil in a saucepan set on a grill over a fire or on top of the stove on medium heat. When the oil is hot, add the garlic and sauté until it's golden. Remove the pan from the heat and let the garlic cool in the oil. Whisk in the ketchup, honey, vinegar, soy sauce, and coffee reduction. Let the mixture simmer over a fire or on the stove for 15 minutes so the flavors blend.

Season each slab of ribs with salt and pepper. Be sure to press the seasonings into the meat on both sides with your hands. Drizzle about 2 tablespoons of olive oil over each rib slab, front and back, and put them in the hot box. Ignite 16 pounds of coals on top of the hot box (see page 146). After 1 hour, get a buddy to help you lift off the ash pan (rest it on the handles of the hot box), and use long tongs to turn all the ribs over. Replace the ash pan, and add another 8 pounds of charcoal to the top. An hour later, lift off the ash pan again, slather all the ribs generously with sauce, and put the ash pan back. Add another 5 pounds of charcoal (you don't need as much as you do for a whole pig). After 30 minutes, take the ribs out of the box, brush again with sauce, and serve.

RECIPE CONTINUES

BABY BACK PORK RIBS
WITH MILANESE RUB (OR PORK²)

Serves 12

This seasoning was inspired by one I tasted in Italy at Peck, a gourmet food store in Milan. Peck is like Dean & DeLuca on steroids. I call this "pork squared," because pork (in the form of finely minced pancetta) is part of the seasoning that goes onto the pork ribs. ❖ Traditionally, for the rub you'd mince the garlic and lemon zest together with a knife, and then add the herbs and mince everything together until very fine. The food processor does this for you in much less time. Put the rub onto the meat 30 to 60 minutes before the ribs go into the hot box.

MILANESE RUB

¾ cup coarsely chopped garlic

5 tablespoons coarsely chopped lemon zest

¾ cup kosher salt

1 cup loosely packed fresh sage leaves, stemmed

1 cup fresh rosemary leaves

1½ cups finely minced pancetta (see Chef's Note)

2 tablespoons freshly ground black pepper

6 racks baby back ribs, 12 to 18 pounds total

FOR THE RUB: In a food processor, pulse to combine the garlic and lemon zest. Add the salt and process until fine. Add the sage and rosemary leaves, and process again. Finally, add the pancetta and pepper, and process until the mixture looks like a very coarse, moist salt rub. Don't over-process, or the rub can turn gummy.

Press the seasoning into the ribs and put them in the hot box. Ignite 16 pounds of coals on top of the hot box (see page 146). About 1 to 1¼ hours later, get a buddy to help you lift off the ash pan (rest it on the handles of the hot box), and use long tongs to turn all the ribs over. Put the ash pan and grate back in place, and pour another 8 pounds of charcoal on top of the hot box. Cook for another 45 minutes to 1 hour, and then test a rib. If they're tender and caramelized, take them out; if not, replace the coal pan, add more charcoal, and cook for another 30 to 60 minutes.

Set out the ribs along with sauce; warn your guests that the ribs will be hot but then step out of the way before they trample you to get to the meat.

CHEF'S NOTE: Put the pancetta in the freezer for 30 to 45 minutes and it'll be easier to slice and mince. Don't freeze for any longer than that; you want *semifreddo* (half-frozen) pancetta, not a pork ice pop.

LAMB RIBS
WITH SALTED MINT SUGAR

Serves 10 to 12

Here's the thinking behind this rub: what if we deconstructed mint jelly and gave lamb ribs a rub with salt, fresh mint, sugar, and lemon zest? It works very well because the sugar caramelizes and the fresh mint adds a great flavor top note and aroma to the meat. ❖ For the lemon zest, I peel a whole lemon with a vegetable peeler (the colored part only, not the white pith). Then I coarsely chop the peel and put it into the food processor with the salt and mint.

SALTED MINT-SUGAR RUB

8 cups loosely packed fresh mint leaves

½ cup kosher salt

3 tablespoons coarsely chopped lemon zest (see headnote)

1½ tablespoons whole black peppercorns

2 cups sugar

6 whole slabs lamb ribs, 6 to 9 pounds total

FOR THE RUB: In a food processor, mix together the mint leaves, salt, and lemon zest until the mint leaves are minced. With the back of a heavy knife, crack the black peppercorns and add them to the food processor. Pour the mixture into a large bowl and fold in the sugar.

Press the rub into the ribs about 30 minutes before they go in the hot box. (They shouldn't sit unrefrigerated for longer than that.) Ignite 16 pounds of coals on top of the hot box (see page 146). About 1 to 1½ hours later, get a buddy to help you lift off the ash pan. Rest it on the handles of the hot box. Turn all the ribs over, replace the ash pan and grate, and pour another 8 pounds of charcoal on top of the hot box. Cook for 45 minutes to 1 hour longer, and then test a rib. If they're tender and caramelized, take them out; if not, replace the coal pan, add more charcoal, and cook for another 30 to 60 minutes.

Set out the ribs right away with sauce and lots of napkins.

CHICKENS FOR TWENTY

Serves 20 people

The hot box is my favorite way to cook up a whole barnyard full of birds. It works well for game birds too—quail, duck, and turkey—but who do you know that doesn't love perfectly roasted chicken? The secret behind the meat's clean, tangy flavor is very thin slices of lemon placed under the chicken's skin just before roasting. I use fresh bay leaves here, because I have a tree in my yard, but dried bay leaves are fine too. ❖ The Caja China hot box—the one I use—comes with a rack. Line up however many chickens you have inside the rack and close it. When it's time to turn the birds over, you can do it in one smooth motion by turning over the entire rack. Have a buddy help you when it's time to lift the hot coal pan. ❖ These birds are great on their own and also good with Coffee BBQ Sauce set on the table so guests can serve themselves as much sauce as they like.

6 to 12 whole chickens, each about 4½ pounds
1 whole lemon per bird, sliced very thinly
2 fresh or dry bay leaves per bird
Coarse sea salt, preferably gray salt
Freshly ground black pepper
Coffee BBQ Sauce (page 149)

Rinse each chicken in cold running water inside and out, and pat dry with paper towels. Gently slide the lemon slices under the skin of each chicken, three or four slices in the breast area and two or three slices in the thighs and legs. Arrange the slices in a thin layer so the entire meat under the breast is in contact with some lemon. Slide in the bay leaves under the skin, one per breast. Sprinkle salt and pepper over all the chickens.

Arrange the birds in the rack (this comes with your hot box). Close up the rack and put it in the hot box. Ignite 16 pounds of coals on top of the hot box (see page 146). After 1 hour, get a buddy to help you lift off the ash pan (rest it on the handles of the hot box). Have the same friend (or a different friend, up to you), help you turn over the rack holding all the chickens. Put the ash pan back in place, and add another 8 pounds of charcoal to the top. Cook for another 45 minutes to 1 hour, and then cut into a chicken (maybe even slice off a bite) to see if it's cooked all the way through. (Yes, you can do this without taking any chickens out of the rack.)

If the chicken isn't done yet, replace the ash pan, add a little more charcoal to the top, and cook for another 25 to 40 minutes.

When the chickens are done, take the rack out of the hot box and let the chickens rest in the rack for 5 minutes. Open the rack, remove the chickens, and cut each bird into quarters using a cleaver. Arrange the pieces on large serving platters, and set out bowls of Coffee BBQ Sauce.

PIG PICKIN'

Serves 25 to 30 people

The high point of a pork feast is that moment when you open the hot box to reveal the whole pig, and then lift it out for the crowd to see. Pork cooked this way is incredibly tender and flavorful; you've never smelled anything as good as this pig during the final 30 minutes of cooking. ❖ I've re-created the flavor of the lechón I loved so much when I lived in Miami. I'm purposely not giving you an amount for dried oregano because I think fresh oregano is better for pork cooked this way. And the cumin is best if you start with whole seeds, toast them in a dry skillet on your stove just until you can smell their fragrance, and then grind them with a clean coffee grinder or spice mill before you use them. After all, you went to all the time and trouble to get a whole pig; you don't want to skimp on the spices and fresh herbs. ❖ The pig is best if marinated for 4 to 6 hours but clear space in the fridge to store it; don't let it sit out unrefrigerated. ❖ Use the rack that comes with the hot box to secure the whole pig; this makes it much easier to turn the pig over and take it off the fire. ❖ The entire meal relies on your choosing a great pig to roast. If you don't know a pig rancher, talk to your butcher, or try Heritage Foods (see Resources, page 218). Even if you don't see what you need on the Heritage website, give them a call. They can usually find what you need or steer you in the right direction. ❖ Restaurant supply stores sell plastic tubs big enough to hold suckling pigs. These do fit in a standard fridge, but plan ahead to make room for it as it takes up a lot of space. Or store the pig and marinate in a heavyweight, double-thick plastic bag or a new 50-gallon plastic trash can, scrubbed inside and out with soap. Ideally, your butcher might hold the pig for you until the day you're ready to cook it.

One whole suckling pig, 30 to 35 pounds

LECHÓN-STYLE MARINADE
1½ cups chopped garlic
¾ cup chopped fresh oregano
¾ cup coarse sea salt, preferably gray salt
4 tablespoons toasted and then freshly
  ground cumin (see headnote)
3 tablespoons whole black peppercorns
2½ cups extra-virgin olive oil

8 cups freshly squeezed lime juice
2 cups freshly squeezed orange juice
8 large yellow onions, peeled and sliced into thin rounds

The butcher should have done most of the work for you, so what you have is a whole animal with all the organs removed. When you order a whole pig, clarify this with your butcher to make sure you're both on the same page. Check to see if the kidneys are still in place. You'll be able to see them attached inside the rib cage, if they're still there. If they are, slice them off and discard or sauté in a hot pan if you like kidneys. Put the pig in a plastic tub or use a double-layered plastic bag or a new 50-gallon plastic trash can (see headnote).

FOR THE MARINADE: In a food processor, mix together the garlic, fresh oregano, salt, and cumin. With the back of a heavy knife (or the bottom of a heavy skillet) crack all the peppercorns and add them to the processor. Process just for a few seconds then scrape the herb mixture into a large bowl and stir in the olive oil.

Rub this mixture all over the pig, inside and out. Let the spices sit on the pig for 15 minutes, then pour on the citrus juices and the onions, pouring some of the juice inside and making sure the onions surround the pig inside and out. Refrigerate for 4 hours or overnight, occasionally turning the pig in the juices.

Take the pig out of the refrigerator and secure it in the hot box rack about 30 minutes before you're ready to ignite the charcoal. Place the pig in the rack inside the hot box. Replace the ash pan and grate and ignite 16 pounds of coals on top of the hot box (see page 146). After 1 hour, add another 8 pounds of charcoal to the top. About 2 hours from the time you placed the pig in the hot box, get ready to turn it over. Have a friend help you lift the ash pan and rest it on the handles of the hot box. Carefully, with a friend's help, flip the rack so the side facing up now faces down in the hot box. Replace the ash pan, and pour another 8 pounds of charcoal on the top.

Let the pig cook for another 2 hours, adding more charcoal after 1 to 1½ hours if you think the coals are burning low. The pig should be ready about 4½ to 5 hours from the time you lit the first batch of charcoal.

Set the ash pan on the hot box's handles, and lift out the pig. Set it on a stable surface and take it out of the rack. (We don't need to tell you it's extremely hot, right?) Let it cool for 15 minutes and then carve it, working from the sides and back.

Let your guests fill their plates and come back for more as often as they like.

PORK SHOULDER
COOKED LECHÓN-STYLE

Serves 16 to 20

For those of you who aren't fired up about roasting a whole pig, here's my version of pork shoulder cooked with the same lechón seasonings. You don't need a hot box to cook this (although you can use a hot box if you have one). This recipe works over a fire or in your oven. Marinate the meat for at least 12 hours in the herbs and lime juice.

LECHÓN-STYLE MARINADE

2 tablespoons coarse sea salt, preferably gray salt

2 teaspoons ground cumin

¼ cup chopped garlic

2 tablespoons chopped fresh oregano

2 tablespoons extra-virgin olive oil

2 cups freshly squeezed lime juice

½ cup freshly squeezed orange juice

1 tablespoon whole black peppercorns

2 large yellow onions, peeled and sliced into thin rounds

One pork shoulder, about 15 pounds total (or two 8-pound pork legs or pork butts)

FOR THE MARINADE: On a cutting board, add the salt and cumin to the garlic and oregano and mash it together with your knife until it forms a paste. Scrape the paste off the board and into a bowl and stir in the olive oil. (See marinade directions in Pig Pickin', page 155; if you have a small food processor, use it to speed up this step.)

Rub the pork all over with the spice mixture.

Combine the lime and orange juices in a bowl. With the back of a heavy knife, crack the peppercorns and add them to the juice. Slide the pork shoulder into a heavy plastic bag and pour in the seasoned citrus juice and the sliced onions. Seal up the bag and let the pork marinate in your refrigerator overnight. Turn the bag over occasionally so the pork gets a good soak all the way around.

Drain off the marinade from the pork shoulder. Save your marinade in the fridge; you'll need it to baste the pork. Put the meat in the hot box. If you don't have a hot box, you can cook the pork over a fire pit or roast it in your oven. (In your oven, start the temperature at 450°F for first 30 minutes, and then decrease the temperature to 250°F.)

Cook the meat for about 1½ hours, until the meat registers 130°F on an instant-read thermometer. Swab down the whole pork shoulder with the remaining marinade and then discard any leftover marinade. Put the pork back in the hot box or over the coals or in the oven. Cook for another 30 to 60 minutes, until the meat registers 160°F on an instant-read thermometer. Let the meat rest for at least 20 minutes before carving.

CHEF'S NOTE: You can slow-roast too. Spread out the coals on top of the hot box when the pork has reached a temperature of 160°F, and let it cook slowly for another 1½ hours. Pig heaven.

HEIRLOOM TOMATOES
WITH
WHIPPED BURRATA, BASIL OIL, SMOKED SEA SALT, AND BALSAMIC REDUCTION

Serves 6

This salad is a departure from the classic tomato-mozzarella-basil caprese because burrata is much creamier than mozzarella and smoked sea salt adds a bolder finish. Burrata differs from mozzarella in how it's made. Burrata cheesemakers form a tiny pouch out of just-made mozzarella and fill the pouch with mozarrella and cream before pinching it closed. Burrata is expensive because it's fragile and requires overnight shipping, but it's worth the cost. ❖ You can buy smoked sea salt (see Resources, page 218) or smoke your own. ❖ I like to use a variety of heirlooms for this salad, in different sizes, but just use what's ripe on the vine or best at the farmers' market on the day you plan to make this.

½ pound burrata

2 tablespoons extra-virgin olive oil

2½ teaspoons Smoked Sea Salt (page 211)

½ cup balsamic vinegar

1½ pounds heirloom tomatoes

2 tablespoons Basil Oil (page 216), or

   substitute 2 teaspoons basil chiffonade (page 43)

Combine the burrata, olive oil, and ½ teaspoon of the smoked salt in the bowl of a food processor, pulsing just until mixed. Set the bowl aside.

Pour the balsamic vinegar into a sauté pan set over high heat. When the vinegar boils, reduce heat to medium-high and cook until the vinegar is reduced to about ¼ cup, approximately 10 minutes. Pour the vinegar into a heat-proof measuring cup to cool. This makes more reduction than you will need for this recipe; the remaining reduction will keep for 1 month in the refrigerator.

While it cools, slice the tomatoes, arrange the slices on a platter, and spoon the whipped burrata in dollops across the top.

Drizzle the salad with the basil oil, and then with 2 tablespoons of the balsamic reduction. Finish by sprinkling on the remaining 2 teaspoons of the smoked salt.

CORN
ON THE COB
ROASTED IN THE HUSK
WITH
RED PEPPER BUTTER

Serves 8

I love this red pepper butter on corn that's been roasted in the husk right on top of the coals. ❖ As with all compound butters, this one is best if made the day before you cook with it. Whenever I have leftover roasted red peppers, I make this compound butter and store it tightly wrapped in my freezer. ❖ Unless I am roasting corn for fifty people, I wouldn't fire up a hot box just for corn; but if you're already cooking ribs or a pig, then use the coals on top of the hot box to cook your corn. At the end of the recipe, we've included directions for roasting the corn on a grill, so you can cook them either way.

ROASTED RED PEPPER BUTTER

3 medium red bell peppers, roasted (see page 215)

2 teaspoons extra-virgin olive oil

2 teaspoons minced garlic

2 teaspoons chopped fresh oregano, or ½ teaspoon
   dried oregano

1 teaspoon balsamic vinegar

1 teaspoon coarse sea salt, preferably gray salt, plus more
   for serving

⅛ teaspoon freshly ground black pepper, plus more
   for serving

1 cup (2 sticks) unsalted butter (cut into large chunks),
   at room temperature

8 ears fresh corn

FOR THE RED PEPPER BUTTER: Peel the roasted peppers, discarding the skin, seeds, and ribs. Coarsely chop the roasted peppers and set them aside.

Heat the olive oil in a small sauté pan over high heat. When the oil is hot, add the minced garlic and decrease the heat to medium-high. Sauté just until the garlic begins to show some color, about 2 minutes. Take the pan off the heat and stir in the oregano. Set the pan aside to cool.

In a food processor or a large blender, combine the red peppers, balsamic vinegar, salt, and pepper. Pulse until smooth. Pour in the warm olive oil with the garlic and oregano and pulse to blend. Add the softened butter and process until the mixture is smooth with a consistent color.

Transfer the butter to a bowl and refrigerate until it's hardened enough to shape into a log, about 30 minutes. Place an 18-inch-long sheet of aluminum foil on a work surface, and spoon the butter lengthwise down the center of the foil. Shape into a log about 1½ inches in diameter, and wrap tightly in the foil.

Refrigerate for 1 week or freeze for up to 1 month.

Fill a bucket with cold tap water and have it handy. First pull out all the corn silk but do it without tearing off the husk. When you pull down the husks of the corn, don't remove the husks entirely. Just pull out the corn silk, discard it, and then smooth the husks back down over the corn. Soak the silk-less corn in their husks for at least 30 minutes before they go over the fire.

You'll want to start roasting the corn about 15 minutes before the ribs or the pork (or whatever you're roasting) come out of the box. To roast the corn on top of the hot box, use long tongs to set the corn on top of the live coals. Let them cook for 8 to 10 minutes, and then take an ear off the coals and test it to see if it's done.

ON A CHARCOAL OR GAS GRILL: Start your gas grill and set it to medium-high. With charcoal or over a campfire, it's best to roast the corn over a fire that is starting to burn down, about half an hour after the coals are at their hottest.

When the grill is at medium heat—when you can hold your hand about 5 inches above the grill rack for 4 to 5 seconds—then put the corn on the grill. Grill until the husks look brown and slightly charred, about 10 to 12 minutes. Take 1 ear off the fire and test to see if it's done.

Pull half of the husks from each ear of corn, slather on some red pepper butter, season with salt and pepper, and serve the corn while it's hot. If you have a crowd, put out a few crocks of the red pepper butter and let everyone spread as much butter on their corn as they like.

APRICOT HAND PIES

Makes 16 pies

When everybody is just about stuffed on pork, ribs, and chicken, a big dessert is not something anyone wants to see. But if you bring out a plate of these small hand pies, watch as people storm your way. There's something about their size that's irresistible. ❖ The mascarpone cheese makes this dough very tender. It's sticky, so use a lot of flour on your work surface before rolling. Handle it lightly and try to work while the dough is cold; it warms quickly and then becomes harder to shape. If the dough becomes too sticky, just cover it with plastic wrap and refrigerate for 15 to 30 minutes to firm it up. ❖ You can make the dough one day ahead. If you can't find mascarpone, substitute an equal amount of cream cheese.

DOUGH

1 cup (2 sticks) unsalted butter, at room temperature

1 cup (8 ounces) mascarpone cheese or cream cheese, at room temperature

2 tablespoons granulated sugar

½ teaspoon coarse sea salt, preferably gray salt

½ cup heavy cream

1½ teaspoons grated lemon zest

2 cups all-purpose flour plus more for dusting

2 eggs, for egg wash

4 tablespoons turbinado sugar

APRICOT FILLING

1 tablespoon unsalted butter

1 dried bay leaf

1 pound apricots, pitted and cut into large dice

1 tablespoon freshly squeezed lemon juice

¼ cup granulated sugar

⅛ teaspoon coarse sea salt, preferably gray salt

¼ teaspoon chopped fresh rosemary

Pinch of ground cinnamon

FOR THE DOUGH: In a food processor, combine the butter, mascarpone, granulated sugar, salt, heavy cream, and grated lemon zest, pulsing until smooth. Add the flour and pulse until a sticky dough forms. Divide the dough into two equal pieces; shape into two balls and cover both in plastic wrap, smoothing the wrap over the dough so no dough is exposed to air. Chill the dough for 3 hours or overnight. Make the filling while the dough chills.

FOR THE FILLING: Either on the stove in a skillet or in a cast-iron pan on top of the grill, melt the butter. When the butter stops foaming, toss in the bay leaf, which will crackle and pop. Add the diced apricots and stir. Add the lemon juice, granulated sugar, salt, rosemary, and cinnamon. Cook over medium heat until the fruit is very tender, 12 to 15 minutes. Take off the heat and allow the filling to cool.

When ready to bake, preheat the oven to 350°F. Line two baking sheets with parchment paper and set aside.

Sprinkle a generous amount of flour on your work surface and take one ball of dough out of the refrigerator. Roll out one of the dough balls to form a rectangle about 10 inches wide by 20 inches long. Using a bowl or the rim of a drinking glass, cut out eight circles, each about 4½ inches wide. Transfer the dough circles to a prepared baking sheet. Spoon about 1 tablespoon of filling in the center of each dough circle.

Beat the eggs lightly in a small bowl. For each filled dough circle, brush half of the outer edge with beaten egg. Fold the dough over the filling to form a half-moon. Press the edges together and use the tines of a fork to press down all the way around the half-circle to seal the dough. Cut four slits in the top of each pie to allow steam to escape during baking. Brush the tops with beaten egg and sprinkle with the turbinado sugar. Repeat rolling, cutting, filling, and sealing with remaining ball of dough. Bake until golden brown, 25 to 35 minutes. Halfway through cooking, switch the top baking sheet to the bottom rack and vice versa, and rotate both baking sheets. Remove to wire racks to cool.

These can be served warm or at room temperature.

CHEF'S NOTE: If you're running short on time, fill each circle of dough with one sliced strawberry and two teaspoons of jam, and skip making the filling.

CHAPTER SEVEN

A SPIN WITH FIRE: THE ROTISSERIE

There's something remarkably peaceful about watching a joint of meat slowing turning above a fire. Maybe it's the lulling movement or the way the meat's fragrance drifts out to the cook.

This method of cooking is different from other methods because it doesn't subject the protein to an onslaught of heat; instead the slow, even exposure to flame results in juicy, evenly cooked chicken, beef, lamb, and pork.

But don't stop with the protein: the rotisserie can add flavor to the unexpected as well: use your rotisserie (with a cage attachment) to give Brussels sprouts a caramelized exterior, roast two butternut squash, or cook a *torta strizzare*—a type of dessert unlike anything you've cooked before. There are more ways to use this tool than you may have imagined.

WHY I USE A
ROTISSERIE

The rotisserie conjures up past-life cell memories for me: While I'm sitting in front of the fire, I can envision a Roman court, with a spit off to one side holding a whole goat, which is being turned constantly with ropes. Goblets are slammed down on huge tables and quickly refilled with wine. You're elbows-on-the-table with your Roman countrymen, a leafy crown on your head. I might be sitting in my backyard wearing shorts and an old T-shirt that says ALWAYS USE A CONDIMENT but in my mind I am a commando in a toga when I put a whole goat on my rotisserie.

HOW TO USE A ROTISSERIE OR A SPITJACK

Most likely you can buy a rotisserie appliance for the gas grill you already own. My favorite form of rotisserie is a spit or a spitjack, an oversize rotisserie that stands alone so you can place it anywhere you want to build the fire. For the stand-alone rotisserie, you need to build the fire near a power outlet or have some extension cords ready. Unless you want to jerry-rig a system of ropes that turn the spit rod (and I have seen this done), then you need electricity for the rotisserie's motor.

The spitjack can hold a whole baby goat or lamb as easily as it can roast a dozen chicken breasts, a tuna loin, or a few turkeys for Thanksgiving Day dinner and part of your side dishes as well. I like to roast whole squash on my rotisserie.

To cook smaller items on a rotisserie, such as Brussels sprouts (see page 172), you'll need a cage attachment. These can be ordered easily online.

See Resources, page 218, for rotisseries, spit, and cage options.

 The most important point to using a rotisserie is to not skewer your own hand. When pushing anything onto a rotisserie or spitjack bar, keep your hands on either side of the spit rod, where they can't be run through if the meat or squash gives way suddenly.

GOAT IS THE NEW LAMB

Bill Niman, who did so much to improve the quality of beef in the United States when he began Niman Ranch, is spending his time these days selling goat to restaurants. This tells you that the goat's day is coming. And that's a good thing because many Americans view a goat as good for cheese and not much else.

What made Niman a national hero to small-scale ranchers, animal lovers, and beef fans is his idea that the better an animal is treated, the better it will taste. These days there are many goat ranchers who bet the farm on this idea; finding good goat meat is no longer the challenge it was a decade ago.

If you don't find any goat farmers at your local farmers' market, get to know Heritage Foods (see Resources, page 218). Like Bill Niman, the folks at Heritage are interested in the welfare of both the animal and the family-owned ranches that practice humane, sustainable animal husbandry. They can sell you a whole or a half goat from a farm where animals are well treated.

If you think of tough, gamey meat when you think about goat, please reconsider. Goat can be delicate. At my house, we roasted a goat over the fire for this year's Easter dinner. The meat was fantastic: tender, flavorful, succulent. My favorite time of year to eat goat or lamb is the spring, when the grass is new and still bright green. As the weather gets warmer and the animals eat more sage, the meat becomes gamier. Roast your goat or lamb in the spring when the meat is sweetest.

BABY GOAT
ON A SPITJACK

Serves 18 very generously

Roasting a whole goat or lamb is like riding a bicycle. The first time you do it is like pushing off on a bike with nobody spotting you—there's a little anxiety but it doesn't take long to master the technique. ❖ It makes good sense to have a friend or two spotting you while you're setting up and maneuvering the meat onto the spin rod. Getting a whole animal onto the spin rod is the hardest part of the meal. I can do this by myself but over the years I've learned that if I wait for a friend to help, the task gets done faster and with a lot less cussing. ❖ You can use this same method to cook a whole lamb or pig. The measures for spices are just a proportion; you might need more of the spice rub or less depending on how big the goat is. ❖ See Resources, page 218, for sources for goat.

One whole baby goat or lamb, 18 to 35 pounds
2 cups olive oil, plus more if needed
2½ cups Fennel Spice Rub (double the recipe on page 208)
1 cup Pimentón de la Vera (sweet, smoky Spanish paprika)
¼ cup kosher salt

BASTING LIQUID
5 cups red wine
12 garlic cloves, minced
4 tablespoons tomato paste
2 tablespoons coarse sea salt, preferably gray salt
2 tablespoons freshly squeezed lemon juice

Small leafy branches of rosemary or oregano
   to use as basting brushes

Make sure the spitjack is assembled, ready to go, and set at least 30 feet from the closest building. Have extension cords to connect the jack to the nearest outlet. Start a fire beneath the spitjack, and prepare the goat while the fire turns to coals.

Rub olive oil over the entire goat, both inside and out. Mix together the spice rub, pimentón, and kosher salt. With your hands, press the spice mixture into the goat, both inside and out.

With the help of a buddy, slide the goat onto the bar of the spitjack from mouth to tail, and secure the bar in place. Let the goat cook for 30 minutes while turning on the spit, before you baste it so the spices have a chance to penetrate the meat. Make the basting liquid when the goat goes over the fire, but have someone responsible stay near the fire.

FOR THE BASTING LIQUID: Combine the wine, garlic, tomato paste, salt, and lemon juice. After the first 30 minutes of cooking, dip rosemary or oregano branches into the basting liquid and swab down the goat, every 10 minutes or so. (If you don't have herb branches, use a silicone brush to baste.)

You'll cook a 30- to 40-pound goat for about 4 to 5 hours. It's done when the skin is crispy and brown and an instant-read thermometer registers 130°F. (You'll find if you insert the thermometer at various points—the haunch or the shoulder—you'll get a different reading for each. That's fine; when most of the readings are close to 130°F, then the goat is done.)

 You and your buddy both need to don some good heat-proof gloves, and then take the entire spit rod off the machine. Before you detach the rod, know where you're going to set the goat.

TO CARVE: Let the goat rest with the spit rod still in place for 15 minutes, then remove the spit rod. Cut away the hind legs at the joint; the meat should be tender enough so this is easy. Next, carve at the shoulder, working down toward the front legs. Cut away the front legs, and then carve the goat one section at a time, working from the ribs toward the backbone. Serve.

I CAN DO THIS BY MYSELF BUT OVER THE YEARS I'VE LEARNED THAT IF I WAIT FOR A FRIEND TO HELP, THE TASK GETS DONE FASTER AND WITH A LOT LESS CUSSING.

TURKEYS
ON A SPITJACK

Serves 12 very generously

These turkeys come off the fire looking like the cover photo for the Thanksgiving issue of a food magazine, and they taste as good as they look. The rotisserie cooks them perfectly all the way through, and the skin is gorgeous, brown, crisp, and crackled. You can cook more than one bird at a time and your oven is kept available for all the side dishes, which makes the entire day easier. ❖ For me, maybe the biggest advantage is cool, fresh air during a holiday celebration. Stand outside by the fire, peacefully watching the turkeys cook, and wait. One by one, your family will come out to stand beside you and take a deep breath of the November air and that wonderful aroma. Cooking a turkey this way makes me even more thankful. ❖ This recipe was written for one medium-size bird. You can easily cook two birds, weighing 12 to 24 pounds, at the same time. Just double the brine recipe. This same method works for goose, duck, and game birds too. ❖ Before you come close to starting the fire, check out your set-up. Will the spitjack be near a power outlet or do you have sufficient extension cords to plug it in? Is there a place near the fire for people to sit? You'll have lots of guests and most likely some children, so review Stay Safe (page 10) at least a few days before the holiday.

BRINE

2 gallons water

1 cup kosher salt

½ cup packed brown sugar (light or dark)

1 tablespoon whole black peppercorns

1½ teaspoons juniper berries

2 bay leaves

One turkey, 12 to 20 pounds

7 tablespoons coarse sea salt, preferably gray salt

Freshly ground black pepper

FOR THE BRINE: Combine all the brine ingredients in an extra-large stock pot. (If you need to cook the brine in two large pots, just put half of each ingredient amount in each pot.) Over high heat, bring the liquid to a boil so the salt dissolves. Let the mixture cool.

Rinse the turkey under cold water. Remove the giblets and discard. Add the turkey to the cool brine mixture and let it rest for 8 to 24 hours in a refrigerator. If you don't have a pot big enough to hold the turkey, you can brine in a double-layered plastic garbage bag. Just check to see that the brine is completely cool before you pour it into the plastic. Make sure the entire bird is submerged in the liquid. If you don't have room in the refrigerator for the bird, you can store it in your garage overnight as long as the temperature stays close to 40°F.

Prepare the spitjack following the manufacturer's directions, and start the fire (see page 26). Have extension cords if necessary to connect the jack to the nearest outlet. When the fire is ready, remove the turkey from the brine and discard the brine. Rinse the bird with cool water and dry it with paper towels. Season the bird inside and out with salt and pepper, and then truss the bird with butcher's twine so the wings don't flap while it revolves.

 Thread the bar of the spitjack through the turkey. You might need to give it some force when the bar is pushing through the neck; please keep your hands on both sides of the bird while pushing. Under no circumstances should you be pushing on the bird with your hand lined up to be impaled by the rod.

Secure the three metal spitjack strips around the bird's breast, midsection, and around the legs. If there are no metal strips, use butcher's twine to secure the bird in place.

Lock the bar onto the two ends of the spitjack, plug in, and turn it on. If you have to step away from the fire, have a responsible grownup stand in for you.

The bird will cook for anywhere from 3½ to 5 hours depending on the size of the bird and the heat of the fire. The turkey is done when it registers about 140°F on an instant-read thermometer inserted into the thigh but not touching the bone.

When the bird is done, you and a buddy both don heat-proof gloves and take the entire rod off the rotisserie. Leave the rod in the bird while it rests for 15 minutes. When the bird has rested, put your gloves back on, use a clean dish towel so your gloves aren't touching the bird directly, and slide the bird firmly off the rod onto a big plate or baking tray.

Move the bird to a clean serving platter, carve it, and serve.

TUNA LOIN
TIED PRIME RIB-STYLE WITH SALSA VERDE

Serves 10 to 12

We're used to seeing tuna as delicate bits of fish, but wrapping a whole loin in caul fat and basting it with salsa verde over a fire brings out what I like most about ahi: the rich texture, the clean flavor, and how beautifully this fish plates up. I like the flavor of garlic with ahi but don't want to overwhelm the fish so I blanch the garlic in hot salted water three times before adding it to the salsa verde. ❖ Caul fat is a way to hold the fish together during cooking while sealing in moisture and holding in the flavor of the herbs that you baste with. Think of caul fat as sort of a natural plastic wrap; the fat melds into the tuna over the heat so by the time the fish is done there's nothing left of it and you won't taste the fat at all on the finished tuna. Ask your butcher to order the caul fat for you and soak it in water for a half hour before you start cooking.

SALSA VERDE

6 quarts water

3 tablespoons kosher salt

2 cups whole garlic cloves

1½ teaspoons finely minced fresh rosemary

2 teaspoons grated lemon zest

4 tablespoons minced fresh flat-leaf parsley

½ teaspoon coarse sea salt, preferably gray salt

¼ teaspoon freshly ground black pepper

¼ cup extra-virgin olive oil

4 sheets caul fat

One tuna loin, about 5 pounds (12 inches long by 3 inches wide by 3 inches high)

1 tablespoon coarse sea salt, preferably gray salt

2 teaspoons freshly ground black pepper

If using a rotisserie over a gas grill, don't turn on the grill until 10 minutes before the fish will go on the heat. If using a stand-alone rotisserie, start the fire and check the rotisserie motor to be sure it's plugged in and working.

 Don't leave the fire unattended; either bring your work tools outside or have another adult stay near the fire while you work indoors.

FOR THE SALSA: In a large saucepan, combine 8 cups of the water, 1 tablespoon of the kosher salt, and the 2 cups of whole garlic cloves. Bring to a boil over high heat. Strain, discarding all the water. Add 8 fresh cups of water to the pan with the garlic and another tablespoon of kosher salt. Bring to a boil again. Again strain and discard the water. For the third time, add 8 cups water and the remaining 1 tablespoon kosher salt to the pan with the cloves of garlic. Bring to a boil and again discard the water.

In a food processor, combine the blanched garlic, rosemary, lemon zest, parsley, ½ teaspoon of sea salt, and ¼ teaspoon pepper until puréed. With the machine running, add the olive oil slowly until the mixture emulsifies. This makes 2 cups. You'll use 1 cup to baste the fish before cooking; refrigerate the remaining salsa verde to serve as a condiment at the table.

RECIPE CONTINUES

Soak the caul fat in cold water for 30 minutes before using it. On a work surface, rub the tuna loin with 1 tablespoon of sea salt and 2 teaspoons of ground black pepper. Use a pastry brush to brush the tuna with Salsa Verde. Pull one sheet of caul fat out of the water and gently squeeze out excess liquid. Lay the caul fat flat on the work surface, and roll the tuna onto the caul fat sheet. Wrap the caul fat around the tuna. Brush more salsa on the tuna and the caul fat and prepare another sheet of the fat to smooth around the tuna loin. Repeat until the tuna is covered with four smoothed sheets of caul fat with a thin coating of salsa between each.

Slide the wrapped tuna loin onto the rotisserie rod, keeping your hands safely on either side of the loin. With butcher's twine, truss the tuna loin prime-rib style, securing it to the bar. Lock the bar into place on your rotisserie, and set it to rotate. Cook until the tuna is medium-rare, 25 to 30 minutes. You can use an instant-read thermometer to check the fish. At 125°F, the fish will be done but still pink at the center.

Carefully slide the loin from the rod. Cut the tuna into 1-inch slices with an electric knife or a very sharp fish knife, plate, and serve with the reserved salsa verde.

BRUSSELS SPROUTS
WITH
LEMONS IN A ROTISSERIE CAGE

Serves 6 to 8

Cooking Brussels sprouts in a rotisserie cage gives them a lot more flavor than you'd get from cooking them in the oven or on the stove. A rotisserie cage lets you roast smaller items—vegetables, small fish, Gypsy peppers—steadily over the flame without having to pick up a spatula even once. This is a great way to roast chile peppers, too, when you need a lot of them. ❖ You can find rotisserie cages online easily, and they usually cost less than thirty dollars. Using a cage is simple. You slide the spin rod through the cage, and secure it. (Usually they click into place.) Then snap the spin rod into place on your grill. Open the cage's hatch and pour in the Brussels sprouts or peppers, or whatever you want to cook. Close up the hatch, start the rotisserie, and you're cooking. ❖ See Resources (page 218) for places to find a rotisserie cage but first check with your grill manufacturer to see if they sell one for your grill.

6 ounces pancetta

4 tablespoons extra-virgin olive oil

¼ cup kosher salt

4 dozen Brussels sprouts

3 lemons

2 teaspoons coarse sea salt, preferably gray salt

¼ teaspoon freshly ground black pepper

Slice the pancetta into 1-inch lardons about ½ inch wide. Make them big enough so they don't fall through the bars of the cage. Pour 2 tablespoons of the olive oil into a large sauté pan over low heat. Add the chopped pancetta. Cook slowly until the pancetta is golden brown, about 6 minutes. Transfer the pancetta to a platter to cool and set it aside while you set up the grill.

If using a rotisserie over a gas grill, don't turn on the grill until 10 minutes before the Brussels sprouts will go over the fire. If using a stand-alone rotisserie, start the fire and check the rotisserie motor to be sure it's plugged in and working. Don't leave the fire unattended; either bring your work tools outside or have another adult stay near the fire while you work indoors.

Inside at your stove, add the kosher salt to a large pot of water over high heat. While the water heats, trim just the barest amount off the stem of each Brussels sprout. You want the head to hold together while turning over the fire so don't trim too much. After trimming, cut an X in the bottom of each stem.

When the water comes to a boil, add the Brussels sprouts and cook just until they start to soften, no more than 5 minutes.

Cut the lemons into quarters. (Don't slice them or the slices could slip out through the cage.) Set aside.

Transfer the Brussels sprouts out of the pot and onto a baking sheet or platter to cool. When they're cool enough to handle, slice them in half from stem to dome. In a large bowl, toss the Brussels sprouts halves with the lemons, pancetta, remaining 2 tablespoons olive oil, salt, and pepper.

Slide the cage into place on your rotisserie bar. Follow the manufacturer's directions: the cage should lock into place on the bar. Spoon the Brussels sprouts into the cage. Lock the bar into place on your rotisserie, and set it to rotate. Cook until the Brussels sprouts show some caramelization, about 20 minutes. Stop the rotisserie, take them out of the cage, and serve.

TORTA STRIZZARE
WITH
MAPLE-PECAN GRAY SALT ICE CREAM

Serves 6 to 8

Strizzare means "twist" in Italian, and this cake is all about the twist. You make the dough, roll it out, cut it into strips, and then wind the strips around a wooden form shaped like a traffic cone. You slide the dough-wrapped cone onto your rotisserie bar and the cake bakes over your grill as it turns, sending out the tantalizing aromas of caramelizing sugar, cinnamon, and butter. ❖ Like monkey bread, when this cake is baked and slightly cooled, your guests get to pull off chunks and pop them into their mouths. ❖ Make sure all the ingredients are at room temperature before you begin making the dough. ❖ See Resources (page 218) for the rotisserie cake form.

6 tablespoons unsalted butter, melted,
  plus extra for brushing the dough during cooking

2 tablespoons sugar

½ teaspoon coarse sea salt, preferably gray salt

1 cup whole milk

2 cups all-purpose flour, plus extra for flouring work surface

1 package (2¼ teaspoons) instant yeast (not fast-acting)

1 egg, plus egg yolk

1½ teaspoons ground cinnamon

2 tablespoons sugar

Maple-Pecan Gray Salt Ice Cream (page 177)

Grease a large bowl with oil; set aside. Melt the 6 tablespoons butter and set it aside.

On the stove in a saucepan or in the microwave in a microwave-safe dish, add the sugar and salt to the milk, and warm it just to lukewarm (105°F to 115°F). Set aside.

Whisk together the 2 cups flour and the instant yeast, and pour it into the bowl of a stand mixer fitted with the paddle attachment or use a hand mixer. Pour in the milk mixture, egg, and egg yolk and run the machine on low speed. With the machine running, very slowly drizzle in the melted butter. Beat on medium-low speed until an elastic dough forms, 5 to 7 minutes.

Transfer the dough to the greased bowl, cover it with plastic wrap or a clean kitchen towel, and set in a draft-free spot for 1 hour to rise.

Slide the wooden cake form onto the rotisserie bar, and secure it in place.

On a lightly floured work surface, gently roll the dough into a rectangle about 16 inches long and 12 inches wide. Cut the dough into strips 16 inches long and about three fingers' width. Combine the cinnamon and sugar; set aside.

RECIPE CONTINUES

Getting the strips to stay in place on the form is tricky. You want to use just a little of the melted butter that you set aside to lightly brush the dough as you roll the strips; if you use too much butter, the strips will slide right off the wooden form, so be sparing with the butter.

THIS PART IS BEST DONE WITH A PARTNER: one person holds the rod and the other gently rolls the strips around the form, pressing the dough into place before adding the next strip of dough. You want to channel those elementary school days when you turned strips of newspaper into papier-mâché. This is the same concept. The nice people who make the wooden cake form have made a homemade video. Watch it and get a sense of how the dough goes on the form: www.twistacake.com.

When all the dough is wrapped evenly around the form, sprinkle it evenly with the cinnamon-sugar. Lock the bar into place on your rotisserie, and set it to rotate. Let the cake bake until brown all the way around with caramelized sugar, 15 to 20 minutes. Let the cake cool on the form for 15 minutes. Gently pull the form out of the cake, and set the whole cake on a platter.

To serve, have guests pull off pieces from the cake to enjoy with bowls of ice cream.

MAPLE-PECAN GRAY SALT ICE CREAM

Makes 1½ pints

Salt, roasted nuts, maple, and cream. This ice cream is simple but—fair warning—it's addictive. ❖ Seek out Grade B maple syrup. It's counter-intuitive, but Grade B maple syrup is actually the best choice when the flavor of each ingredient matters.

¾ cup chopped pecans
⅔ cup Grade B maple syrup
2 cups heavy cream
⅔ cup whole milk
¼ teaspoon coarse sea salt, preferably gray salt

In a cast-iron skillet over the fire, toast the nuts, shaking the pan to keep them from burning. As soon as you can smell them, pour the nuts out of the skillet and onto a plate to cool. (You can also toast the nuts on a baking sheet in a 325°F oven for 10 to 15 minutes, taking care that they don't overcook.) Set the nuts aside to cool.

Indoors at the stove, in a large saucepan over medium heat, bring the maple syrup just to a boil. Decrease the heat to low and simmer for 5 minutes to thicken.

Take the pan off the heat and whisk in the cream, milk, and salt. Transfer the mixture to a bowl to cool to room temperature. If you want the mixture to cool faster, set the bowl in an ice bath (a large bowl of ice water). Refrigerate the mixture, covered, for at least 1 hour or up to 3 days.

Freeze the mixture in an ice-cream maker according to the manufacturer's directions. When the ice cream is almost at the desired consistency, stir in the nuts and continue freezing another 5 minutes.

In an airtight container, this can keep in your freezer for weeks—although it never lasts that long at my house.

BACKYARD CAMP-OUT BREAKFAST

Breakfast over a campfire is the best. It's great when you're backpacking through the mountains but it's equally great in your own backyard. This is a breakfast I made when some of my son's friends spent the night. One thing I know for sure: if a half-dozen kids are sleeping in tents in your backyard, you're not going to get the best night's sleep.

This meal is easy enough for sleep-deprived parents but we've added some campfire tricks that kids will love.

PAIN PERDU
(FRENCH TOAST)

Serves 6

The better the bread, the better the toast! Try breads such as challah, raisin-walnut, or breads with dried sour cherries or other dried fruit. This French toast is great when made from day-old bread slices.

Many folks can't imagine French toast without real maple syrup, and I agree that's good, but lately I've been pouring apple cider syrup over my French toast and pancakes for a nice change of pace.

I've added a splash of rum. Leave it out if you like, but it adds just a hint of flavor and any alcohol burns off during cooking.

4 eggs

¾ cup heavy cream

½ teaspoon ground cinnamon

¼ teaspoon ground ginger

1 teaspoon grated orange zest

1 tablespoon dark rum (optional)

3 tablespoons light brown sugar

1 teaspoon pure vanilla extract

2 tablespoons unsalted butter

2 tablespoons peanut or canola oil

6 thick slices country bread, preferably slightly stale

1½ cups real maple syrup or apple cider syrup, warmed in the microwave

In a large bowl, whisk together the eggs, cream, cinnamon, ginger, zest, rum (if using), brown sugar, and vanilla. Pour the mixture into a shallow bowl or baking dish.

Start a fire or ignite charcoal. If using a gas grill, start it about 10 minutes before you're ready to cook. (Make sure there's an adult watching it; don't walk away from a lit grill.) Preheat a plancha or a cast-iron pan over the fire or on the grill, or heat a skillet at the stove. Add 1 tablespoon of the butter and 1 tablespoon of the oil to the hot pan. (If using a plancha, add all the butter and all the oil, and cook all the slices at one time.)

Have a warmed platter ready for the cooked French toast.

Slide the bread slices into the egg mixture and turn so the egg soaks both sides. If you like you can let the bread soak in the egg mixture for 5 minutes but if the kids are hungry, forget about the soak and just cook. Place as many slices as can fit onto the hot pan. Cook until the bread is golden brown on the bottom, about 2 minutes. Turn and cook until the other side is browned, another 2 minutes.

With tongs or a spatula, transfer the toast to the warmed platter. Add the remaining butter and oil to the pan and cook the remaining slices if needed. Set out warmed syrup in a small pitcher.

SAUSAGES COOKED ON LONG FORKS

Serves 6

Nothing is as fun as holding a long fork or stick over a fire while browning a sausage or roasting a marshmallow. I buy the best mild sausages I can for the kids (with a few spicy Italian sausages for me) and poach them in hot water in the house before I bring them out to the fire. You can also buy cooked sausages, if you like, which only need heating.

2 dozen sweet Italian sausages (or any link sausage you like)

Poach the sausages in simmering water until they're done, about 5 minutes. Outside, slide a sausage (or several if you have multi-prong forks) onto the end of a long-handled fork and hold it over the fire until the skin is crisp and brown all the way around.

BROWN-BAGGED EGGS AND BACON

Serves 6

Cooking bacon and eggs in a paper bag is my campfire version of the classic technique *en papillote*—cooking in a parchment-paper packet. The old-school method is to rub some raw bacon inside the bottom of a brown paper bag, spread out the raw bacon to cover the bottom, and crack open an egg and drop it down on the bacon. Then you fold up the bag, poke a stick through the fold, and hold the bag by the stick over the coals until the bacon and eggs have cooked. This can take a half an hour, which is fine if you're sitting at the top of a mountain range with a couple of old friends drinking coffee. For a group of six-year-olds (and the dad in charge) thirty minutes equals infinity and beyond.

Out of sheer necessity (to ward off insanity), here's the faster method: cook the bacon in a cast-iron skillet or a plancha until it's about three-quarters done but not yet crisp. Grease the inside of the sacks with a few slices of raw bacon. With tongs, line up the partially cooked bacon in the bottom of each kid's bag. (Don't let the kids fool around near the hot bacon grease; I'm just sayin'.) Ask each kid if he wants one egg or two in his bag, and then crack each egg and drop it onto the warm bacon, fold up the bag, put it on a stick, and let each kid hold his sack over the fire. Warn them that if they get the bag too close to the fire it'll flame up. Expect flame-ups and have plenty of bacon, eggs, and brown bags on hand.

18 slices (give or take) of thick-cut bacon, plus 2 slices for greasing the sacks
1 or 2 eggs for every kid, plus extra
6 plain school lunch–size brown bags, plus extra
6 sturdy sticks, each about 1 yard long, for holding the bag over the fire

Build a fire (if you don't already have one going from the French toast). Preheat a cast-iron skillet or a plancha over the fire. Cook the 18 slices of bacon until they show color but aren't yet crisp. While the bacon cooks, set up a brown bag for each kid on a stable surface. Grab two slices of raw bacon, kind of roll them a little, and use them to grease the inside of each sack. (Those two slices should grease up all the bags, no problem.) With tongs, transfer three slices of mostly cooked bacon into the bottom of each greased sack.

For each bag, crack an egg into a small bowl or dish (you can let the kids do this) and then use the bowl to slide the egg into a bag so it sits on top of the warm bacon. Don't leave the bowl in the bag. It's okay if the egg yolk breaks.

Fold the top of each bag at least three times. Cut a hole through the fold and slide the bag onto a long stick.

 Don't skimp on the stick—you want the kids sitting a good distance from the fire.

Let each kid hold their bag over the fire. Warn them about eighty times that the bag will burn if they get it too close to the coals. Watch as several of the bags burn, and have someone responsible sitting beside the kids while you replace the bacon and egg sacks that are sacrificed to the coals.

When the eggs are done, after 10 to 15 minutes, peel the brown bag away from the bacon and eggs, or just hand the kids some forks and let them eat right out of the bag. When the kids are finished eating, I give our dog Dash any leftover bacon and eggs (there's usually not much) and then burn the emptied bags right on the fire.

MELON, TWO WAYS

MELON PLATTER (FOR KIDS) AND
MELON SALAD WITH RICOTTA SALATA
AND TORN MINT (FOR GROWN-UPS)

The kids don't need a formal salad; they'll be happier with a platter of sweet, ripe melons cut up into triangular slices. (Leave on the rind so the wedges are easier to pick up.) If you like, add some ripe strawberries to the platter.

For the grown-ups swinging by to pick up their children, why not toss together a gussied-up but quick version of a melon salad. It's so simple you can be pretty casual about amounts: For 6 servings, put about 6 cups melon cubes in a bowl, toss on about ¾ cup crumbled or grated ricotta salata cheese, and add some hand-torn fresh mint leaves. Drizzle on 2 tablespoons olive oil and some sea salt and black pepper, toss to combine, and head on outside.

CHEF'S NOTE: When it comes to melon, don't get hung up on the idea that you have to have the triple play of watermelon, cantaloupe, and honeydew. Look for varietals such as Tuscan melons when at the farmers' market and buy the melons with the best fragrance.

MALTED HOT CHOCOLATE WITH FIRE-TOASTED MARSHMALLOWS

Serves 8

Hot chocolate with marshmallows that you toast over a fire—I can't think of a better drink for a sleepover breakfast.

You can pour the milk and chocolate pieces into a pan and set it over the fire. (Bring along a whisk to froth it up.) You can also heat the milk at your stove and pour the hot chocolate into a thermos so you don't have to go back in the house to reheat it.

One thing I've learned through experience: One kid will taste this, thunk his mug down on the table, and say, "I don't like malt." You'll have a small stare-down and he will win. Keep the malt powder nearby and let the kids spoon it into their own cups. A good rule of thumb is either 2 tablespoons of malt powder or 2 teaspoons of sugar per 8 ounces of milk—but don't add both the malt powder and sugar.

4 ounces bittersweet chocolate,
　preferably 72 percent cacao
8 cups whole milk
Malted powder (such as Ovaltine) or sugar
16 to 24 large marshmallows

Chop the chocolate into small pieces (see Chef's Note, following). In a large pan, heat the milk over medium-high heat. Add the chocolate to the milk. Whisk constantly until the chocolate is all melted and the milk is foamy, 1 to 2 minutes. When the chocolate is hot (but don't let it boil), pour into mugs. Let each kid stir in his or her own malt

powder (or sugar) but try to limit them to 3 tablespoons of malt powder per mug or 2 teaspoons of sugar.

Top with two or three marshmallows that have been held over a campfire until they're golden and toasty—or charred black outside, if that's your marshmallow preference.

CHEF'S NOTE: When chopping a solid bar of chocolate, use a chef's knife and start at one corner, moving the blade from a corner of the bar at a 45-degree angle and chopping inward toward the middle of the bar. Then turn your cutting board and chop in the opposite direction so you have tiny chocolate chunks that melt easily.

Here's a quick rule of thumb for measuring chocolate: 1 ounce of solid chocolate equals about 4 tablespoons when finely chopped. You want 2 tablespoons (or ½ ounce) of chocolate per cup of milk.

CHAPTER EIGHT

THE LAST OF THE FIRE:
COALS AND EMBERS

When I read the book *Seven Fires*, by Argentine chef Francis Mallmann, it had a profound impact on me. Here was this internationally renowned chef, stripping away all the nonessential elements from his cooking, and harnessing fire to create the most beautiful, soulful foods. I especially loved to see how Francis cooked in coals and embers, a technique he calls *rescoldo*. He wrote, "Like country folk all over the world, the Indians of Argentina believed that nothing should be wasted. This includes fire—as long as it can be used for cooking, one should use it."

This struck a chord with me because the country folk in Italy who are my relatives felt and still feel this belief strongly: fuel is an expensive commodity for southern Italians and it can never be wasted. Even as a child, I knew that it was wrong—it was throwing away good money—to not use every bit of the wood.

Ember roasting calls for a different mind-set than for cooking over fresh wood or charcoal. Ember roasting cannot be for the dinner you're cooking now. It requires some thought about the next day's meals. When the fire is burning down, after your last guest has left, when the last glow of the coals is almost hidden by the ash, then you can push eggplants and onions into the embers, and start to plan what you will make the next day: lamb burgers sweetened with the roasted onion, or maybe a squash soup. How about pumpkins as you've never seen them before?

This method isn't meant for fresh fuel. Don't anger the charcoal gods by starting a fire just to use the embers. If you need roasted onion purée but don't have dying coals to use, see the alternate method that lets you make a purée from onion slices grilled over live coals.

EMBER-ROASTED
ONION PURÉE

Makes about 1½ cups purée

I love using the last of a fire to roast vegetables for the next night's dinner. Please don't start a charcoal fire just to roast veggies. You can burn through pounds of charcoal trying to roast a few onions that cost dimes to dollars what you paid for the fuel. ❖ Instead, think about what you have inside the house when you're done with a fire. Bring out the red peppers, the onions, the eggplant, a few small squash, or a small pumpkin. Bury what you have in the hot coals. Within 20 to 40 minutes, they'll be done and you can set them aside and plan how you'll use them the next day. ❖ Any onion will work for this method. I like to use sweeter onions such as Vidalias but regular yellow onions are wonderful, if that's what's on hand. ❖ How do I use this purée? I put some under the skin of a chicken before roasting. I add it to ground lamb for burgers (see page 70), or I use it to make a crust for a roast or pork loin. I add it to soup, and I make a damned good vinaigrette out of it, facing page.

2 large whole yellow onions, with skin intact

When the coals show only a hint of red and you can feel with your hands that the fire's heat has died down, use a poker or long tongs to push the onions into the embers and rake or shovel coals on top. They're done when a skewer slides easily into the onion, 20 to 40 minutes, depending on the heat of the coals.

Peel the onions and discard the peels. The onion itself will be very soft; take care to keep as much ash out of it as possible. Put the onions in a food processor or blender, and process until there are no large chunks.

In an airtight container, the purée will keep for 3 days in your fridge or for up to 1 month in your freezer.

PURÉE FROM
GRILLED ONIONS

Makes about 1½ cups purée

If you need the onion purée for the lamb burgers or the vinaigrette and you don't have a charcoal fire that's mostly burned down, peel and cut the onions into thick rounds, drizzle with olive oil, salt, and pepper, and grill until the slices show some brown on both sides. We did a taste test between the ember-roasted onion purée and one made from grilled onions: The purée from onions roasted in coals is a pale, creamier color because their skins keep them free of ash. Purée made from grilled onion slices was much darker in color and sweeter from the caramelization as well as smokier. ❖ You can grill thick onion slices right on the grill rack, but if your slices are a little thinner use a grill basket so you don't sacrifice too much onion to the fire.

2 yellow onions, sliced into ½-inch-thick rounds
3 tablespoons extra-virgin olive oil
1 teaspoon coarse sea salt, preferably gray salt
½ teaspoon freshly ground black pepper

Drizzle the onion slices with olive oil on both sides, and sprinkle with salt and pepper. Put on a grill (use a grill basket if the rounds begin to slip apart) or cook on a hot grill pan over high heat on your stove.

Cook the onions over a hot fire for 8 to 10 minutes, and then turn the slices (or the basket) and grill the other side until the slices show a lot of char but still have some juice in them, another 6 to 8 minutes.

Let the onions cool for at least 30 minutes and then process the slices in a food processor or blender until a smooth purée forms.

In an airtight container, the purée will keep for 3 days in your fridge or for up to 1 month in your freezer.

PURÉED ONION
VINAIGRETTE

Makes about 1½ cups

Because the grilled onions were salted before roasting, don't add salt or pepper until you've mixed the vinaigrette. Then taste and see if it needs more seasoning. ❖ Pour this over a winter salad of oranges and fennel or tangerines and radishes. In the summer, I use this to dress a salad of strawberries, organic greens, and blue cheese.

1 cup Ember-Roasted Onion Purée (facing page)
3 tablespoons white balsamic vinegar
1 tablespoon water
¼ cup extra-virgin olive oil
Coarse sea salt (if needed), preferably gray salt
Freshly ground black pepper, if needed

In a food processor or a blender, combine the onion purée, vinegar, and the 1 tablespoon water. With the machine on, slowly pour in the olive oil until the dressing emulsifies. Taste before seasoning.

Covered, this will keep in the fridge for 2 weeks but you may need to stir it before pouring.

EMBER-ROASTED
GARLIC

Even if you have nothing else to roast in a dying fire, bring out your garlic. Whole heads of garlic are ideal to roast in the embers. You don't need a recipe. Just give each head a good drizzle of olive oil and a sprinkle of sea salt and pepper. Double-wrap in foil and bury the packets in the coals. Low embers are better for these—if the fire is too hot the garlic can burn and turn bitter. ❖ Leave the packets in the fire for an hour or so, then take them out, and let the garlic cool. Squeeze the garlic paste out of each clove just as you would with oven-roasted garlic. ❖ I generally roast four whole heads of garlic this way, and then make Roasted Garlic Paste (page 212). It freezes well and you'll be glad to have a stash of it.

EMBER-ROASTED
EGGPLANT
PURÉE

Makes about 3 cups purée

At Bottega, we fold this silky eggplant purée into ground lamb that is shaped onto skewers as spiedini and grilled. At home, I like to use this as the base for baba ghanoush (see page 190) because the smokiness suits the eggplant's texture. I've also included an alternate method for roasting the vegetables in the oven.

2 Italian eggplants with stems and peel intact
1 large yellow onion with peel
2 tablespoons extra-virgin olive oil
½ teaspoon chopped fresh thyme
1 tablespoon coarse sea salt, preferably gray salt
Pinch of freshly ground black pepper

Pierce the eggplants four or five times with a skewer; don't pierce the onion. When a wood or charcoal fire has burned down to glowing coals that are just beginning to lose their red color, use a poker or long tongs to push the onions and eggplants into the embers and rake or shovel coals on top.

Cook until the onion and eggplants are soft and a skewer slides in easily, about 20 minutes for the onion and 30 to 40 minutes for the eggplants, depending on the heat of the coals. When you take them out of the coals, set them aside until they're cool enough to handle.

Halve the eggplants lengthwise and scoop out the flesh directly into the bowl of a food processor. Take care not to get ash in the flesh. Peel the onion, discard the peel, and place the onion in the food processor with the eggplant. Purée until smooth.

Heat a large sauté pan over medium-high heat and pour in the oil. When it's hot, add the thyme and then immediately add the 2 cups of the purée, salt, and pepper. Sauté until the mixture is almost dry. Now here comes the tedious part: Push the mixture through a medium sieve with the back of a wooden spoon. This is slow work but worth the effort for the silken, smooth result.

IN THE OVEN: You can roast the eggplants and onions in your oven if you prefer. Preheat the oven to 500°F, and be sure to pierce each eggplant four or five times. Set them on a rimmed baking sheet, and roast until a skewer slides easily into the eggplant, about 40 minutes. Let them cool, then continue with the recipe.

BABA GHANOUSH
WITH
TOASTED PINE NUT TAHINI AND SOCCA

Serves 6 as an appetizer

The best eggplant dip—baba ghanoush—starts with ember-roasted eggplant. As a twist, here it's mixed with aromatic pine nuts, toasted and ground, in place of the usual ground sesame seed in Middle Eastern tahini paste. ❖ *Socca*, made with chickpea flour, are like pancakes but they're savory and lighter in texture. In Nice, where socca is popular street fare made by vendors cooking over smoking grills, they spread the batter thin and make their socca large. Cook socca on a plancha or cast-iron skillet over a fire, in your hearth, or on a gas or charcoal grill. You can make socca in your oven but it lacks something when it's not cooked over a fire.

SOCCA

1 cup chickpea flour (see Resources, page 218)

1 cup plus 1 tablespoon Chicken Broth (page 217) or water

¾ teaspoon coarse sea salt, preferably gray salt, plus extra for finish

2 tablespoons extra-virgin olive oil, plus more for the pan

1 teaspoon freshly squeezed lemon juice

½ teaspoon minced garlic

BABA GHANOUSH

¼ cup extra-virgin olive oil

¼ cup pine nuts

3 sprigs fresh rosemary, plus more for garnish

2 cups Ember-Roasted Eggplant Purée (page 189)

1 garlic clove, minced

1 teaspoon freshly squeezed lemon juice

Coarse sea salt, preferably gray salt

Freshly ground black pepper

Drizzle of your best extra-virgin olive oil, for finish

FOR THE SOCCA: In a medium bowl, mix together the chickpea flour, broth, the ¾ teaspoon salt, 2 tablespoons of the olive oil, lemon juice, and garlic. Mix well, cover, and let the batter rest for 1½ hours at room temperature.

Warm a large platter and have it ready before you start cooking. You'll probably want to cook these on a fire you're using to cook other foods, too. Set a plancha or large cast-iron skillet to heat over a medium-high fire or on your gas grill for at least 10 minutes. If baking the socca in your oven, preheat to 500°F. Pour the socca batter into a pitcher or a measuring cup with a spout.

When the plancha or pan is blazing hot—hot enough so droplets of water scatter on the surface—brush the surface with a little olive oil. Pour batter onto the hot plancha or pan, to form cakes about 3 inches across. Cook until the tops show large bubbles around the edges, about 30 seconds. Flip all of the socca with a spatula and cook just until golden brown, another 20 seconds or so.

Transfer to the warm platter and cover; continue cooking until you've used all the batter. They're best served warm off the fire, but if you need to, cover the socca and keep them warm in a 200°F oven until ready to serve.

FOR THE BABA GHANOUSH: Line a plate with paper towels. Heat a small sauté pan over high heat on the stove or on your grill. Add the olive oil. When it's hot, add the pine nuts. Toast them until they're golden brown (don't overcook them). As soon as they begin to show color, slide them out of the pan and onto the paper-lined plate to cool. Toss the rosemary sprigs into the hot pan to crisp them. Take them off the heat, and let them cool. Mince the leaves of the rosemary. You'll need just 1 tablespoon of the minced toasted rosemary.

When the pine nuts are cool, grind them in a small food processor or with a mortar and pestle until they form a paste.

In a large bowl, fold the pine nut paste into the eggplant purée, and stir in the garlic, lemon juice, and 1 tablespoon of the minced toasted rosemary. Taste and season with salt and pepper. Refrigerate until ready to serve.

To serve, spoon a few tablespoons of the baba ghanoush on one side of a serving plate, and use the back of the spoon to form an artful smear. Drizzle some of your best olive oil over the smear. Arrange the socca on the other side of the plate—cut several of the socca in half just for visual contrast—and garnish the plate with fresh rosemary if you like. Serve while still warm.

BRUSCHETTA
WITH
COAL-ROASTED GARLIC
AND GRILLED TOMATOES

Serves 6

Bruschetta comes from the Roman word *bruscare*, which means to roast over coals. For at least 800 years, Romans and Italians have been crisping up bread over the heat. I don't see this going out of fashion during my lifetime. ❖ The raft of grilled bread can hold just about any topping but this one is a classic: warm, soft garlic and some grilled tomatoes on bread toasted over a fire . . . sit back, pour yourself some wine, and be happy.

6 to 8 medium to large ripe tomatoes, preferably heirloom

Drizzle of extra-virgin olive oil

Coarse sea salt, preferably gray salt

Freshly ground black pepper

A sprinkle of chopped fresh thyme, fresh flat-leaf parsley, or fresh oregano

6 slices from a country loaf of bread, cut about ½ inch thick

Ember-Roasted Garlic (page 187) or Roasted Garlic Paste (page 212)

Have ready a campfire or a charcoal fire that's beginning to burn down so the coals are mostly gray or turn a gas grill to high. When it's hot, clean the grill rack and then decrease the gas grill's temperature to medium-high.

Cut an X in the base of each tomato and coat each lightly with olive oil. Place the tomatoes on the hot grill, X-side up, and season with salt and pepper.

Let the tomatoes cook for 8 to 10 minutes. With tongs, turn the tomatoes X-side down and cook for another 3 to 5 minutes. If using a gas grill, keep the lid down while the tomatoes cook. When they're soft but still firm enough to stand on their own, take the tomatoes off the heat with tongs.

Wait until they're cool enough to handle, then seed and peel the tomatoes and chop coarsely. Sprinkle with herbs and taste. Add more salt and pepper if you like.

Skewer each piece of bread on a stick and hold it over the fire or lay the bread slices on the hot grill rack. Give it just a minute and then turn them over so the bread is toasted on both sides but not dried out in the center.

Spread each slice with some roasted garlic, spoon on tomatoes, sit back, and enjoy.

I DON'T SEE THIS GOING OUT
OF FASHION DURING MY LIFETIME.

SMASHING PUMPKINS
WITH
MINT PESTO
AND GOAT CHEESE

Each pumpkin serves 4 people

Big fires mean big smoldering piles of embers; that's when it's time to bury pumpkins in the ashes. If you think of pies when you think about eating pumpkin, this will change your point of view. ❖ Forget about those big pumpkins that beg to be carved into jack-o'-lanterns. Choose small flavorful varieties with tender flesh, such as Sugar Pie pumpkins. The farmers' market is a good place to scope out some heirloom breeds such as Small Sugar, Wintery Luxury, Snow White, or Baby Pam. This is also a good recipe to make with kabocha squash from Japan.

2 small heirloom pumpkins, about 3 pounds each
1¼ cups Mint Pesto (page 32)
16 ounces fresh goat cheese
Coarse sea salt, preferably gray salt
Freshly ground black pepper

You'll want to cook pumpkins at the very end of the fire, when there's some red showing in the embers but mostly it's burned down to gray ash. First saw off the pumpkins' stems so they don't flame up in the coals. Bury the pumpkins in the hot embers, shoveling hot coals on top to cover them completely. Cook until an instant-read thermometer slid into the side of one of the pumpkins registers 150°F. Take the pumpkins out of the embers, and let them cool for at least 30 minutes.

Now comes the fun part: breaking the pumpkins into pieces. Wear heat-proof gloves and long sleeves. With a firm but controlled motion, slam the pumpkin into a sharp object: I use the corner of my stone table but for a little more drama you could use a small axe or hatchet to give each pumpkin a hard knock.

In a perfect world the pumpkin breaks into two more-or-less even hemispheres, but if it breaks into pieces, just go with it. Scrape off most of the seeds (don't worry about a few stragglers) and serve the pumpkin with the inside facing up; you don't need bowls or plates because the pumpkin is the plate. Spoon some of the pesto right onto the flesh, top with cheese, and sprinkle with sea salt and pepper. If you like you can add an airy salad or keep it simple with just the cheese and pesto.

Eat right from the gourd, with two people sharing each half. Use a spoon to scrape up some of the tender roasted flesh with each bite.

CHEF FRANCIS MALLMANN
INSPIRED THIS SOULFUL
METHOD OF COOKING PUMPKINS.

CHAPTER NINE

FIRE AND ICE:
COLD DRINKS

An ice-cold drink to go with whatever you're cooking over the fire—
that's a given. The cocktails that I serve outdoors are different from my
indoor cocktails. I make them with bolder flavors, and give some a hit
of smoke. Even when you start with classic cocktails—a Bloody Mary
or a margarita—you can shake things up, and add a little interest. Here's
proof that cocktails can be sparked by the same creativity that you
bring to your cooking.

The most important party ingredient during hot weather is ice; have
plenty of ice in coolers before the party starts. One pound of ice per
person is a good starting point.

GRILLED ZINFANDEL SANGRIA

Makes about 5 cups

Grilling lemon and orange slices and halved grapes intensifies the fruit and gives the sangria a smoky, rich flavor. You can increase the amount of this drink easily by following this proportion: for every 1 cup of red wine pour in 1 ounce of brandy and 1 ounce of simple syrup. ❖ If you like, grill extra fruit and set up a small sangria bar where people can garnish their drink with as much fruit as they like. ❖ Make this at least 4 hours in advance to give the wine time to absorb the flavors of the fruit.

2 oranges, cut into ½-inch-thick slices with peel

2 lemons, cut into ½-inch-thick slices with peel

1 large cluster of grapes, fruit cut in half

4 cups Zinfandel

4 ounces Simple Syrup (page 32)

4 ounces brandy

On a clean grill rack over a gas grill or a charcoal fire that is half burned down, grill the citrus slices. Put the grape halves in a fine-mesh grill basket. Grill until the citrus slices show some brown, about 2 minutes per side. Shake the grill basket every 30 seconds or so to allow the grapes to cook evenly. Take all the fruit off the fire when it's juicy and smoky; don't let it develop too much black char. Put all the fruit in the fridge to cool.

In a large glass pitcher or decanter, mix together the Zinfandel, simple syrup, and brandy. Add the fruit to the pitcher and chill until ready to serve. Add ice to the pitcher, but not until your guests are there and you're starting to pour.

BLOODY MATADOR

Makes 1 cocktail

A Bloody Bull is a classic cocktail that combines beef bouillon and tomato juice. We've revved it up by grilling the tomatoes before juicing and then reducing beef stock so it's a little higher octane. I serve this jet cold in small rice bowls with a tiny dice of celery, cukes, and tomatoes in the bottom. (A brunoise is a chef's trick where you dice the veggies into tiny neat cubes.) The drink is full flavored and the final taste of crunchy, raw vegetables is a cool, refreshing surprise at the end.

1½ ounces vodka

2½ ounces Grilled Tomato Bloody Mary Blend (page 214)

1½ ounces beef stock reduction (see Chef's Note)

¾ teaspoon brunoise dice of heirloom tomatoes

¾ teaspoon brunoise dice of celery

¾ teaspoon brunoise dice of peeled, seeded cucumber

In a cocktail shaker, pour the vodka, tomato blend, and beef stock reduction over ice. Shake until cold. Add the diced vegetables to a small bowl and pour the drink through a strainer onto the vegetables. Serve right away.

CHEF'S NOTE: To make the reduction, pour 2 cups of Beef Stock (page 216) into a saucepan over medium-high heat. Cook until the stock is reduced to just ½ cup, about 10 minutes.

ROASTED APRICOT PURÉE

Makes about 1¼ cups

I cook the apricots on a cast-iron pan or plancha set on the grill because I want to heat them until they're so soft they barely hold their shape. Don't use any oil with these because oil would overwhelm the subtle notes of the Prosecco in the cocktail.

1 pound fresh apricots (about 8 to 10 fruit), halved and pitted

Set a cast-iron pan or plancha over a hot grill rack over medium to medium-high heat. Place the fruit on a hot surface and grill until they're browned and very, very soft, 6 to 8 minutes on each side. Let the fruit cool for at least 15 minutes.

In a blender or food processor or with an immersion blender, purée the fruit (with skin) until it's a little smoother than applesauce. Chill the purée for at least 1 hour. If covered tightly, with plastic wrap smoothed across the top, this will keep in your fridge for 2 days.

ROASTED APRICOT BELLINI

Makes 1 cocktail

Roasting the fruit brings a whole new attitude to the classic Bellini, which I make with Prosecco instead of Champagne. ❖ This drink will have flecks of black char from the fruit, which I like.

1 ounce Roasted Apricot Purée (preceding)
¾ ounce Simple Syrup (page 32)
5 ounces Prosecco

Pour the apricot purée and simple syrup into a tall, chilled glass. Stir and pour on the Prosecco.

DAN DUCKHORN'S FIRST-NIGHT COCKTAIL

Makes 1 cocktail

1 jigger premium vodka

1 dash celery salt

3 dashes Worcestershire sauce

¼ teaspoon prepared horseradish, plus more if you like

Coarse sea salt, preferably gray salt

Freshly ground black pepper

1 dash jalapeño hot sauce or Tabasco sauce

4 to 6 ounces Clamato juice

1 pickled green bean (optional)

Fill a tall glass halfway with ice cubes. Pour in the vodka, celery salt, Worcestershire, horseradish, salt, pepper, and hot sauce. Fill the glass the rest of the way with Clamato juice. Stir vigorously and garnish with a pickled string bean if you like.

RED BEER

Makes 1 cocktail

This is my favorite drink on a hot day. It's a proportion of 25 percent Bloody Mary blend to 75 percent beer. You can eyeball it—you don't really need to measure. I like a Corona-style beer for this one instead of a microbrew, and I pour this drink always, always into a tall, ice-cold glass.

1 lime wedge

Coarse sea salt, preferably gray salt

2 ounces Grilled Tomato Bloody Mary Blend (page 214)

6 ounces ice-cold beer, such as Corona

Rub the lime on the rim of a tall, chilled glass, and dip the rim into sea salt. Pour the tomato mix into the glass, taking care not to splash the salt. Pour on the beer, and enjoy . . . preferably in a hammock beside a lake.

CITRUS VARIATION: If you don't want to make up the Bloody Mary blend, serve wheat beer with grilled slices of orange or lemon instead.

TEQUILA MARGARITA

Makes 1 cocktail

Smoking the tequila gives the liquor a mescal-like flavor that I love. I also roast the lemons and limes before juicing them. Hold the orange peel over a flame for about 5 seconds before adding it to the drink. ❖ For the rim, try either Smoked Chardonnay Salt or Smoked Sea Salt (page 211) to add another hit of smoke flavor.

Smoked Chardonnay Salt (see Resources, page 218),
 Smoked Sea Salt (page 211),
  or coarse sea salt, preferably gray salt
1 lime wedge
½ ounce juice from roasted lemon (see headnote)
½ ounce juice from roasted lime (see headnote)
2 ounces smoked tequila
 (see The Smoking Gun, at right)
¾ ounce Simple Syrup (page 32)
3-inch length of orange peel, colored part only,
 no white pith (see headnote)

Pour the salt into a saucer and rub the lime wedge around the glass rim. Dip the glass rim in the salt. Carefully add ice to the glass and set it aside.

Pour the lemon juice, lime juice, smoked tequila, and simple syrup into a cocktail shaker full of ice. Shake until cold. Pour the drink over the ice in the salted glass, taking care not to splash the salt. Flame the orange peel just for 2 to 5 seconds by holding the peel either over the gas flame on your stove or over a live fire, then drop the flamed peel into the drink.

THE SMOKING GUN

The handheld motorized cold-smoker is my favorite off-fire tool for infusing foods with a smoky flavor. There are several types of smoking guns; the one I use is battery-operated with a small recess in the top to hold wood chips. You pack the recess with any kind of wood chip you like: hickory or mesquite for very strong flavors, apple wood or any fruit wood for a subtler smoke.

To smoke, you attach the hose to the gun's nozzle and then light the wood chips in the top of the gun with a lighter. The motor pulls the smoke into the hose, so you can aim a stream of smoke wherever you like.

This tool is fantastic when you're making cocktails. I use it to smoke tequila and I even smoke water to freeze into smoky ice cubes. When smoking a liquid, you need to create a kind of smoke chamber. You can use a bell jar if you have one; if not, use any clear container (so you can see the smoke inside) and seal it with plastic wrap over the top.

The smoking gun motor isn't very strong; if you submerge the hose in the liquid you'll get very little smoke out of the hose. Here's a better way: pour the liquid into a glass container such as a large baking dish. A shallow container gives the liquid more exposure to the smoke. Place the smoking gun hose into the container but don't light the gun yet. Cover the container and the tip of the hose with plastic wrap so the smoke will fill up the space above the liquid. Fire up the gun and get a good amount of smoke on top of the liquid. Pull out the hose and seal up the plastic wrap with the smoke inside. Let the liquid sit and absorb the smoke flavor for 5 to 10 minutes.

If making ice cubes from the smoked liquid, freeze them as soon as you've finished smoking.

See Resources (page 218) for where to buy a smoking gun.

HIGHWAYMAN'S
MOJITO

Makes 1 cocktail

Guarapo de cana can refer to either fresh juice from sugar cane or a syrup made from the juice; either way it's very popular in Cuban and South American cocktails. See Resources, page 218, for where to find guarapo de cana in a can. ❖ A true Miami-style mojito is simply rum poured into guarapo, preferably from a flask. (Maybe you have to be twenty-one years old to truly appreciate that version. We've upgraded the drink here with fresh mint and tarragon.) To taste the true version of this drink, made with fresh guarapo, seek out a Cuban grocer, who could probably find guarapo for you; otherwise, go to Chowhound.com and ask if anybody near you knows where to buy it. If you can't locate guarapo, you can substitute an equal amount of simple syrup.

6 sprigs fresh mint

1 stem fresh tarragon

1 ounce freshly squeezed lime juice

1½ ounces rum, either light or dark

1 ounce guarapo de cana or Simple Syrup (page 32)

In a cocktail shaker or a sturdy bar glass, muddle the mint and tarragon with the lime juice. When you can really smell the herbs, pour in the rum and guarapo. Strain and pour the drink into a chilled martini glass or pour the cocktail, leaves and all, into a chilled tumbler.

MEYER LEMON
VERBENA WATER

Makes 2 quarts

Everyone appreciates ice-cold flavored water on a warm day. By adding herbs and lemon slices to water, you've made it more refreshing but kept the calories and sugar out of the mix. We made this with lemon verbena because I had bushels of it in my yard. Mint and lemon water, cucumber water, orange water, and raspberry water are all welcome additions to a party.

2 whole Meyer lemons, thinly sliced with peel

2 cups fresh lemon verbena

2 quarts cold water

Combine the fruit, herbs, and water in a large decanter and chill. Serve cold with lots of ice.

ROASTED STRAWBERRY LEMONADE
WITH HERB SYRUPS

Makes about 2½ gallons

I love lemonade that's not too sweet. When I make lemonade, I don't add sugar. Instead, I set out bottles of herb-infused simple syrups and let people sweeten their own. Roasting the strawberries gets rid of their tartness and intensifies their flavor. You can roast the strawberries the day before, and then refrigerate them. Purée and add to the lemonade just before serving. ❖ On a hot day, lemonade flows like water at my house. I make a lot of it, setting out a 3-gallon glass decanter with a spigot and stashing plenty of extra lemonade in the fridge before the party starts.

16 lemons, cut into ¼-inch slices
1 cup freshly squeezed lemon juice
4 quarts cold water
4 quarts club soda
Roasted Strawberries (page 90), puréed
Basil Simple Syrup (following)
Balsamic Simple Syrup (following)
Mint Agave (following)

Put the lemon slices on the bottom of a large decanter. Pour on the lemon juice, the cold water, and the club soda. Add the strawberry purée, and stir. Chill well.

When you're ready to start the party, set out all the flavored syrups, label them, and let guests sweeten their own lemonade.

BASIL SIMPLE SYRUP

Makes about 2¼ cups

Follow these directions with any leafy herb. My favorites include lemon verbena, mint, and the leaves from a rose geranium.

2 cups water
2 cups granulated sugar
12 big whole fresh basil leaves, plus 8 small
   tender leaves for basil confetti

Pour the water and sugar into a medium saucepan and bring to a boil over high heat. Stir. When all the sugar is dissolved, take the pan off the heat and toss in the 12 big basil leaves. Either let the mixture cool naturally or set the pan in an ice bath (water and ice cubes) if you need it to cool faster.

When the syrup has cooled, remove the 12 basil leaves and discard. Cut the remaining 8 leaves into chiffonade (see Chef's Note, page 43). Then turn your cutting board and slice the ribbons crosswise into tiny, neat squares. Stir this confetti into the basil syrup. It will float to the top but just shake the bottle before pouring the syrup into your lemonade.

BALSAMIC SIMPLE SYRUP

Makes about ½ cup

½ cup white balsamic vinegar
6 tablespoons granulated sugar

Heat the balsamic vinegar and sugar in a small saucepan over medium-high heat. Bring to a boil and let cook until reduced by half, 6 to 8 minutes. (The process speeds up toward the end, so don't walk away from it.) Take the pan off the heat and let the mixture cool. Skim off any foam.

MINT AGAVE

Makes about 3 cups

3 cups (or one 23.5-ounce bottle) agave syrup
2 big fistfuls of fresh mint, stems and leaves
   (about 8 leafy stems)

Pour the agave into a medium saucepan and bring to a boil over high heat. As soon as the syrup boils vigorously, take the pan off the heat. Toss in all the mint, stir, and let the syrup cool.

CHAPTER TEN

OIL, SALT, AND SPICE:

SEASONINGS, SAUCES, AND DRESSINGS

The recipes in this chapter are building blocks, basics that I use as the foundation in many of my meals. In addition to methods, I've listed a few ways in which you can use each of these go-to recipes.

Any time you make a spice rub or seasoning, choosing super-fresh spices is key. For where to find the best fresh spices, see Resources, page 218.

FENNEL SPICE RUB

Makes about 1¼ cups

It's been about two decades since I first mixed this blend, and it's still my favorite spice combination. I sprinkle this on everything from grilled goat cheese (see page 45) to roasted whole goat, roasted chicken, and many different vegetables. Try rubbing this on fresh butterflied prawns just before grilling.

1 cup fennel seeds

3 tablespoons coriander seeds

2 tablespoons whole white peppercorns

3 tablespoons coarse sea salt,
   preferably gray salt

Put the fennel seeds, coriander seeds, and peppercorns in a small heavy skillet over medium heat. Toss the seeds so they toast evenly. As soon as you begin to smell them, take them off the heat. Don't let them get darker than a light brown.

Turn the spices out onto a plate to cool. (If you try to grind them while they're warm, they will gum up the blades of your blender or spice mill.)

Pour the cooled seeds into a blender or spice mill. Blend until the spices are about the same size as the salt, and then add the salt. Blend to a powder, removing the blender pitcher from its stand and shaking occasionally.

Store in an airtight container in a cool, dark place for 4 months or store in your freezer for up to 1 year.

TOASTED SPICE RUB

Makes about 1 cup

I love this blend on lamb, shrimp, and fish. I sprinkle it over a pot of beans or rice while they're cooking or on omelets and scrambled eggs.

¼ cup fennel seeds

1 tablespoon coriander seeds

1 tablespoon whole black peppercorns

1½ teaspoons red pepper flakes

¼ cup pure California chili powder

2 tablespoons kosher salt

2 tablespoons ground cinnamon

Put the fennel seeds, coriander seeds, and peppercorns in a small heavy skillet over medium heat. Toss the seeds so they toast evenly. As soon as the fennel seeds turn light brown, work quickly: Turn on the exhaust fan, add the red pepper flakes, and toss, toss, toss. After three tosses, turn the spices out onto a

plate to cool. (If you try to grind them while they're warm, they will gum up the blades of your blender or spice mill.)

Pour the cooled seeds into a blender or spice mill, and add the chili powder, salt, and cinnamon. Blend until the spices are evenly ground, removing the blender pitcher from its stand and shaking occasionally.

Store in an airtight container in a cool, dark place for 4 months or store in your freezer for up to 1 year.

CHEF'S NOTE: If you have a spice grinder or clean coffee mill (that you use only for spices), you can grind just the fennel seeds and coriander seeds with the peppercorns and red pepper flakes and then toss with the remaining ingredients.

COCOA SPICE RUB

Makes about ¾ cup

Cocoa powder gives this spice rub a dark, rich flavor that works well with chicken and vegetables, but is especially good with pork or sprinkled over sweet potatoes before roasting. ❖ When I make this, I use Scharffen Berger cocoa powder but any naturally processed cocoa powder works in this recipe. Avoid Dutch-processed cocoa powder, which may be darker in color but sometimes has an alkaline aftertaste.

1 tablespoon whole white peppercorns

1 tablespoon whole coriander seeds

4½ tablespoons ground cinnamon

2 teaspoons ground nutmeg

1 teaspoon ground cloves

3½ tablespoons unsweetened cocoa powder

4 tablespoons coarse sea salt, preferably gray salt

In a dry medium saucepan over medium heat, toast the white peppercorns and coriander seeds until they begin to pop. Remove the pan from the heat and transfer the spices to a plate to cool. (If you try to grind them while they're warm, they will gum up the blades of your spice mill.) Grind the spices to a fine powder in a spice mill or coffee grinder that's used only for spices. Mix the ground pepper and coriander with the ground cinnamon, nutmeg, cloves, cocoa powder, and salt.

Store in an airtight container in a cool, dark place for 4 months or store in your freezer for up to 1 year.

CHEF'S-STYLE BALSAMIC REDUCTION

Makes about 1½ cups

I've been reducing balsamic vinegar for decades but Rob Hohmann, Bottega's chef de cuisine, taught me this trick for making a better reduction. When you reduce a vinegar, you can subtly alter its flavor, and not always in a good way. By adding an equal amount of inverted sugar before simmering, the reduction keeps the flavor of the original liquid even when it's cooked down by a good percentage.

1½ cups balsamic vinegar

1½ cups inverted sugar (recipe follows)

In a large saucepan, bring the vinegar and inverted sugar to a boil over medium-high heat. Decrease the heat to medium and let the mixture simmer, bubbling quietly but not at a roiling boil, until reduced by half.

CHEF'S NOTE: You can replace the inverted sugar with corn syrup, but this will make the reduction slightly sweeter than if you use inverted sugar.

INVERTED SUGAR

3 cups sugar

1½ cups water

¼ teaspoon citric acid (available in health food stores), or use 2 teaspoons freshly squeezed lemon juice

In a large saucepan, bring the sugar, water, and citric acid (or lemon juice) to a boil over medium-high heat. Decrease the heat to keep the mixture medium-low; adjust the heat as needed to keep the liquid at a lively simmer until it's reduced by half, about 30 minutes.

SMOKED
OLIVE OIL

THIS IS A GREAT WAY TO ADD GRILLING FLAVOR TO FOODS OFF-SEASON.

Makes 6 cups

I was filming *Next Iron Chef All-Stars* in New York, out at Montauk Point on the tip of Long Island, and didn't have enough time to perfectly smoke the fluke on the menu. I poached the fish instead in smoked olive oil. This is a great way to add grilling flavor to foods off-season. ❖ You'll need two roasting pans for this recipe that can stack one on the other—the bottom one will be half-full of water, the top pan will hold the olive oil. (You want a good amount of surface area so more of the oil is exposed to the smoke.) You'll rest the pan holding the olive oil on top of the pan holding water. Wood chips added to a hot fire will provide the smoke and the flavor. ❖ Use a vegetable peeler to get good wide swaths of orange peel to flavor the oil.

6 cups extra-virgin olive oil

1 tablespoon juniper berries

Rind from 1 large orange

  (peel only, no white pith; see headnote)

2 bay leaves

1 tablespoon coarsely chopped fresh thyme

Put two big handfuls of wood chips in a bowl or bucket of water and let them soak for about 30 minutes while you start the fire.

Ignite charcoal in a grill with a cover. (You could put wood chips in a metal container in your gas grill; many grill manufacturers sell wood chip holders but I think a wood or charcoal fire offers more smoke flavor than doing it on your gas grill.) When the coals are ready, spread them on the grill. Fill a roasting pan half full with water. Pour the olive oil into a second roasting pan, and add the juniper berries, orange peel, bay leaves, and thyme. With your hand, take the soaked wood chips out of the water and flick them to shake off some excess liquid. Add the wood chips to the coals.

Close the grill and let it fill with smoke. Open the grill, and put the water-filled pan on the grill rack. Rest the pan filled with oil and aromatics on top of the water-filled pan. Close the lid and let it smoke for 5 to 7 minutes for a subtle smoke essence or 10 to 15 minutes for a smokier oil. (If it becomes too smoky for your taste, simply dilute with a little more olive oil.) Take both pans off the coals and set them aside to cool.

When cool, pour the olive oil through a paper coffee filter or fine-mesh sieve into a glass jar. Cover tightly, and store in a cool, dry place. The smoky flavor will dissipate over time but it will hold the flavor for a good month.

SMOKED
OIL DRESSING

Makes about 1½ cups

The subtle smoke flavor is a way to add summer flavor when the season has passed. You can also use this recipe for any olive oil left over from Grilled Vegetable Antipasti Sott'Olio (page 49).

2 teaspoons coarse sea salt, preferably gray salt

¼ teaspoon freshly ground black pepper

2 tablespoons fresh roasted lemon juice

  (see page 117) or roasted orange juice

1 tablespoon Champagne vinegar

½ cup Smoked Olive Oil (preceding)

Whisk together the salt, pepper, lemon or orange juice, and vinegar. While whisking, slowly pour in the smoked oil. This will keep in your refrigerator for 2 weeks.

SMOKED SEA SALT

Makes 1 cup

You can find smoked sea salt in gourmet stores (see Resources, page 218), but it's easy to make. I'm going to give you two methods: smoking it with a smoking gun or smoking it over charcoal in your grill.

1 cup coarse sea salt, preferably gray salt

WITH A SMOKING GUN: If you have a smoking gun (see page 201), follow the manufacturer's directions. Spread out the salt in a shallow baking dish and cover the dish with plastic wrap, leaving a small opening for the nozzle. Slide the end of the nozzle beneath the plastic wrap and above the salt; light the wood in the gun's chamber. You'll see smoke fill up the space between the salt and the plastic wrap. When there's a good amount of smoke, pull out the nozzle and seal up the plastic. Let the salt sit in the smoke for at least 15 minutes.

If you want a more intense smoke flavor, stir the salt and repeat the smoking once more.

WITH A CHARCOAL GRILL: To smoke salt in your grill, start a charcoal fire. (You could put wood chips in a metal container in your gas grill; many grill manufacturers sell wood chip holders but I think a wood or charcoal fire offers more smoke flavor than doing it on your gas grill.) When the fire is hot and all the coals are well ignited, spread out the salt in a baking dish, and add some good damp wood chips to the fire. I like fruit wood chips but any hardwood chips will do. Close the lid to the grill and let the salt absorb the smoke flavor for 5 to 10 minutes.

Store house-smoked salt in an airtight container in your pantry for about 2 months or in your freezer for 6 months.

CHEF'S NOTE: I soak wood chips in cool water for 30 minutes. Some folks like to put the chips in a strainer to drain. I don't. I take a fistful of chips out of the soaking water, give them a few good shakes to throw off excess water, and then put them right on the fire.

CITRUS-ROSEMARY SALT

Makes about 1 cup

This is perfect with the quail and grape salad on page 85. I also use this for a straight-up roasted chicken when I need an easy Tuesday night dinner.

1 cup coarse sea salt, preferably gray salt
2 teaspoons freshly grated lemon zest
2 teaspoons freshly grated orange zest
1 teaspoon minced fresh rosemary

In a bowl, blend the salt with the zests and the rosemary. Stored in an airtight container, this will keep for 4 months in your pantry or for 1 year in your freezer.

ROASTED GARLIC PASTE

Makes ¾ cup

This flavorful paste freezes well. I always have some on hand in my freezer for piadines, pizzas, garlic bread, or the dressing recipe following.

4 heads roasted garlic (Ember-Roasted Garlic, page 187)
⅓ cup extra-virgin olive oil
3 sprigs thyme, chopped
Coarse sea salt, preferably gray salt
Freshly ground black pepper

Squeeze the garlic paste from each clove of the roasted heads into a bowl. Whisk in the olive oil and thyme. Season with salt and pepper. Store covered in the fridge for 1 week or freeze for up to 2 months.

ROASTED GARLIC DRESSING

Makes about 2¼ cups

If you love roasted garlic, this may become your go-to dressing.

1 cup Roasted Garlic Paste (preceding)
1½ teaspoons coarse sea salt, preferably gray salt
¼ teaspoon freshly ground black pepper
¼ cup Champagne vinegar
½ cup water
1 tablespoon Dijon mustard
2 tablespoons minced fresh tarragon
½ teaspoon minced shallots
1 cup extra-virgin olive oil

Stir together the garlic paste, salt, pepper, vinegar, the ½ cup water, mustard, tarragon, and shallots. While whisking continuously, slowly drizzle in the olive oil.

Store covered in your refrigerator for up to 3 days.

RED WINE VINAIGRETTE

Makes ¾ cup

This vinaigrette will only be as good as your red wine vinegar. Choose the best-tasting vinegar you can find. You can add a teaspoon of chopped fresh herbs such as thyme, tarragon, or chives to this vinaigrette if you like.

¼ cup top-quality red wine vinegar
½ cup top-quality extra-virgin olive oil
1 teaspoon coarse sea salt, preferably gray salt
½ teaspoon freshly ground black pepper

Whisk together the vinegar and oil. Add the salt and pepper, taste, and add more seasoning or fresh herbs if you like.

HONEY-APPLE CIDER VINEGAR DRESSING

Makes 1¼ cups

The Italian term *agrodolce*—meaning sour and sweet—describes this flavorful blend. Try it with different varieties of honey and cider vinegar, or even substitute hard apple cider and then reduce it just a bit.

2 tablespoons honey
¼ cup top-quality apple cider vinegar
1 cup light or "pure" olive oil
Coarse sea salt, preferably gray salt
Freshly ground black pepper

Warm the honey and vinegar. Whisk in the olive oil, and season with salt and pepper. Store covered in the refrigerator for 1 week.

GRILLED RED ONION DRESSING

Makes about ½ cup

You can grill the onions on a preheated grill rack or griddle them on a hot plancha. Either way, they give this dressing a lot of flavor.

2 medium red onions, cut into ½-inch-thick slices
3 tablespoons extra-virgin olive oil
1 teaspoon coarse sea salt, preferably gray salt
¼ teaspoon freshly ground black pepper, plus a pinch
¼ cup freshly squeezed orange juice
1 tablespoon Champagne vinegar

Turn a gas grill to high or ignite charcoal. When the grill is hot, clean your grill rack. Decrease the temperature to medium-high, and brush or wipe a little olive oil on the grill rack. If using a plancha, place it on the grill rack and heat for at least 10 minutes.

Drizzle the onion slices with 2 tablespoons of the olive oil, ½ teaspoon of the salt, and about ¼ teaspoon pepper.

When the grill is hot, use tongs to place the onions on the grill rack or a preheated plancha and cook the slices until they show dark brown grill marks, about 8 minutes per side. Set the onions aside to cool. When the onions are cool, dice them fine. Measure 1 cup of diced onions for the dressing; any leftover diced onion can be added to your salad if you like.

Whisk together the 1 cup of diced onion, orange juice, vinegar, the remaining 1 tablespoon olive oil, and remaining ½ teaspoon of salt and pinch of pepper. This will keep in the fridge for 1 week.

PASSATA

In Italian, *passata* means "to pass," in this case to pass tomatoes through a press or a sieve. I buy passata imported from Italy whenever I spot it. If I can't find it, I make my own from canned tomatoes.

One 28-ounce can of whole organic peeled tomatoes along with all the juice

In a blender or food processor, purée the tomatoes. Measure what you need and refrigerate the rest. Passata will keep for 1 week in the fridge.

GRILLED TOMATO
BLOODY MARY
BLEND

Makes 3½ cups

I pour this blend into beer (see page 200) and use it as the start of a great Bloody Matador (page 198). A juice extractor such as a Magimix is the quickest way to go from whole veggies to a cocktail blend.

4 pounds ripe tomatoes

Coarse sea salt, preferably gray salt

Freshly ground black pepper

1 juicy lemon, halved

2 cups celery pieces cut in 1-inch lengths (preferably from inner stalks)

2 teaspoons Worcestershire sauce

4 dashes hot-pepper sauce (such as Crystal or Tabasco), more if needed

Turn a gas grill to high or ignite charcoal. When the grill is hot, for both gas and charcoal grills, clean your grill rack. For a gas grill, decrease the temperature to medium-high, and brush or wipe a little olive oil on the grill rack.

Core each tomato and cut an X in its base. Season very lightly with salt and pepper. Place the tomatoes on the hot grill, X-side up and away from direct heat. Cover the grill and cook for 8 to 10 minutes. With tongs, turn the tomatoes X-side down and cook for another 3 to 5 minutes. During the last few minutes of cooking, add the lemon to the grill, cut-side down. With tongs, transfer the tomatoes and roasted lemon off the heat and into a large heat-proof bowl. Let them cool to room temperature.

Take the lemons out of the bowl, and add the celery and a sprinkle of salt and pepper. Toss the tomatoes and celery and then put the contents of the bowl with all the juices through a juicer, and squeeze the lemon juice from the lemon halves into the juicer as well.

Stir the Worcestershire sauce and hot-pepper sauce into the juice blend. Refrigerate for at least 30 minutes or until ready to serve. Stir before serving, taste, and add more salt, pepper, hot-pepper sauce, or lemon juice if needed.

TOMATO VINEGAR

Makes about 1¼ cups

I like the concept of tomato "squared," with a bright tomato vinegar finishing a tomato salad.

¾ pound vine-ripened tomatoes

2 tablespoons extra-virgin olive oil

½ teaspoon minced garlic

½ teaspoon coarse sea salt, preferably gray salt

⅛ teaspoon freshly ground black pepper

¼ cup Champagne vinegar or herbal vinegar flavored with basil

¼ cup water, if needed

1 tablespoon finely chopped fresh basil

Turn a gas grill to high or ignite charcoal. When the grill is hot, for both gas and charcoal grills, clean your grill rack. Decrease the temperature to medium-high (on a gas grill only), and brush or wipe a little olive oil on the grill rack.

Toss the whole tomatoes with 1 tablespoon of the olive oil and grill them (following the steps on facing page under Grilled Tomato Juice, but don't juice them). When the tomatoes are cool enough to handle, peel them, discard the peel and seeds, and dice the tomatoes, reserving all the juice that you can.

Indoors on the stove, heat the remaining 1 tablespoon of olive oil in a saucepan over medium-high heat. When the oil is hot, add the garlic. Sauté just until the garlic is light brown, slightly less than 1 minute. Add the tomatoes and tomato juice, and bring to a boil. Decrease the heat to medium and simmer until the sauce is thick, about 3 minutes. Season with salt and pepper. Take the pan off the heat and let the mixture cool for at least 30 minutes.

Working in batches if necessary, purée the tomato mixture in a blender until smooth. Add the Champagne vinegar and thin with water if necessary. Add the basil and purée.

You can use this right away or store it in a bottle or jar with a nonmetallic lid. This will keep for 1 week in the refrigerator.

GRILLED
TOMATO SAUCE

Makes about 3½ cups

Grilling the tomatoes and roasting the red pepper gives this sauce an underlying flavor that I really like. I tend to double this recipe and freeze what I don't need. I'm always glad to have this sauce on hand. ❖ It's best to grill tomatoes over charcoal or a wood fire that's about 30 minutes past its hottest point. I like to use a plancha but you can use a cast-iron pan or grill the tomatoes directly on the grill rack.

3 pounds vine-ripened tomatoes

1 large red bell pepper

4 tablespoons olive oil

2 teaspoons coarse sea salt, preferably gray salt

½ teaspoon freshly ground black pepper

1 cup minced onion

1 tablespoon minced garlic

1 tablespoon finely chopped fresh oregano

2 tablespoons red wine vinegar

2 tablespoons finely chopped fresh flat-leaf parsley

Core each tomato and cut an X in it's base. In a bowl, toss the tomatoes and bell pepper with 1 to 2 tablespoons of the olive oil; season with 1 teaspoon of the salt and ¼ teaspoon of the pepper. Place the tomatoes on the hot grill, X-side up and away from direct heat, with the red pepper. Cover the grill and cook, turning the bell pepper to char evenly all over. Cook the tomatoes for 8 to 10 minutes. When the bell pepper's skin is blistered and blackened all the way around (about 15 minutes), put the pepper in a bowl and cover to steam and loosen the skin. Take the tomatoes off the heat and let cool to room temperature.

Peel the grilled vegetables. Halve the tomatoes horizontally and squeeze out the seeds into a sieve suspended over a bowl to catch the juices. Finely chop the tomatoes. Return the tomato pulp and any juices from the chopping board to the bowl holding the tomato juices.

Seed the bell pepper and slice off the ribs; discard the seeds and ribs. Finely dice the bell pepper; set aside. Heat the remaining 2 tablespoons olive oil in a cast-iron skillet (if you're cooking at the grill) or in a large sauté pan (if you're working at your stove) over medium heat until hot. Add the onion, season with ½ teaspoon of the salt, and sauté until softened, about 2 minutes. Add the garlic and oregano and stir. Add the tomatoes and their juice and bring to a boil over high heat. Decrease the heat to medium and simmer until thickened, about 10 minutes. Add the bell pepper and simmer for another minute. Add the vinegar. Season to taste with the remaining ½ teaspoon salt and ¼ teaspoon pepper and finish with parsley.

Keep warm until ready to serve or let cool, cover, and refrigerate. Store this in an airtight container in your fridge for 4 to 5 days or in your freezer for up to 2 months.

GRILLED
TOMATO JUICE

Makes about 3 cups

A juice extractor such as a Magimix makes quick work of juicing fresh tomatoes that you've grilled. You can also use a juicer to make a killer Bloody Mary blend (facing page).

4 pounds ripe tomatoes

Coarse sea salt, preferably gray salt

Freshly ground black pepper

Turn a gas grill to high or ignite charcoal. For both gas and charcoal grills, clean your grill rack. Decrease the temperature to medium-high, and brush or wipe a little olive oil on the grill rack. Core each tomato and cut an X in its base. Season very lightly with salt and pepper. Place the tomatoes on the hot

grill, X-side up and away from direct heat. Cover the grill and cook for 8 to 10 minutes. With tongs, turn the tomatoes X-side down and cook for another 3 to 5 minutes. Take the tomatoes off the heat and put into a large heat-proof bowl. Let the tomatoes cool to room temperature.

Pass the contents of the bowl—the tomatoes and all their juice—through a juicer. Refrigerate until ready to use, and stir before serving.

BASIL OIL

Makes about 1⅓ cups

Use these steps with parsley, cilantro, tarragon—any fresh herb that's abundant and at its peak. I first made this oil from basil in the '90s when a farmer backed up to the restaurant with a truck bed full of basil. We were making so much pesto that it was inevitable we would overlook a batch and leave it out overnight. Disgusted with the waste, I decided to try to salvage something from the basil leaves and this oil was born. ❖ This is a condiment oil, something to drizzle on at the last second; don't try to cook with an herb oil because heat will destroy all those garden-fresh flavors.

4 cups firmly packed fresh basil leaves

2 cups olive oil

In a blender, combine the basil and olive oil, processing until the mixture is completely smooth. Pour the mixture into a saucepan set over medium heat. When the oil reaches a simmer, let it cook for another 45 seconds. Remove it from the heat and then pour it through a fine-mesh sieve into a bowl. Tap the strainer lightly to coax the oil through but don't press on the solids with a spoon.

Let the oil settle as it cools and ladle off the top into a flat-bottomed paper coffee filter while the oil is still warm. The easiest way to do this is by layering coffee filters three deep in a large strainer, with the strainer placed securely over a heat-proof container. Warm oil will pass through the paper more quickly. When most of the oil has gone through, you can pick up the filters if you like and use your fingers to squeeze out the remaining oil, but be careful not to tear the filter paper.

Let the filtered oil settle for a few hours and then pour it into a clean container, leaving any sediment or cloudy liquid behind. Kept in an airtight jar set within a cool, dark spot, this oil will hold its bright flavor for at least 1 month.

BEEF STOCK

Makes 4 quarts

Beef stock gives the Bloody Matador on page 198 some power. I also add this to bean soups and stews. This recipe is simpler than the beef stock I make in my restaurant but it still packs a flavor punch. This is a stock, not a broth, because it's made from bones, while a broth is meat-based—a rule I've followed since my student chef days.

5 pounds beef bones

1 pound stew meat, cut into cubes

2 cups dry red wine

One 12-ounce can whole tomatoes, with juices from the can

1 large yellow onion, quartered

2 large carrots, cut into thirds

2 celery stalks, cut into thirds

8 sprigs flat-leaf parsley

2 bay leaves

1 tablespoon whole black peppercorns

Preheat the oven to 400°F. Put the beef bones in a roasting pan and roast until they are browned, about 40 minutes.

When the bones are roasted, put them in a large stockpot with the cubed stew meat, red wine, tomatoes, onion, carrots, celery, parsley, bay leaves, and peppercorns. Bring the mixture to a boil over high heat, then decrease the heat to low and keep at a slow simmer. Skim the top every 20 minutes or so with a wire-mesh skimmer. Simmer for about 3 hours. You want the bones always submerged: add water if the stock drops below the bones.

Strain the stock through a colander and then strain again through a chinois or fine-mesh sieve and discard all the bones and solids. Let the liquid cool to room temperature, store in airtight containers, and refrigerate for up to 3 days or freeze for up to 3 months. If you'd like to reduce the stock by 50 percent to save room in your freezer, you can. Just rehydrate with water when you use it.

CHICKEN BROTH

This chicken broth is very meaty, so it can be used anywhere you'd use stock. ❖ I use the entire bird: the wings and feet contribute gelatin for better body, the neck and the drumsticks both contribute to the broth's meaty flavor. You want every bit of flavor that you can coax into the liquid. ❖ Don't pour hot water from your tap over the chicken. Warm water that's been sitting in your hot-water heater can add a mineral aftertaste to your stock. Plus classically trained cooks believe that you get a clearer broth with cold water because it doesn't seal in the protein. ❖ Beautiful, fresh, crisp vegetables add significant flavor, especially when they're cut on the bias because this exposes more cut surface to the water. ❖ Skimming the surface clarifies the liquid. You're taking out the imperfections and leaving pure, clear flavors. Add the chicken, vegetables, and water to the pot first. Add the herbs and spices after the first few skimmings so you don't skim them off with the foam. This calls for a very large pot—at least 12 quarts. If you don't have an extra-large stock pot, halve the recipe.

2 pounds chicken necks

4 pounds chicken wings (cut each wing into 3 sections)

2 pounds chicken drumsticks

4 cups coarsely chopped yellow onions, about 4 large onions

2 cups chopped celery (about 4 ribs), cut on the diagonal into 1-inch pieces

2 cups chopped carrots (about 3 large carrots), cut on the diagonal into 1-inch pieces

2 gallons cold water

1 packed cup fresh flat-leaf parsley, coarsely chopped

¼ cup fresh thyme, leaves and stems

2 tablespoons whole black peppercorns

12 lightly crushed juniper berries

6 bay leaves

Add the chicken parts, all the vegetables, and the water to a large heavy pot. Over high heat, bring the liquid to a boil, and then reduce the heat to medium-low and bring the liquid to a simmer. Watch the heat; a low simmer gives you better flavor than boiling your stock.

Skim off the foam that rises to the top with a mesh skimmer. After about 20 minutes of cooking and skimming, add the parsley, thyme, peppercorns, and juniper berries. Add the bay leaves, crumbling them over the pot. After 4½ hours of cooking, remove the broth from the heat. With tongs, gently remove the pieces of chicken from the pot to avoid clouding the liquid. (Set the chicken aside to cool. Later, pull the chicken off the bone and reserve it for another use such as chicken salad, chicken ravioli, or chicken soup.) Strain the broth through a colander and then strain again through a chinois or fine-mesh sieve.

Allow the broth to cool completely and then store in air-tight containers and refrigerate or freeze for up to 3 months. If freezer space is tight, reduce the broth by 50 percent to make a concentrate and then rehydrate with water as needed.

CHEF'S NOTE: I don't add salt to my broths and stocks because if I reduce a salted liquid significantly, it becomes too salty.

CRÈME FRAÎCHE

Make crème fraîche by combining cream and buttermilk. Live cultures in the buttermilk react with the cream, creating a light, thin version of sour cream that's delicious and heat-stable.

1⅔ cups heavy cream

1 tablespoon buttermilk

Whisk together the heavy cream and buttermilk and pour into a large clean glass jar or bowl. Cover it with two layers of cheesecloth, secure with a rubber band, and just let it do its thing on your countertop at room temperature for up to 24 hours.

After that, seal the jar with plastic wrap and refrigerate if you don't plan to use the crème fraîche right away. It will keep for up to 1 week in the refrigerator.

RESOURCES

FOOD

Anson Mills
www.ansonmills.com
Fine-ground polenta

Bob's Red Mill
www.bobsredmill.com
Chickpea flour and masa harina

Charbay
www.charbay.com
Meyer Lemon Vodka and other
infused spirits

Chiarello Family Vineyards
www.chiarellovineyards.com
Wine

Cooking Enthusiast
www.cookingenthusiast.com
Butcher's salt

Cuban Food Market
www.cubanfoodmarket.com
Guarapo de cana (sugar
cane juice)

Dean and Deluca
www.deandeluca.com
Tomato vinegar

Fabbri North America
www.fabbrinorthamerica.com
Wild cherries in amarena syrup

Gioia Cheese Company
www.gioiacheeseinc.com
Burrata cheese

Giusto's Vita-Grain
www.giustos.com
Organic flour and fine-ground
polenta

Heritage Foods
www.heritagefoodsusa.com
Humanely raised goat, lamb,
and pig

Hog Island Oysters
www.hogislandoysters.com
Oysters

Katz & Company
www.katzandco.com
Artisan oils, vinegars, and honey

King Arthur Flour
www.kingarthurflour.com
Ascorbic acid and sheet gelatin

Manna Foods
www.mannafoodsinc.com
A variety of meats

NapaStyle
www.napastyle.com
Calabrian chile paste, olive oils,
rubs, salts, spices, and vinegars

Nuts
www.nuts.com
Chickpea flour

Osprey Seafood
(415) 291-0156
Seafood

Penzeys
www.penzeys.com
Spices

Preferred Meats
www.preferredmeats.com
A variety of meats

Rancho Gordo
www.ranchogordo.com
Heirloom beans (varieties vary
by season)

The Spanish Table
www.spanishtable.com
Pimentón de la Vera
(smoked Spanish paprika)

Williams-Sonoma
www.williams-sonoma.com
Smoked olive oil

EQUIPMENT, TOOLS, AND KITCHENWARE

Anchor Hocking
www.anchorhocking.com
Glassware

BBQ Guys
www.bbqguys.com
Hibachis and
tabletop charcoal grill

Churrascoshop.com
www.churrascoshop.com
Lances for steak

Conair Corp/Cuisinart
www.cuisinart.com
Electric knife
and food processor

Duralex
www.duralexusa.com
Tempered glassware

Emile Henry
www.emilehenryusa.com
Pizza stone and cookware

Fire Sense
www.firesense.com
Grills, fire pits, and urban grills

Fox Run Brands
www.foxrunbrands.com
Grilling accessories
and thermometers

GrillPro
www.grillpro.com
Grilling accessories

John Boos
www.johnboos.com
American-made cutting boards,
cutting block oil

**La Bella Terra Custom
Wrought Iron**
www.ironworksnapavalley.com
Custom fire pit grates

La Caja China
www.lacajachina.com
Hot box

Lazzari
www.lazzari.com
Lump charcoal

Lodge Cast-Iron Products
www.lodgemfg.com
Cast-iron cookware, plancha, and
the Lodge Logic Sportsman's Grill

Napa Cooking Steel
www.napagrilling.com
Iron cross and metal stands
for roasting lamb

NapaStyle
www.napastyle.com
Cutting boards, fire pits, grills,
grill and hearth tools, hearthside
lever roaster, hot box, pizza stone,
plancha, and Tuscan grill

Polder Housewares
www.polder.com
Thermometers, scales,
and timers

Root Candles
www.rootcandles.com
Candles

Rösle
www.rosleusa.com
Grills and tools

Spitjack
www.spitjack.com
Rotisserie equipment

Tutto Mio
www.tuttomio.biz
Dishware

Twista Cake
www.TwistaCake.com
Wooden cake form for rotisserie

Weber-Stephen Products
www.weber.com
Grills and grill accessories

Williams-Sonoma
www.williams-sonoma.com
Cataplana, grill baskets, plancha,
and smoking gun

Wings in Things
www.wingsinthings.com
Rotisserie cage

INDEX

The exact equivalents in the following tables have been rounded for convenience.

Liquid/Dry Measurements

U.S.		METRIC	
¼	teaspoon	1.25	milliliters
½	teaspoon	2.5	milliliters
1	teaspoon	5	milliliters
1	tablespoon (3 teaspoons)	15	milliliters
1	fluid ounce (2 tablespoons)	30	milliliters
¼	cup	60	milliliters
⅓	cup	80	milliliters
½	cup	120	milliliters
1	cup	240	milliliters
1	pint (2 cups)	480	milliliters
1	quart (4 cups, 32 ounces)	960	milliliters
1	gallon (4 quarts)	3.84	liters
1	ounce (by weight)	28	grams
1	pound	448	grams
2.2	pounds	1	kilogram

Oven Temperature

FAHRENHEIT	CELSIUS	GAS
250	120	½
275	140	1
300	150	2
325	160	3
350	180	4
375	190	5
400	200	6
425	220	7
450	230	8
475	240	9
500	260	10

Lengths

U.S.		METRIC	
⅛	inch	3	millimeters
¼	inch	6	millimeters
½	inch	12	millimeters
1	inch	2.5	centimeters